Enlightenment Aberrations

Error and Revolution in France

DAVID W. BATES

Cornell University Press

ITHACA AND LONDON

First published 2002 by Cornell University Press

Printed in the United States of America

Library of Congress Cataloging-in-Publication Data

Bates, David William.
   Enlightenment aberrations : error and revolution in France / David W. Bates.
     p. cm.
   Earlier versions of some chapters have appeared in the journals Representations, Eighteenth-Century Studies, and The Eighteenth Century, Theory and Interpretation.
   Includes bibliographical references and index.
   ISBN 0-8014-3945-0 (alk. paper)
   1. France—History—Revolution, 1789–1799. 2. Error. 3. Enlightenment—France. I. Title.
  DC158.8 .B38 2002
  944.04—dc21   2001004681

Cornell University Press strives to use environmentally responsible suppliers and materials to the fullest extent possible in the publishing of its books. Such materials include vegetable-based, low-VOC inks and acid-free papers that are recycled, totally chlorine-free, or partly composed of nonwood fibers. For further information, visit our website at www.cornellpress.cornell.edu.

Cloth printing   10 9 8 7 6 5 4 3 2 1

Contents

v

Preface

> Truth is nothing without the opposed error that corresponds to it.
>
> F. L. ESCHERNEY, *Les lacunes de la philosophie* (1783)

 Why write a conceptual history of error? And why write a history of error during the Enlightenment? The answer is not immediately obvious. Not only is it difficult to imagine error as a subject in its own right, freed from its dependence on conceptions of truth; it seems especially strange to focus on the problem of error in the Enlightenment, a period defined in many ways by its attack on error in all forms. And yet a careful study of eighteenth-century thinking about error shows just how critical this concept is for any understanding of the Enlightenment, and, as a result, for any understanding of the development of modernity. Error, in other words, will lead us not only to a new reconceptualization of the Enlightenment itself, but more important, toward a critique of those powerful historical and cultural narratives that look back to the eighteenth century as a way of explaining the incredible triumphs as well as the horrendous disasters of our modern, enlightened world.

How will a study of the seemingly marginal concept of error accomplish this difficult task? A simple observation can serve as a starting point. At its heart, philosophy is not about truth. Or at least, philosophy begins to think about truth only when it arises as a problem. Historically, truth became a problem for philosophical inquiry only when error was recognized to be an endemic condition, a recurrent possibility. The search for truth, a search that defines philosophy from its origin in ancient Greece at least to the modern era, begins really with a definition of error.[1] Since all philosophy is predicated on the absence—or at least potential absence—of truth, philosophy must begin in error. However truth may be defined, there is no need for the very technology of thought if the mind is not prone to error. And so any conceptualization of philosophical inquiry relies on a prior understanding of error. It would be possible, and I think highly desirable, to rewrite the history of philosophy as a history of error, to demonstrate how "truth" is really parasitic on its supposed negation.[2]

What makes the European Enlightenment so important for a history of error is that for the first time in the West the very ideal of "truth" was being put into serious question. Of course skepticism had been a philosophical possibility since ancient times. Still, skepticism defined human failure in terms of an idealized truth that was understood to be beyond human capabilities. By the time of the Enlightenment, however, knowledge was being restructured in a radically new way. Emerging as an essentially *probabilistic* process of discovery, knowledge was not measured by the standard of perfect certainty. In this period intellectuals fashioned entirely novel epistemologies that aimed less at the revelation and possession of a total truth than the discovery of a limited understanding of the natural and human world. This turn was a response to the seventeenth-century Scientific Revolution, which was of course immensely successful in its application of mathematical and experimental techniques to the study of nature. At the same time, it is important to emphasize just how radically disorienting this epistemological turn was, for the methodology of careful experimentation, observation, and logical

1. Some reference points for this position can be found in Marcel Detienne, *The Masters of Truth in Archaic Greece*, trans. Janet Lloyd (New York, 1999); J. P. Levet, *Le vrai et le faux dans la pensée grecque archaïque* (Paris, 1976); Alexander Mourelatos, *The Route of Parmenides: A Study of Word, Image, and Argument in the Fragments* (New Haven, 1970); Page du Bois, *Torture and Truth* (London, 1991); Nicolas Denyer, *Language, Thought, and Falsehood in Ancient Greek Philosophy* (London, 1990); Adi Ophir, *Plato's Invisible Cities: Discourse and Power in the Republic* (Savage, Md., 1991).

2. Among works that help frame this historical problem are Giora Hon, "Going Wrong: To Make a Mistake, to Fall into an Error," *Review of Metaphysics* 49 (1995): 3–20, and "Towards a Typology of Experimental Error: An Epistemological View," *Studies in History and Philosophy of Science* 20 (1989): 469–504; Deborah Mayo, *Error and the Growth of Experimental Knowledge* (Chicago, 1996); G. R. Evans, *Getting It Wrong: the Medieval Epistemology of Error* (Leiden and Boston, 1998); Susan James, *Passion and Action: the Emotions in Seventeenth-Century Philosophy* (Oxford, 1997); Theodore M. Porter, *The Rise of Statistical Thinking, 1820–1900* (Princeton, 1986); Stéphane Callens, *Les maîtres de l'erreur: Mesure et probabilité au XIXᵉ siècle* (Paris, 1997); Carlo Sini, *Images of Truth: From Sign to Symbol*, trans. Massimo Verdicchio (Atlantic Highlands, N.J., 1993); Colleen Lamos, *Deviant Modernism: Sexual and Textual Errancy in T. S. Eliot, James Joyce, and Marcel Proust* (Cambridge, 1998).

organization was grounded on a *denial* of any privileged, immediate human insight. Truth had, since the Renaissance at least, been progressively secularized, understood to be something discoverable through the study of the finite world, available to the human mind without divine intervention. By the time of the Enlightenment, however, the human mind did not have much in the way of help for this quest: confined to the data of the senses and the faculty of reason, human beings would discover only the limited form of truth appropriate to their limited form of understanding.

The empirical bent of Enlightenment inquiry led to a redefinition of truth as a goal rather than as a prized possession. For truth was in fact endlessly deferred in this intellectual context, given both the extreme limitation of the operations of the human mind and the admitted uncertainties of all sensible observations. It was here, perhaps for the first time in modern thought, that error assumed a significant role not just in the definition of knowledge but in the very search for knowledge itself. Within the largely empirical framework of Enlightenment thought, error was not going to be "corrected" with certain techniques or revelatory insights. Once truth was articulated as a *destination*—and not a sure possession of some kind, guaranteed by a higher order of being—the horizon of knowledge could be infinitely expanded. Truths that were now defined in terms of a purely human and therefore variable system of thought could hardly ever act as stable norms for the evaluation of all error. The very emphasis on probability and epistemological modesty in eighteenth-century thought, its rejection of comprehensive philosophical systems and supposedly foundational "truths," its turn to theories of indefinite progress—all these characteristic marks of the Enlightenment express a frank admission that error is an important aspect of human understanding. Error was, in other words, understood to be a necessary risk of any pursuit of knowledge, given that traditional sources of certainty had been all but dismantled or destroyed and no firm replacements were seen to be available.

The acknowledged provisionality of truth in any scientific mode of inquiry was the starting point for the most serious reflection on the nature of error in eighteenth-century thought. While the crudest errors, those obvious "mistakes" of reason, certainly could be, and were, confidently attacked by Enlightenment figures, the more radical risk of error that haunted any search for knowledge was understood to be much more problematic and therefore attracted serious philosophical attention. This kind of radical error, linked to an inevitable "errancy" of the human mind, could be identified only in the light of future discovery. This was of course the very heart of the Enlightenment idea of progress—the truths of one generation of investigators would be identified as errors only in the context of an expanded future knowledge.

It is important to note here the function of error in this progress toward truth. Truth, in this temporalized epistemology, *relies* on the specificity of the error for its realization. Errors form the foundation of knowledge, and these errors can be corrected only within the movement of thought in its historical totality. This meant that error, at least the most radical kind of error, was the site of both risk and promise in the Enlightenment. The dangers of mental aberrations were never to be ignored, of course, but they could never be predicted and controlled in advance, since one never adopts an error knowing it to be an error—that would simply be madness.[3] An error is valued because it is believed at that moment to be the truth. At the same time—and this is something that has rarely if ever been noted—the error holds out the promise of its own correction. Illuminated by the light of some future truth, error would be defined and overcome. Which means that in the absence of any clearly visible truth (an absence that grounds any modern empirical epistemology), error becomes in the Enlightenment a potential site of truth's appearance, even though the promise of that appearance is deferred, perhaps infinitely. Still, what is crucial for any understanding of the Enlightenment is an awareness that the promise of error lies hidden, in its capacity for leading to a truth that would never have been gained without the error of the original inquiry. The uneasy coexistence of risk and promise structures the concept of error in the Enlightenment, something we will see in a variety of contexts. Error was intimately linked, and not just negatively, to the truth.

In the eighteenth century there were repeated attempts to exploit the complex temporal structure that linked truth with error. The error itself, related to some future knowledge that framed it as an aberration, provided special insight into the nature of a truth that was never fully present to limited human minds. The Enlightenment introduced, then, what I call an epistemology of error. Human knowledge was figured as an aberration. And if knowledge itself was always a potential error, then the deviation that was error might very well point the way to new truths. The search for truth (whether philosophical, political, or scientific) was

---

3. Michel Foucault quotes the following passage from François Boissier de Sauvages's 1772 treatise on nosology: "We call madmen those who are actually deprived of reason or who persist in some notable error; it is this *constant error* of the soul manifest in its imagination, in its judgments, and in its desires, which constitutes the characteristic of this category." See *Madness and Civilization: A History of Insanity in the Age of Reason*, trans. Richard Howard (New York, 1964), 104.

in essence an attempt to disentangle (without any sure guide) the merely accidental deviation from the more *productive* aberration that held out the promise of some future discovery.

To think of Enlightenment knowledge as structured by error, of error as the site of both risk and promise, is to undermine some of the most dominant interpretations of the Enlightenment. Both relentless critics and passionate defenders of the Enlightenment project emphasize that it is founded on the power of *reason*. Many have praised the Enlightenment for its defense of reason against superstition, ignorance, and oppressive tradition—all the accumulated errors of human history. They invoke reason as an antidote for the madness of irrational belief, the source of so much conflict, repression, and violence, not only in early modern Europe but also in our own world. Of course, for many critics of the Enlightenment an obsessive faith in reason is itself a kind of madness that has repeatedly caused its own deadly violence. By refusing to recognize its own essential limits, these critics allege, reason has been forced to destroy in the name of progress. For both critics and defenders, the Enlightenment was defined by its confidence in reason. The question concerning the essence of the Enlightenment is really a question of reason and its role in modernity: can reason truly eradicate error and prepare the way for a more sane and orderly world, or is reason itself a kind of dangerous error responsible for many of the disastrous effects of a technologically and socially advanced civilization?

The close analysis of error offered in this book is meant to reconceptualize the Enlightenment in an entirely new framework. By looking at how eighteenth-century figures conceived of error and its relationship with knowledge and truth, we can begin to see how complex, how *ambivalent* the idea of reason was in the Enlightenment. On one level, the conceptual history of error in eighteenth-century France will provide a new understanding of the period, one that goes beyond any simplistic critique or defense of the Enlightenment project. This rereading then raises a more difficult question: How does an understanding of error and enlightenment alter our understanding of the subsequent history of modernity? The answer is not so clear. It must be admitted that the great power of the strongly partisan interpretations of the Enlightenment lies in their identification of a pathology of modern culture and the suggestion of a potential cure for the ills of our own civilization. On the one hand, enlightenment is the cure for the "disease" of irrationality, and on the other, enlightenment itself is the pathogen that must be combated with alternative concepts of truth and identity. A portrait of the Enlightenment that emphasizes its essential complexity and ambivalence might provide a historically subtle account, but at the risk of evading the very questions that make the Enlightenment such a critical point of departure for so many intellectuals across different disciplines.

The history of Enlightenment error offered here is in fact meant as both a critique of prevailing interpretations of eighteenth-century intellectual history and a fundamentally new answer to the broader question of enlightenment and its relation with the advent of modernity itself.

This project has evolved over a number of years. The University of Chicago, the University of British Columbia, the University of Saskatchewan, and the University of California, Berkeley, have all provided me with indispensable resources. The Bibliothèque Nationale and the Bibliothèque Mazarine in Paris, as well as the Bodleian library at Oxford, offered me their inexhaustible collections and professional assistance. The Mellon Foundation, the University of Chicago, the Social Sciences and Humanities Research Council of Canada, and the University of California, Berkeley, have all offered critical financial support for research at various stages of my career.

Students in Canada and California have been forced to engage with many of the ideas in this book, and I thank them for their enthusiasm and their insights. I was especially fortunate to work with an eclectic group of students and faculty in the Arts One Humanities Program at the University of British Columbia, where a substantial part of the book was written—many interesting questions were both raised and answered while I was teaching there. My current interdisciplinary home in the Department of Rhetoric at Berkeley has been the perfect space to complete this project—my thanks especially to Judith Butler and David Cohen for their contributions.

A constant flow of people has made this book possible. The entire Lejay family—especially Henri and Marie-Thérèse Lejay—made us feel more than at home in France. Research in Paris was eased considerably with help from the late François Furet, who also gave his critique of some chapters. Ed Hundert and Keith Baker gave me much needed support, both intellectual and professional, at critical points in the writing of this book; their own work also provided exemplary models of intellectual historical scholarship, from which I have no doubt deviated considerably at times. Paul Nelles, Susan Crane, Jan Goldstein, Giora Hon, Nick Hudson, Ernie Hamm, Jürgen Trabant, Daniel Brewer, Julie Hayes, Dan Gordon, Larry Stewart, Howard Brown, Carla Hesse, Pheng Cheah, and many others have helped me conceptualize enlightenment, error, and revolution in particular. And for providing much needed inspiration in the last stages of writing, my thanks to Lorna Hutson, Nancy Ruttenberg, and especially Vicky Kahn.

Steven Wolfe helped lay the foundations of this project many years ago in Chicago, and since then he has always been willing to share his own work and insights, from which I have benefited deeply. Michael Geyer has been a constant—if absent—presence while I was writing this book; his astute critique and his unfailing support have, I hope, been redeemed here in part. I owe a great debt to Harvey Mitchell, who not only has read and commented on virtually the entire manuscript (in more than one version) but has also generously shared his deep knowledge of the period with me for years now. For all his support, I can't thank him enough, but what I appreciate the most is his genuine enthusiasm for this project. Finally, I thank my entire family for their varied and complex contributions: my parents and sisters; the constellation of in-laws; my children, Heather and Graeme; and especially Ann, for being there from the start.

Earlier versions of some chapters have appeared in the journals *Representations, Eighteenth-Century Studies,* and *The Eighteenth Century: Theory and Interpretation,* and I thank the University of California Press, The Johns Hopkins University Press, and Texas Tech University Press for permission to use this material here.

Enlightenment Aberrations

)

CHAPTER 1

Aberrations of Enlightenment

Instead of assuming a derogatory air, we must take courage and measure our powers against those of the Enlightenment, and thus find a proper adjustment. The age which venerated reason and science as man's highest faculty cannot and must not be lost even for us. We must find a way not only to see that age in its own shape but to release again those original forces which brought forth and molded that shape.

ERNST CASSIRER, *The Philosophy of the Enlightenment* (1932)

Before any new reading of the Enlightenment can be offered, any new interpretation of its role in the history of modern civilization, it is essential to recognize that the very problem of enlightenment is itself the product of a historical development. For this reason, it is only by tracing the history of this question that it is possible to see what any new approach will accomplish. Only then, after clarifying exactly what is at stake in the ongoing conflict over the legacy of the Enlightenment, will we be in a position to understand how a conceptual history of error in this period might address these difficult and complex problems in a productive way. We can take as a starting point for this discussion a troubling and persistent paradox in our age: Why has our supposedly advanced enlightened civilization been continually disrupted by repetitions of mass violence, mass death, and mass destruction, on a scale never before seen in human history? The repeated juxtaposition of violence with ideals of progress in modern history demands an interrogation of the origin of modernity and the identification of its enemies.

ENLIGHTENMENT AND PATHOLOGY

The problem of enlightenment emerged most forcefully in the aftermath of the French Revolution, in a Europe haunted by the spectacle of the Terror, new forms of international war, and civil breakdown. Many early critics of the Revolution, seeking to explain the extreme and disruptive violence it spawned in France and beyond, identified the Enlightenment itself as the pathogen that led to the crisis. Figures as diverse as Edmund Burke, Joseph de Maistre, and G. W. F. Hegel all looked critically at the "arrogance" of Enlightenment rationality to explain the collapse of order and the rise of violence in revolutionary Europe (and its globalized zones of influence). According to these conservative critics, the unfettered power of human reason in the Enlightenment, and in particular the French Enlightenment, did not recognize its own very real limitations, and when the forces of enlightenment attempted to rationalize humanity on the abstract model of natural science, it was forced to correct as errors the inevitable resistances of concrete individuals and cultures, thereby unleashing its own uncontrollable violence—uncontrollable because reason acknowledged no legitimate opposition. Of course, the defenders of the Enlightenment, those who wanted to uphold its central values in an era of radical instability, saw the French Revolution and its violent aftermath as a failure of reason, a move away from enlightenment. For early liberals, then, the origin of revolutionary and social violence was located in those irrational forces that now had to be moderated precisely by the dictates of reason, enforced by an enlightened social and political elite.

In the early nineteenth century, liberals and conservatives refought the battles of the Enlightenment and the Revolution, with liberals emerging victorious in the largely bourgeois economic and political order of postrevolutionary Europe. However, the rise of socialism as a powerful opponent of liberalism in a newly industrialized world provided a whole new perspective on enlightenment. Socialists tied the obsession with instrumental rationality and radical individuality characteristic of eighteenth-century thought less to a blind philosophical confidence in reason than to omnipresent, if often disguised, economic interests. This was an important development for the understanding of enlightenment in modern culture, for unlike so many conservative critics, socialists often adopted the explicit ideals of eighteenth-century thought (liberty and equality, for example) even as they criticized the aberrant ideologies and practices of the bourgeoisie who were merely pretending to institute those ideals in the political sphere. And so various forms of socialism and fields of inquiry, such as sociology, that emerged in its wake, along with the liberal doctrines, all could trace theoretical roots to the eighteenth-century Enlightenment.[1] The result was that the legacy of the Enlightenment became increasingly complex as widely diverse intellectuals and political theorists battled over the question of "modernity" and the critical role the eighteenth century played in its development.

Although the intricate history of just how the Enlightenment was understood and criticized in late nineteenth- and early twentieth-century Europe remains to be written, there is no question that our contemporary understanding of the problem of enlightenment and modernity has been overwhelmingly influenced by the trauma of the Second World War. Even though the question of enlightenment figured in the critique of mass industrial society that followed the Great War, it was the experience of even greater technological destruction, alongside mass death and genocide, that sparked the most intense reflection on the nature of modernity. In the postwar world, the idea of enlightenment came to play a critical role in thinking (and rethinking) all the horrors and the achievements of modernity.

Just as in the violent revolutionary period, Europeans in the 1930s and 1940s were able to link violence, war, and death both to the collapse of Enlightenment values in the face of new errors and superstitions *and* to the very essence of the Enlightenment project, the essential madness of an instrumental rationality that had technologized life and death equally. Not surprisingly, the intellectual history of the Enlightenment, often called the Age of Reason in the postwar period, became an incredibly confrontational zone, tied as it was to highly politicized positions on the very nature of modern Western culture.

For many scholars, particularly in the Anglo-American world, the fight against Nazism and then communism was taken to be a repetition of the battles fought by the Enlightenment in the eighteenth century: a liberal and rational democratic culture was pitted against "irrational" views that were held responsible for the most violent and repressive twentieth-century states. Typical of this approach is perhaps the most famous postwar survey of eighteenth-century thought, Peter Gay's two-volume textbook *The Enlightenment: An Interpretation*, which appeared in the 1960s. In his conclusion, Gay wrote:

> We have known horrors, and may know horrors, that the men of the Enlightenment did not see in their nightmares. Yet, though few are today inclined to believe it, none of this impairs the permanent value of the Enlight-

1. Wolf Lepenies, *Between Literature and Science: The Rise of Sociology* (Cambridge, 1988), 13–14.

enment's humane and libertarian vision, or the permanent validity of its critical method. . . . It remains as true today as it was in the eighteenth century:
the world needs more light than it has, not less.[2]

Gay defined the Enlightenment's "humane and libertarian vision" as a
profoundly realistic perspective. David Hume is revealed to be the perfect representative of the Enlightenment philosophes because, as Gay
tells us, Hume "makes plain that since God is silent, man is his own master: he must live in a disenchanted world, submit everything to criticism,
and make his own way."[3] Hume, in other words, was "willing to live
with uncertainty, with no supernatural justifications, no complete explanations, no promise of permanent stability, with guides of merely probable validity." We might say that enlightenment is, according to Gay, the
ability to face the condition of possible error with courage, and to respect
the solidarity of all people condemned to this position. This particular
interpretation of the Enlightenment had a wide appeal in this era, and
one can find a number of texts (and textbooks) that echo Gay's eloquent
defense of the philosophes. To take one example, one of the most notable
eighteenth-century specialists of Gay's generation, Lester Crocker, introduced a selection of Enlightenment texts with this grand claim: "It was
the Enlightenment," he wrote, "that opened the consciousness of modern man . . . to the fact that he is lost among the stars, with no meaning to
his existence except the meaning he creates; that he must therefore be his
own guide, his happiness and well-being on earth his only lodestar."[4]

How exactly did "man" find his way in the world, according to these
admiring views of the Enlightenment? The "rise of modern science," as
Alfred Cobban once noted, was the most influential new intellectual development of the period.[5] As Gay and many other liberal scholars also
emphasized, the methods and principles of the new science framed the
Enlightenment's bold philosophical vision. What distinguished the Enlightenment from the Scientific Revolution was the extension of this
epistemology into a general theory of human nature and understanding.
Enlightenment philosophes sought the answers to psychological, social,
economic, and political problems in the observed laws of human behavior—as Gay explained in volume 2 of his study, subtitled *The Science of
Freedom*. The eighteenth century saw the emergence of economic theory,

2. Peter Gay, *The Enlightenment: An Interpretation,* vol. 2: *The Science of Freedom* (New York, 1969), 567.
3. Ibid., vol. 1: *The Rise of Modern Paganism* (New York, 1966), 418–19.
4. Lester G. Crocker, ed., *The Age of Enlightenment* (New York, 1969), 30.
5. Alfred Cobban, *In Search of Humanity: The Role of the Enlightenment in Modern History* (New York, 1960), 29.

anthropology, psychology, social science, political science, a general rationalization of the individual and society to parallel the achievements of natural science. Therefore, however varied it may have been in its internal structure, the Enlightenment was often described, as Hayden White wrote in 1967, as a "dedication to human reason, science, and education as the best means of building a stable society of free men on earth."[6] What Gay often called the "dialectic of Enlightenment"[7] was for many in this period a movement that pitted the relentlessly secular humanism of classical thought against Christianity and other traditional forces, but in the new context of a scientific worldview. This "dialectic of Enlightenment" produced something called "modernity"—that rational spirit that faced a "disenchanted" world with a courageous and humanitarian brand of stoicism.

For Gay, and for so many other liberal academics of the postwar era who traced stable political and social order to the ideals of the eighteenth-century philosophes, the Enlightenment was resolutely decoupled from the violence of the Revolution and the Terror. If at times the Enlightenment would be aligned with the constitutionalism of the American republic or the ideals of early moderate revolutionaries in France, eighteenth-century philosophy was never implicated in the drastic disruptions and disorders of the revolutionary era. Like earlier figures such as Ernst Cassirer, whose 1932 classic *The Philosophy of the Enlightenment* ignored the Revolution, postwar defenders of the Enlightenment were looking to protect the emancipatory possibilities of a purely human reason, to avoid the ethical and epistemological extremes that were often linked (especially by new existential philosophies) to a cognitive subject abandoned to its own limited experiential world. Cassirer wrote his own defense of the Enlightenment as an explicit response to philosophers such as Heidegger (who had clashed with Cassirer over the legacy of Kant in a famous 1929 debate in Switzerland),[8] those thinkers who elaborated the darker side of human finitude, its relationship with death and profound existential limitation. According to neo-Kantians such as Cassirer, the symbolic faculties of the human mind—language, myth, concepts—were the means by which humanity made contact with some "infinite" reality, not through traditional philo-

6. Hayden White, "Editor's Introduction," in Robert Anchor, *The Enlightenment Tradition* (Berkeley, 1967), ix.

7. Gay, *Enlightenment*, 1: xiii.

8. An English translation of the lecture notes (by Francis Slade) is available in *The Existentialist Tradition: Selected Writings*, ed. Nino Languillo (Garden City, N.Y., 1971), 192–203.

sophical investigations of some supposedly objective reality.[9] The Enlightenment for Cassirer was a moment of transition, when metaphysical conceptions of the infinite were being systematically criticized (leading to skeptical positions like Hume's) and the structure and potential of human understanding itself were just beginning to be understood.[10] For Cassirer, the return to a metaphysics of Being in Heidegger's work was a grave mistake, a backward movement.

But if Cassirer looked to Kant and Lessing as the culmination of an Enlightenment that began with a critical spirit but ended with an almost mystical aesthetic theory, Anglo-American scholars would, in the starker postwar world, highlight the critical spirit of the classic Enlightenment, the more "skeptical" strain of thought found in figures such as Hume and Voltaire. In particular, liberal scholars emphasized the political discourse of rights and humane reform that this critical movement spawned. Yet even in this context, the potential dangers of enlightenment were often recognized. Isaiah Berlin, for example, introducing a large collection of Enlightenment writings, praised eighteenth-century philosophy for its critical and rational spirit, but also warned against the desire to become "engineers of human souls and human bodies," an extremely dangerous tendency that ran through much of Enlightenment thought.[11] Even Peter Gay hinted occasionally at the potential dark side of the Enlightenment. In his discussion of the modern, rational perspective of the world Gay explained that the eighteenth-century philosophes, following Newton and the experimental science of the seventeenth century, had self-consciously *limited* the scope of human reason. But this limitation marked a paradoxical turn. As Gay writes, "the philosophes' manner of philosophizing increased man's power by mitigating his claims. This is what Bacon and, after him, the Enlightenment meant by saying we master nature by obeying her."[12]

ENLIGHTENMENT AND DICTATORSHIP

It is difficult to believe that Gay, himself an exile from Nazi Germany, had not read the famous opening lines of Max Horkheimer and

9. See Cassirer's "Kant and the Problem of Metaphysics," trans. Molte S. Gram, in *Kant: Disputed Questions*, ed. Gram (Chicago, 1967), 131–57, where these questions are discussed with reference to Heidegger's own work on Kant.

10. The importance of Heidegger for Cassirer's interpretation of the Enlightenment is well explicated in Daniel Gordon's concise "Ernst Cassirer," in the *Oxford Encyclopedia of the Enlightenment*, ed. Alan Kors et al. (New York, forthcoming).

11. Isaiah Berlin, "Introduction," in *The Great Ages of Western Philosophy*, vol. 4: *The Age of Enlightenment—The Eighteenth-Century Philosophers*, ed. Berlin (New York, 1957), 29.

12. Gay, *Enlightenment*, 1: 186.

Theodor Adorno's version of the "dialectic of Enlightenment"—their book *Dialektik der Aufklärung,* written in Los Angeles and published in Holland in 1947, after circulating in manuscript form since 1944.[13] In their first chapter, "The Concept of Enlightenment," the two authors took aim at precisely this technological domination characteristic of modern scientific rationalism, revealing its rather sinister implications:

> In the most general sense of progressive thought, the Enlightenment has always aimed at liberating men from fear and establishing their sovereignty. Yet the fully enlightened earth radiates disaster triumphant. The program of the Enlightenment was the disenchantment of the world; the dissolution of myths and the substitution of knowledge for fancy.[14]

What follows is a long quote from none other than Bacon, whom Voltaire called the "father of experimental philosophy," as Horkheimer and Adorno note. Their goal is to question this "mastery" of nature, which was, as Gay himself recognized, eventually extended to include mastery of human life itself beginning in the eighteenth century. The two exile writers, in another famous statement, attack the very heart of Gay's Enlightenment vision by showing that this vastly successful mastery is predicated on a fundamentally violent repression of difference and individuality. "Men pay for the increase of their power with alienation from that over which they exercise their power. Enlightenment behaves toward things as a dictator toward men. He knows them in so far as he can manipulate them" (9). The Enlightenment ideal is the system, we are told, which relies on an underlying homogeneity and unity in order to function at all. The modern method of scientific *abstraction* is "totalitarian" because, like the dictator, it understands the object only in terms of the knowing subject, and not as a unique reality. Science must convert the dissimilar into the similar (via quantitative mathematical techniques) in order to impose its rational order on what is, for Horkheimer and Adorno, a fundamentally heterogeneous world. "Abstraction, the tool of Enlightenment, treats its objects as did fate, the notion of which it rejects: it liquidates them" (13).

From this perspective, Enlightenment is no longer confined to its eighteenth-century European form, and functions more or less as a name for human knowledge itself. The techniques of abstraction that one meets in the Scientific Revolution turn out to be merely one stage of the development of an Enlightenment process that begins in myth, or even perhaps

---

13. See James Schmidt, "Language, Mythology, and Enlightenment," *Social Research* 65 (1998): 807–38.

14. Max Horkheimer and Theodor Adorno, *Dialectic of Enlightenment,* trans. John Cumming (London, 1971), 3. Further page references are in the text.

with the intellectual formation of the concept, which itself is linked with the very foundation of human language. Myth is already enlightenment for Horkheimer and Adorno, because myth attempts to explain the unknowable through an abstraction of the unique moment and unique event; myth, like enlightenment and science, attempts to predict what is fundamentally unsystematic and thus unpredictable: nature and the human. The concept is linked with myth because it manifests a similar form of control. "The concept," they write, "has from the beginning been . . . the product of dialectical thinking in which everything is always that which it is, only because it becomes that which it is not"(15). The concept is an aberration, a distortion of the real in a structured framework of the unreal—thought itself, that is.

In the end, Horkheimer and Adorno can define enlightenment as a certain relationship toward error. Enlightenment masters the unknown not by eliminating it so much as *controlling* it; there is no error in the radical sense, for any disruptive element will be made to fit the system, it will be integrated or liquidated—it is mere mistake. Once this systematizing spirit is extended to human social and economic life (and therefore the political life of human beings), the unique individual person is necessarily repressed in order to function as a repeatable element in the machine that is mass society. Enlightenment *creates* a systematic unity of human beings that can then be understood systematically (that is, scientifically), but only once the radical heterogeneity of humanity is forgotten, or more likely destroyed, in the name of correction.

Horkheimer and Adorno suggested that a whole people can be destroyed in an "enlightened" modern society, as the Jews were in Nazi Germany, not because of some genuine confrontation of heterogeneous elements, or even hatred of the other, but because fascism, like enlightenment, projected a delusion of systematicity, a delusion shared by the omnipresent forms of modern technological capitalism. "Jews are being murdered at a time when the Fascist leaders could just as easily replace the anti-Semitic plank in their platform by some other just as workers can be moved from one wholly rationalized production center to another"(207). For enlightenment, the true individual (unique and unrepresentable) is a form of error, a mistake that must be corrected in terms of the system. For Horkheimer and Adorno, the "error" of individuality, sacrificed to the enlightened truth of the conceptual abstraction, must in some ways be redeemed in the postwar world.

The rather esoteric critique of modernity launched by the Frankfurt theorists gained a new kind of power in the 1960s and 1970s, as it became allied with attacks being made against social, political, and intellectual "regimes." From poststructural philosophy came renewed interest in the ungrounded nature of rational totalities, and the critique of "classical" (that is, post-Cartesian) positions on language, self, and society. From feminist theorists came criticism of "patriarchal" reason, a tool that defined as aberrant the feminine processes of thought and understanding. Critical theory in different guises exposed the contradictions of the liberal democratic culture, the myth of individualism and rights, which were now seen as a mere cover for the systematic repressions of alternate identities (of race, for example, as well as class and culture).[15] Postcolonial theory, meanwhile, linked capitalism and Enlightenment philosophy with the "othering" of non-white, non-European civilization.

Not only was the legacy of the Enlightenment in the modern world attacked from a variety of perspectives, but the traditional space for the defense of the Enlightenment vision—intellectual history, that is—had itself become rather marginalized, swept up in a general professional turn to social history, which was often opposed to the elite concerns of the history of ideas. While this turn meant an increased interest in the French Revolution, the Enlightenment was specifically ignored in this context in favor of class or social conflicts. Perhaps the most influential scholar of the Enlightenment in this era was Robert Darnton, whose research on the margins of eighteenth-century intellectual life (pornography, satire, hack writers of Grub Street) served to undermine the authority of the so-called high Enlightenment.[16]

Some of the most influential work on the Enlightenment, understood as an intellectual movement, was done by the French philosopher Michel Foucault, who took Horkheimer and Adorno's conceptual perspective and historicized it in his own account of modernity as the emergence of dominating and repressive institutional norms. Foucault (along with others of this generation) deconstructed the enlightened humanism so dear to scholars such as Gay and Crocker by showing how the "light" of eighteenth-century reform concealed the development of ever more comprehensive systems of control and observation in modern society. Looking at the tight discursive and institutional connections among philosophy, language theory, medicine, penal reform, and economic doctrine, Foucault showed us how the Enlightenment (the "Classical" age, in his terminology) was in effect a period when any individuality or difference was inevitably perceived as deviant, an aberration, and subject

15. An example here is Lucien Goldmann, *The Philosophy of the Enlightenment: The Christian Burgess and the Enlightenment,* trans. Henry Maas (London, 1973), esp. 25–32, on individualism in the eighteenth century.

16. The classic essay is Robert Darnton, "The High Enlightenment and the Low-Life of Literature," which can be found in his *Literary Underground of the Old Regime* (Cambridge, Mass., 1982).

to control or subjugation.[17] This systematic repression was no less severe—just the opposite—for being grounded in a rational scientific methodology. For Foucault, truth and falsity in science were not so much epistemological categories as historically conditioned "distributions"; that is, "the effects of power that different societies and different institutions link to this division" between truth and error.[18] Reason fabricated the very errors that it set out to contain and destroy.

Much sophisticated work in intellectual history and the history of science has emphasized a similar turn in the eighteenth century to "totalitarian" epistemologies. Lorraine Daston, for example, has been charting the emergence of "objectivity" in the Enlightenment in a way that is hardly incompatible with the positions put forward by Horkheimer and Adorno or Foucault. In a work on wonders (written with Katherine Park) Daston shows how "monsters," the aberrant objects of early modern fascination, became normalized and subject to functional standards in the eighteenth century, a move that indicated "a particular view of the natural order as absolutely uniform and not subject to exceptions." The Enlightenment, as Daston explained in an earlier book on the history of probability theory, was obsessed with calculation, even in political and moral domains. This calculation, Daston points out, implied "a system of converting all the possible outcomes to a homogeneous medium that made comparisons of degree possible," a phrase that would not be out of place in *Dialectic of Enlightenment*. This vision of homogeneity was shattered by the trauma of the French Revolution, Daston argued, to be replaced by the idea that error and difference could be accepted as empirical expressions of transcendent realities.[19]

Yet as academic postmodernism took shape in the 1980s and 1990s, especially in the United States, much of the criticism of the Enlightenment moved away from these complex historical questions, toward overly simplistic deconstructions aimed at reaffirming the significance and dignity of what was so often labeled "aberrant" or "deviant" in earlier cultures. Enlightenment was persistently invoked in this context as the originary evil of rational totalitarianism and the demand for absolute

17. The key texts include *The Birth of the Clinic: An Archeology of Medical Perception*, trans. A.M. Sheridan Smith (New York, 1973); *The Order of Things: An Archeology of the Human Sciences* (New York, 1970); and *Discipline and Punish: The Birth of the Prison* (New York, 1979).

18. Michel Foucault, "Introduction," in Georges Canguilhem, *On the Normal and the Pathological*, trans. Carolyn R. Fawcett with Robert S. Cohen (Dordrecht, 1978), xix–xx.

19. Lorraine Daston and Katherine Park, *Wonders and the Order of Nature, 1150–1750* (New York, 1998), 205; Lorraine Daston, *Classical Probability in the Enlightenment* (Princeton, 1988), 376.

uniformity.[20] This postmodern critique at times reached the level of absurdity—witness the book *Hitler as Philosophe,* John Gray's sweeping dismissal of enlightenment and modernity, and Jonathan Glover's effort to link figures such as Pol Pot and Stalin to Enlightenment humanism.[21] Of course, "Enlightenment" was often rather loosely defined (and usually poorly understood) in many of these fashionable arguments.[22]

It is important to note, though, that in this mad rush to denigrate the Enlightenment and the errant madness of "reason," and to rehabilitate the repressed margins or silenced "aberrations" that were seen as the victims of modernity, an important question was being evaded. How could we ever recreate a world based on the rejection of reason and enlightenment?

THE RETURN TO ENLIGHTENMENT

As Horkheimer and Adorno saw so clearly, the world of the Enlightenment, with all its defects and dangers, is still our own world, and not some aberration that could be corrected and then replaced by some simplistic pluralism, deconstructive irony, or a return to unsystematic thinking (whatever that might be). While condemning enlightenment, the two German exiles did not believe that it was an isolated pathology that could be fought with a particular cure. "They did not seal off the life-worlds and death-worlds of the twentieth century into separate compartments. . . . They took seriously the presence of violence in the midst of civility."[23] In *Dialectic of Enlightenment,* the very evil of enlightenment, the threat of conceptual abstraction, the unreality of thought, are perennial dangers. Although exiled from their own culture, Horkheimer and Adorno did not (unlike so many postmodern intellec-

20. An example: "Nothing is so simple that it avoids being cross listed on complex grids of overlapping taxonomies, or so complex that its intricacies cannot be clearly diagrammed": Grant Holly, "The Allegory in Realism," in *Enlightening Allegory: Theory, Practice, and Contexts of Allegory in the Late Seventeenth and Eighteenth Centuries,* ed. Kevin L. Cope (New York, 1992), 150.

21. Lawrence Birken, *Hitler as Philosophe: Remnants of the Enlightenment in National Socialism* (Westport, Conn., 1995); John Gray, *Enlightenment's Wake: Politics and Culture at the Close of the Modern Age* (London, 1996); Jonathan Glover, *Humanity: A Moral History of the Twentieth Century* (London, 1999).

22. Recent critical surveys of this literature include James Schmidt, "Civility, Enlightenment, and Society," *American Political Science Review* 92 (1998): 419–27; and Daniel Gordon, "On the Supposed Obsolescence of the French Enlightenment," *Historical Reflections/Réflexions historiques* 25 (1999): 365–85.

23. Michael Geyer, "Germany, or, The Twentieth Century as History," *South Atlantic Quarterly* 96 (1997): 671–72.

tuals) exempt themselves from responsibility for its effects. What they were suggesting, however tentatively, was not the elimination of some Enlightenment other, a celebration of errancy opposed to truth, but rather the rediscovery of our own modernity and the refashioning of enlightenment as a self-conscious and therefore undeluded and less murderous mode of being. It is often forgotten, especially by the postmodern critics who obsessively quote *Dialectic of Enlightenment*'s most denunciatory aphoristic passages, that this famous book was conceived as the first of two volumes. The sequel to *Dialectic of Enlightenment*, never written, was supposed to outline a "positive" program that would, in the words of Horkheimer, "rescue" enlightenment for the modern world.[24]

The "illness" of reason itself, Adorno once suggested, must play a role in this rediscovery.[25] Adorno's new "dialectic of Enlightenment" turned out to be a theory of *negative* dialectic, one that tried to preserve the essential "nonidentity" of the content that is subsumed by the unifying powers of the concept and of language. It is especially interesting, in this context, to note that although Adorno continued to criticize eighteenth-century formulations of the rational concept in *Negative Dialectics*, he also used as an example of his own critical method one of the major representatives of Enlightenment thought, the *Encyclopédie* of Diderot and d'Alembert. Adorno wrote that "Encyclopedic thinking—rationally organized yet discontinuous, unsystematic, loose—expressed the self-critical spirit of reason."[26] This self-critical spirit, an Enlightenment without content, was an Enlightenment capable of living in the postmodern world. Even Foucault's late essay on the Enlightenment explicitly resurrected this eighteenth-century ideal of "criticism," as has the work of another arch postmodern philosopher, Richard Rorty.[27] Enlightenment reason as a negative force might be recuperated.

Like Adorno, Horkheimer looked for ways of reconceptualizing the Enlightenment. Although he never fully developed the idea, Horkheimer suggested that the function of speech in human life might be reconsidered. If language could never be an adequate representation of some reality, given its radical *unreality* as thought (as outlined in *Dialectic of Enlightenment*), it could, as a specifically human capacity, open up certain humanistic possibilities. "To speak to someone," wrote Hork-

24. Schmidt, "Language, Mythology, and Enlightenment," 811.
25. Ibid., 822.
26. Theodor Adorno, *Negative Dialectics*, trans. E. B. Ashton (New York, 1973), 29.
27. See Michel Foucault, "What Is Enlightenment?" trans. Catherine Porter, in *The Foucault Reader*, ed. Paul Rabinow (New York, 1984), 32–50; Richard Rorty, *Contingency, Irony, and Solidarity* (Cambridge, 1989).

heimer to Adorno in 1941, "is, basically, to recognize them as a possible member of the future association of free human beings. Speech establishes a shared relation to truth, and is therefore the innermost affirmation of another existence."[28] The authors of *Dialectic of Enlightenment*, then, "did not lose hope in enlightenment—not as relentless progress toward a perfect world, but as infinite struggle for public-mindedness as the source of all liberty."[29] As some people are now arguing, this fundamental "recognition" of the other as human (via the capacity of speech and reason) is the genuine legacy of the Enlightenment, one that needs to be defended in a modern world suffused with the often antihumanistic norms and obligations of technological nation-states. Jürgen Habermas, most famously, has continually called for the completion of the Enlightenment project, even though he relentlessly criticized the limitations of eighteenth-century bourgeois notions of reason and universality.[30] Habermas, in a way not dissimilar to Horkheimer and Adorno's, sees the danger of enlightenment in the temptation to substitute a particular conceptual organization for a universal "reality." However, the *promise* of enlightenment lies in the ideal of a genuine consensus based on a shared understanding, a consensus of independent rational individuals. In this public space, the coercive demands of social, political, and economic systems could be excluded (even if they could never be eliminated).

Partly as a result of Habermas's own more philosophical work on reason and the spaces of the public sphere, the Enlightenment as an object of historical study has undergone some important transformations. Instead of focusing on the instrumental reason that postmodern intellectuals like to target, cultural and intellectual historians have looked more and more to the actual practices and institutions of sociability and discourse in the Enlightenment, to see how modern ideals of consensus can be traced back to eighteenth-century forms.[31] Work on salons, democratic societies, coffeehouse culture, Masonic lodges, newspapers, publishing networks, and other forms of the public sphere, has shown that the Enlightenment cannot be reduced to certain privileged theoretical

28. Quoted and translated in Schmidt, "Language, Mythology, and Enlightenment," 823.

29. Geyer, "Germany," 672.

30. Jürgen Habermas, *The Structural Transformation of the Public Sphere: An Inquiry into the Category of Bourgeois Society,* trans. Thomas Burger with Frederick Lawrence (Cambridge, Mass., 1989).

31. See the essays in W. Daniel Wilson and Robert C. Holub, eds., *Impure Reason: Dialectic of Enlightenment in Germany* (Detroit, 1993), pt. 1, "Twentieth-Century Critiques of Enlightenment."

texts or epistemological procedures.[32] Clearly, though, the rehabilitation of Enlightenment sociability evades the serious question posed by Horkheimer and Adorno: What caused the turn from enlightenment to mass death in the modern world? Is violence something that can be framed only as the unpredictable irruption of error? The Manichean vision of history is preserved here.

In a somewhat different move, scholars sympathetic to the postmodern perspective have looked again at Enlightenment intellectual culture and, resisting a simplistic condemnation, have revealed eighteenth-century culture to be marked by subversion, dialogue, and often very unsystematic intellectual play. If postmodernists such as Lyotard, for example, rejected the *grands récits* of modern progress that are supposed to have originated in the Enlightenment, others can show in great detail how certain key Enlightenment figures constantly subverted the coherence of narrative in favor of the unique and unrepeatable moment.[33] The postmodern critics, in other words, have not looked closely enough at the eighteenth century. While "aberrations in language, body, and imagery incarnated unenlightenment in the Age of Enlightenment," and many rational philosophes did think that reason should cut through error and superstition, for an alternative visual culture the paradigm of totality was merely "phantasmal," and error was not condemned as "irrational erring" but instead celebrated as "errant knowledge pursuing the free-hand filigrees of life."[34] Other Enlightenment specialists have shown how error could be understood as an "epistemological tool."[35] Even the most rational enlightenment can be redefined in a way that echoes the postmodernism of its most persistent critics: the Enlightenment is not so much the imposition of monological totalitarianism as "the recognition that a labyrinth is perpetually available within the most

---

32. Some of the best work in this area includes Dena Goodman, *The Republic of Letters: A Cultural History of the French Enlightenment* (Ithaca, 1994); Margaret Jacob, *Living the Enlightenment: Freemasonry and Politics in Eighteenth-Century Europe* (New York and Oxford, 1991); Joan Landes, *Women and the Public Sphere in the Age of Enlightenment* (Ithaca, 1988); Daniel Gordon, *Citizens without Sovereignty: Equality and Sociability in French Thought, 1670–1789* (Princeton, 1994); Mona Ozouf, "'Public Opinion' at the End of the Old Regime," *Journal of Modern History* 60, Supplement (1988): 3–21. For a broader view, see Thomas Kaiser, "This Strange Offspring of *Philosophie*: Recent Historiographical Problems in Relating the Enlightenment to the French Revolution," *French Historical Studies* 15 (1988): 549–62.

33. Thomas Kavanagh, *Esthetics of the Moment: Literature and Art in the French Enlightenment* (Philadelphia, 1996).

34. Barbara Maria Stafford, *Body Criticism: Imaging the Unseen in Enlightenment Art and Medicine* (Cambridge, Mass., 1991), 36, 82, 205–6, 209, 213.

35. Wilda Anderson, "Error in Buffon," *MLN* 114 (1999): 701.

carefully conceived geometric space, within every system and every language; that within the general system, fiction and seduction are ineluctably bound to knowledge of self and of the world." In its very "complexity and instability," then, the systematic discourse of the Enlightenment harbored its own "potential subversiveness."[36]

This rediscovery of the complexity of the Enlightenment, and especially the Enlightenment's own sense of its complexity, is in one sense a welcome turn in intellectual and cultural history. Still, much of the recent postmodern rehabilitation of the Enlightenment, like the rehabilitation of its inherent sociability, has been aimed at showing that enlightenment is *not* responsible for the "totalitarian" logic of modernity invoked by so many of its critics. Again, this means that we are still faced with the question of violence. A sociable, complex, antisystematic Enlightenment, defined by its indeterminacy and open-endedness, is effectively distanced from the violence of the French Revolution and the violence of modernity itself. Violence becomes an *aberration* of the newly defined Enlightenment project, an irruption of the antimodern. We are left with an unsatisfactory set of options: while the critics of the Enlightenment fail to explain the very real value of rationality in the modern world even as they locate the origin of its essential violence, the recent rehabilitation of the Enlightenment, like the earlier liberal interpretation of the period, is marked by a refusal even to think about the relationship of reason, sociability, and violence.

ERROR AND ENLIGHTENMENT

This is exactly the point where my own study of error will trace a new path. Error introduces an undeniable complexity in eighteenth-century thought, but I will show how this very complexity prepares the way for the conflict generated in the political and social spheres in the French Revolution. Rather than tracing that extreme conflict and subsequent violence to some pathological spirit of rational systematicity, or alternatively seeing violence as necessarily the manifestation of the irrational, I am suggesting that the Enlightenment concept of error can help explain the intimate juxtaposition of deadly violence and idealism. The recognition of error, the awareness of the essential risk of human inquiry, made dogmatic claims of total and absolute truth impossible. But Enlightenment error did not lead to a peaceful pluralism, for the essential *promise* of error, its potential as a site of truth's appearance, meant that

---

36. Julie C. Hayes, *Reading the French Enlightenment: System and Subversion* (Cambridge, 1999), 191, 21.

whatever the dangers, some concrete space for truth must be discovered and protected from any adversaries.

The confrontation with error in French thought traced in the following chapters awakened a desire to control the most dangerous extremes of aberration, even as the *mark* of aberration—truth itself—remained profoundly mysterious. The Enlightenment faced the challenge of human error and forged a novel epistemology, one that inhabited a space between certainty and ignorance. The logic of Enlightenment error made conflict inevitable. The boundaries of error, marked only by the borders of truth itself, were never given in advance. And yet the promise of truth demanded an attempt to forge a path, to cut through established zones of knowledge and interest, despite the lack of any foundational legitimation.

So even as the revolutionaries sought political truth in 1789, as heirs to the Enlightenment they knew that this truth was anything but simple and straightforward. The life-and-death conflicts of the Revolution were, in many ways, conflicts over what path, what kind of preparation, would lead to this elusive truth. Tracing the political variants of the Enlightenment concept of error, we will see that revolutionaries in France knew that political forms had to be constructed not according to some model of truth but with the problem of error at the center. It was understood by many political figures, who represented a variety of political and social perspectives, that the inevitable gap between the "people" and the state created the potential for deviation or aberration. Yet without the state, the people's voice lacked a clear organ. So revolutionary politicians faced a version of the epistemological problem of error and "progress." How to identify and correct error in the absence of any normative guide? In politics as in epistemology, the necessity of investigation and judgment was predicated on the absence of the goal itself. And yet, as we will see, the potential error haunting any concrete political form held out the hope for future success, even as it made pathological deviation possible. Politics, in the early phases of the Revolution at least, was about creating and defending spaces that would protect the nation from unproductive error as much as possible, even while it was acknowledged that any political truth (however defined) was never given in advance.

The failures of the Revolution, or at least the perceived failures of this violent and deadly era, provoked a radical rethinking of truth and error. But as my analysis of certain counter-revolutionary thinkers will show, what was rejected in this period was not the complex Enlightenment structure linking error with truth but instead the specific paths to truth adopted and defended in eighteenth-century philosophy and later in revolutionary political theory and practice. For those living through the traumatic and disruptive revolutionary period, those who experienced—directly or not—the constant violence of the revolutionary *journées*, the civil wars, the Terror, the destructive European wars that dragged on for years and years, and the often brutal realities of Napoleonic conquest, any interest in the subtleties of early revolutionary political thought soon yielded to an overwhelming concern with suffering and death. The reaction to the French Revolution, one that laid the foundations for both conservative and Romantic doctrines in the nineteenth century, is usually understood as a break from the Enlightenment and especially its faith in human reason as a social and political tool— the eighteenth-century position that was taken up, in modified form, by the liberals and social scientists of the nineteenth century. In numerous ways, the values and the intellectual assumptions of counter-revolutionary reactionary thinkers are of course in stark contrast to those of earlier Enlightenment figures. Separated by the rupture of the Revolution, these two eras mark an obvious break in intellectual history. Still, by following the conceptual thread of error through these reactionary forms of thought, it is possible to see early responses to the violence of Revolution as a *transformation* of sorts of the Enlightenment understanding of truth and error.

The essential structural relationship between error and truth developed in eighteenth-century thought persists in radically new contexts in the postrevolutionary era. Specifically, the idea of living in error while seeking an endlessly deferred truth became, in early nineteenth-century thought, an explicitly historical concept. The violence of the Revolution, for example, came to be seen as a kind of punishment for error on a grand social scale. Here, whole nations, humanity itself even, were understood to be in error, yet still on the way to truth in the stages of historical development. And here again, in this radically new context, intellectuals looked to exploit the elusive but very real link between concrete forms of error and the absent truth that would be capable of defining it. In key French writers such as Maistre and Ballanche, for example, theological structures of thought mask some essential continuities with Enlightenment philosophical discourse and revolutionary concepts. Subsequent developments like the turn to the historical specificity of error, so important to nineteenth-century philosophy from Hegel on, or the emergence of statistical models in mathematics and sociology, where truth reveals itself only through a mathematical analysis of concrete error and aberration, all of these can be linked to eighteenth-century conceptualizations of the symbiotic relation between error and truth.

Error in the Enlightenment was defined as the aberration from something that *must itself remain absent*. If there is of course no error without a truth to define it, at the same time there is no need to think about truth in the absence of error. As the site of both risk and promise, a moment of both the negation and the incarnation of truth, error was inherently unstable and subject to multiple interpretations. There is no one exemplary figure of the Enlightenment in my account, because the *structure* of error is the real subject of analysis here. By tracing the variations of error in French thought, we can see how the Enlightenment's secular faith in an absent truth generated differing, even opposing conceptions of knowledge. The Enlightenment was therefore not about consensus, it was not about systematic unity, and it was not about the deployment of instrumental reason: what was developed in the Enlightenment was a modern idea of truth defined by error, a modern idea of knowledge defined by failure, conflict, and risk, but also hope.

CHAPTER 2

Wandering in the Space of Knowledge

W hen we read eighteenth-century French texts, it is striking how many Enlightenment figures address the most crucial epistemological questions by using topographical metaphors and imagery. The philosophical forms of "error" can, as a result, hardly be disentangled from the complex imagery that articulates what might be called a space of knowledge in this period, that moment when error seems to be specifically identified as the one true enemy of truth. The epistemological implications of these powerful and dominant metaphorical systems need to be carefully unraveled if the problem of truth and error is to be properly understood. To understand the topographical complexities of eighteenth-century *erreur*, its linguistically dense history needs to be taken into account, for error, through much of its history, was not necessarily linked with conceptions of truth (*vérité*).[1] Error was not, in fact, even exclusively framed as an intellectual operation.

ERROR AND ERRANCY

Historically and etymologically, the French words associated with error (the noun *erreur*, the verb *errer*, and the adjective *errant*) are connected less with the idea of discrete mental mistakes than with the very real action of wandering. And it is very important to note that *er-*

---

1. It is interesting to note that the Latin *verus*, the root of *vérité* in French, "veritable" in English, and *Wahrheit* in German, originally seems to have meant simply "not false," according to the *Dictionnaire étymologique de la langue latine: Histoire des mots* (Paris, 1932), s.v. "verus." Truth emerges conceptually only when the counterfeit is recognized.

rare, the Latin root of "error" in all its forms, originally meant two quite different things: first, "to go this way and that, to walk at random," and also, in a crucial variation, "to go off the track, to go astray," with the subsequent extension "to be mistaken."[2] There is, etymologically, an ambivalence at the heart of error, a tension, that is, between merely aimless wandering and a more specific aberration from some path. This often repressed ambivalence has, in fact, significant implications for the epistemological forms of error in France, for this etymological complexity did not at all disappear over the course of the historical development of specifically French linguistic forms of "error." Even in a dictionary of modern French, for example, *erreur* can still be defined as a "sinuous and unpredictable path [*parcours*]."[3] And in the early modern period, the words associated with error signified to a much greater extent than today an actual movement in space; only metaphorically, or derivatively, did error come to mean a wandering of the mind or a straying from truth. In the sixteenth century, not only could the word *erreur,* for example, denote "the action of erring this way and that," as in the original Latin form *errare,* it would also be used to denote "an excursion," or "a voyage involving adventures."[4] Error in France was not, in the early modern period at least, wholly determined by the epistemological structure of truth. Error had a certain independence conceptually, and this meant that error was not always deployed in an entirely negative context once it migrated into the epistemological terrain.

By the time we reach the seventeenth century, definitions of *erreur* do become more psychologically rooted, dominated by references to intellectual aberrations, defined by normative standards—error is "taking true for false (or vice versa); illusion; mistake." And yet at the same time, error is still being defined as "a vagabondage of the imagination, of the mind that is not subject to any rule."[5] Clearly the etymological traces of spatial errancy persist here in this psychological context. *Erreur* is still understood to be a very concrete mode of travel, an actual movement of wandering or deviation—the epistemological idea of error cannot but rely heavily on this "proper" sense of the term. Quite literally, then, error is originally not at all a static or parasitic concept, defined simply as a distance from truth. The vitality of error as a kind of motion is even more apparent in the history of the word *errant,* which is a complex linguistic form that in fact conceals two distinct roots: both the Latin *iterare* (to

2. *Grand Larousse de la langue française,* 6 vols. (Paris, 1972), s.v. "erreur." Cf. *OED,* s.v. "error."
3. *Trésor de la langue française (1789–1960)* (Paris, 1985), s.v. "erreur."
4. *Grand Larousse,* s.v. "erreur."
5. Ibid.

journey) and *errare* (to stray).[6] The two most powerful early examples of the use of "errant" reveal just how ambivalent the attitude was toward this "wandering journey." The *chevalier errant*, or "knight errant," for example, traveled in quest of some great goal, his journey a heroic effort in the face of great dangers. In contrast, the wandering Jew (*juif errant*) literally embodied, for Christian Europeans, the individual separated from the truth, condemned to wander with no redemption, no final goal. The journey was entirely unproductive, a punishment and not an opportunity for insight. Only later, in the seventeenth century, did the word "errant" become a noun that indicated a person who had "deviated" from truth.[7] Still, as late as 1778, in that year's edition of the dictionary of the French Academy, though the "errant" individual was defined as one who is literally "in error" in matters of faith, he is also, possibly, someone who just simply "travels ceaselessly." And *errer* still means "to wander [*vaguer*, the root of "vagabond"] from side to side, to go here and there *à l'aventure*," as the entry puts it, implying at least the possibility of reward.[8] The hidden duality of error, a duality that persists into the modern period, hinges on this crucial distinction between "wandering" and "deviation."

THE LIGHT OF REASON AND THE GHOSTLY FORMS OF ERROR

In the French Enlightenment, the progress of philosophical inquiry was likened to the blazing of new trails and the mapping (not to mention conquest and exploitation) of territory. Significantly, truth was not a possession but instead a destination. This perspective on knowledge greatly complicated the approaches to intellectual aberrations. Here the problem of error could be framed in two very different ways. On the one hand, it is possible to see the destruction of prejudice and superstition, the elimination of entrenched errors, as an Enlightenment effort to destroy illegitimate and fanciful "maps," so that they could be replaced with careful and accurate representations constructed only after extensive, and often collaborative, exploration. Yet on the other hand, Enlightenment philosophers faced the challenge of entering radically unknown and dangerous zones of inquiry in this epistemological topography. In this context, error emerged as a more complex difficulty. No longer simply the mistaken map that had to be replaced, error was un-

---

6. See *OED*, s.v. "errant," where the French forms of this word are discussed in detail.
7. *Grand Larousse*, s.v. "errant(e)."
8. *Dictionnaire de l'Académie française*, 2 vols. (Nismes, 1778), s.v. "errant(e)" and "errer."

derstood to be a kind of errancy, a more radical wandering that threatened the journey of discovery. As Locke once noted, human reason is a light that does not lead us "straight and without fail" toward the truth—literally, in Latin, without any error (*sine omni errore*)—but it does help us achieve a certain level of certainty without any external aid whatsoever.[9] The light of reason is linked significantly with both the risk of error and the promise of truth. Truth is the destination of a potentially errant journey, a journey guided only by the limited illumination of the human mind. True exploration began without a clear vision of the destination. The leap into the unknown constituted a genuine risk. In this space, without any guide, wandering could not really be defined in a systematic way. If human reason could dissipate certain kinds of errors, those "missteps" of past thought, Enlightenment thought also recognized that the mind, with its limited scope, was always threatened by a tendency to stray from the proper path. The challenge for eighteenth-century thinkers was to find a way to control or even exploit these more radical aberrations of enlightenment. Here I will trace, in the metaphorical spaces of epistemological inquiry, a certain line of thought that revealed how the "errancy" of the intellect was in fact closely connected with its ability to discover new paths to truth.

The Enlightenment's epistemological confrontation with error was a direct result of a reconceptualization of truth taking place as European intellectuals experienced severe disorder in their world. In many ways, Enlightenment thought was a response to a profound intellectual crisis occasioned by political, religious, and civil disruptions. The emergence of modern science, for example, a development that prepared the way for the Enlightenment, had shattered the long-established and intimate connections among God, nature, and human experience, however these were defined in various eras and milieus. So while the new mathematical models of natural law may have opened up truly revolutionary insights, they also had the effect of alienating the human mind from the immediacy of nature and the very presence of the divine "signature." Nature was transformed, no longer a book to be read but a complex text that had to be carefully translated into a series of quantitative signs to be understood at all. Of course, right through the seventeenth century, reason was considered a divine gift, and this reading of nature was still a privileged act. The insights of the human mind could, for many pre-En-

9. John Locke, *Essays on the Law of Nature*, ed. W. von Leyden (Oxford, 1988), 123 (Latin text 122).

lightenment thinkers, establish a firm foundation for explanatory systems rigorously deduced from these conceptual origins. The problem, of course—one that became particularly acute by the seventeenth century—was that these rigorous systems of thought (whether philosophical, political, theological, or scientific) were constantly being questioned and their universality was being undermined by contradictory insights. Agreement on first principles was noticeably lacking. Significantly, the last great efforts to salvage the deductive system of knowledge tried valiantly to use this very disagreement as a new certain origin. Descartes, for example, argued that the very instability of opinion at least guaranteed the existence of the thinking subject, which could found a new system of thought, while Hobbes, in a similar fashion, declared that the very relativity of human sensual experience was itself a certain proposition that could lead to a rigorously deduced political philosophy. However, the gradual dominance of a whole new epistemological framework cleared the way for the Enlightenment.

For theologically oriented "rationalists" like Descartes and his follower Malebranche, sensory experience from the material body was considered with suspicion; it was something that could cloud reason or induce error, and was perhaps an essential limit to human knowledge. For the experimental science of the late seventeenth century, however, this experience became the very origin of all knowledge. Reason had the new role of *organizing* the data of experience. According to this new epistemology, reason did not gain insight into pure disembodied truths; rather, it illuminated empirical observations in order to discover a truth inherent in the operations of the world itself.[10] Reason was essentially secondary and thus instrumental. The earliest expressions of the Enlightenment, for example in Voltaire's work, were popularizations and generalizations of this empirical methodology. Increasingly, Enlightenment thought effected a transformation of Newtonian scientific methodology into a comprehensive theory of mind and nature.[11] The Enlightenment recast the foundations of knowledge that had guided inquiry for centuries: the search for certainties was replaced by the notion of the ongoing path of probabilities. It was possible to map out the contours of the natural world without an a priori vision of the whole. Although this is not usually recognized by scholars of the period, the Enlightenment idea

10. See Simon Schaffer and Steven Shapin, *Leviathan and the Air-Pump: Hobbes, Boyle, and the Experimental Life* (Princeton, 1985).
11. A process well explicated in Keith M. Baker, *Condorcet: From Natural Philosophy to Social Science* (Chicago, 1975), esp. pt. 1.

of indefinite progress was in fact grounded on the inevitability of error and the provisionality of all "truth."[12] The desire for a complete, higher truth was in fact scorned in the eighteenth century as a ridiculous product of passion. Those who sought these heights were criticized as "the men who walk in the shadows."[13] The genuine philosopher was someone who worked his way patiently and methodically through the intellectual wilds.

But *how* did the mind move through this epistemological wilderness toward new truths? During the Enlightenment, as we see in so many visual and metaphorical representations, the light of reason would guide the way, gently dissipating the mists and shadows of error and superstition.[14] However, like the theologian who must explain both the nature of good and the presence of evil, Enlightenment philosophers of truth had to account for what caused the mind to stray from the methodical path—and the eighteenth century was, in a profound way, obsessed with error, the darker side of understanding.[15] Inevitably, the sharp distinction between the light of reason and the shadow of error would break down. Within this topographical frame, the mind did not simply move out of error and into truth in one singular movement. The mind, according to many thinkers, was easily misled by deceptive appearances as it moved into unmapped territory. In the metaphorical landscape, the mind could be led astray by something called *false* lights. The baron d'Holbach, one of the more radical philosophers of the French Enlightenment, pointed this out in his *Système de la nature*. He noted that errors should be considered to be more than mere obstacles or veils, easily distinguished from the light of rational insight. Errors, he said, are better understood to be ghostlike *forms* of truth and highly deceptive for that reason. Errors did not just refract or obscure light, they often imitated it, much like "those misleading lights travelers encounter during the night," as Holbach wrote. (These lights, in French known as *feux follets*, or "foolish fires," a

12. An exception is Jean Ehrard, *L'idée de nature en France dans la première moitié du XVIIIᵉ siècle*, 2 vols. (Paris, 1963), 1: 759.

13. *Encyclopédie*, s.v. "philosophe," 12: 509.

14. See Rolf Reichardt, "Light against Darkness: The Visual Representations of a Central Enlightenment Concept," *Representations* 61 (1998): 95–148.

15. See Balduin Schwarz, *Der Irrtum in der Philosophie: Untersuchungen über das Wesen, die Formen und die psychologische Genese des Irrtums im Bereiche der Philosophie; mit einem Überlick über die Geschicte der Irrtumsproblematik in der abendländischen Philosophie* (Münster, 1934), 275–77. Another history of error written at this time is Leo W. Keeler, *The Problem of Error from Plato to Kant: A Historical and Critical Study* (Rome, 1934); the French Enlightenment is completely ignored in this survey. Victor Brochard, in his *De l'erreur* (Paris, 1879), offers a similarly limited historical approach, but has a remarkably rich conceptual understanding of the philosophical problem of error.

translation of the Latin *ignus fatui*, are phosphorescent particles that recede as one approaches, only to disappear and reappear with alarming unpredictability.[16]) Although Holbach advised, rather sensibly, that "it is important to destroy unworldly illusions that only lead us astray,"[17] there remained the immense difficulty of figuring out how to recognize the misleading light—how to distinguish it, in other words, from the genuine illumination of rational thought.

At this critical juncture, Holbach's text is not very helpful. We are in error, he says, "when we suppose nonexistent beings to exist."[18] Holbach returned to this problem in another text, again noting that truth consists in "seeing things such as they are." Error he defined as "the opposition of our judgments with the nature of things."[19] But of course the problem is that these ghosts of truth, the "hideous phantoms and seductive chimeras"[20] that are the structures of error, lead us astray precisely because they look so much like the truth. Ghosts, as the *Encyclopédie* tells us, are "images that make us imagine corporeal bodies outside of us that are not at all there." These complex images, it is suggestively noted, are caused by both light and shadow, and cannot be easily dissipated by any one source of illumination.[21]

In the complex epistemological topography marked out in Enlightenment philosophical texts, error is a dangerous deception because it induces errancy, by seducing us away from the path to truth. Error is explicitly defined in this way in the *Encyclopédie*. There it is said that error is "a wandering of the mind that induces it to make a false judgment."[22] Error is not the actual mistake but a more complex form of intellectual errancy. These various aberrations, described in the *Encyclopédie* as, once again, "specters and phantoms," are a kind of "contagion" that afflicts weak minds (the old, the young, females) most severely. But no mind is really immune. Following Bacon's earlier description of the different "idols" of the understanding, the Encyclopedists say here that the human mind is like a "magic mirror" that disfigures the objects of our perception, presenting us with only "shadows and monsters."[23] Error results when human minds "take shadows or the appearance of things for

---

16. *Encyclopédie*, s.v. "feu," 6: 613.

17. Baron d'Holbach, *Système de la nature, ou Des lois du monde physique et du monde morale*, 2 vols. (Paris, 1821), 1: v–vi.

18. Holbach, *Système de la nature* (London [i.e., Paris], 1771), 141.

19. Holbach, *La morale universelle* (Amsterdam, 1776), 44.

20. Holbach, *Système de la nature* (1771), 453.

21. *Encyclopédie*, s.v. "fantôme," 6: 404.

22. Ibid., s.v. "erreur," 5: 910.

23. Ibid., s.v. "préjugé," 13: 284.

the things themselves, and the phantom formed for the truth they believe they discern."[24] For this reason, truth must be something that can overcome this congenital aberration. Unfortunately, this kind of clarity is fleeting. "Truth shines sometimes amid our confused and contradictory notions, but it lasts only an instant, like the sun at midday, in the sense that one sees it without being able to seize it or follow its course." Again, we find this complex imagery: the light of the truth is hidden despite the light, for the error deceives the mind with its own play of light.[25] This is made explicit in the *Encyclopédie* article on metaphysical truth. There it is said that truth consists in "perceiving things as they are in themselves"; yet it is also admitted that just as "strong daylight [*le grand jour*] is less conducive to the theatrical performance than the lamp [*lumière*], so for most men *truth* is less pleasurable than error."[26] There is, perhaps, something overwhelming about the brilliant clarity of truth. Living as we do in the shadowy world of uncertainty, we find the phantoms of error and the "feeble and imperfect glow" of opinion actually easier to behold.[27]

It is not surprising, then, that the genuine philosophe, the one who loves truth and seeks it out, is someone who can heroically avoid the deceptions of error; who resists, that is, the appearance of the phantoms that may lead away from truth, however promising these images may appear in the darkness. "Truth, for the philosophe, is not a mistress that corrupts his imagination, and that he believes he finds everywhere; he is contented with the ability to disentangle it where he perceives it." This rather mythical figure is therefore able to distinguish clearly between the true, the doubtful, and the deceptive. This emblematic Enlightenment traveler, who "walks in the night, but . . . is preceded by a torch,"[28] will not be led astray by those misleading *feux follets* that are in German called *Irrlichten,* or "err-lights."

In this rather dangerous topography, this torch is obviously critical to epistemological success. Yet the torch is also highly problematic. For Enlightenment philosophers, the torch of human reason was a rather limited tool, defined as the ability to organize experience gained from concrete sensory observations. As the great mathematician and encyclopedist d'Alembert once wrote, the general instrument of logic, the process of ordering thought and sensations, was the "torch that must guide us" in the pursuit of knowledge.[29] But how was it possible to be *preceded*

24. Ibid., s.v. "vraissemblance," 17: 483.
25. Ibid., s.v. "préjugé," 13: 285.
26. Ibid., s.v. "vérité métaphysique," 17: 71.
27. See ibid., s.v. "opinion," 11: 507.
28. Ibid., s.v. "philosophe," 12: 509.
29. Jean Le Rond d'Alembert, *Essai sur les éléments de philosophie, ou Sur les principes des connoissances humaines,* in *Oeuvres de d'Alembert* (Geneva, 1967), 1: 180.

by a torch that in effect organizes, only *after* the fact, these experiences of the intellect? If we reflect on this image, we see that the philosophe celebrated in the *Encyclopédie* seems to be walking backward.

D'Alembert, for one, did not evade this rather strange predicament. In his own work on the philosophical foundations of knowledge, he carefully followed all of the implications suggested by this particular spatial metaphor. He ended up suggesting that the ideal philosopher is in fact one who is at least figuratively blind, and therefore able to explore the spaces of knowledge in the most limited, and hence most circumspect, way. The "light" of reason was paradoxically described here as a kind of productive blindness. The intellect, so constructed, would be able to avoid all the dangerous effects of any luminescent "phantom." The desire for the direct illumination of foundational "first truths" is in fact, for d'Alembert, the very origin of intellectual aberration.

> The human mind, occupied for so long by a search for these first truths, probing a thousand paths to achieve success, not finding them, and tiring itself out in sheer wasted effort by turning on itself in this way, resembles a criminal locked up in a shadowy cell, unnecessarily spinning around in all directions to find an exit, and yet dimly perceiving a feeble light through some narrow and tortuous cracks that he tries in vain to widen. If there are in these shadows some objects scattered here and there that might possibly strike us, it is only by touch, and consequently quite imperfectly, that we can know them, moreover we must approach them only step by step, and with a wise and careful circumspection; by throwing ourselves on these objects, we would risk being injured by them and knowing them only through the pain they would make us feel. Sadi recounts that someone asked the wise Lochman to whom he owed his wisdom: *To the blind,* responded this Indian philosopher, *who do not step any place without being assured of the solidity of the earth.*[30]

As another Enlightenment text would put it, only the blind man knows his way in the fog.[31] Instead of being seduced by deceptive imagery, philosophers assured themselves by limiting their exploration to touch, which can never be deceived in this way (at least in this metaphorical topography). Crucial here is the awareness of limitation, and the willingness to suspend all judgment in the absence of solid evidence. As d'Alembert advised, the method of enlightenment consists in making solid connections between actual observations, "of not filling in by a false genealogy the places where connection is lacking, of imitating, fi-

30. Ibid., 148.
31. Saint-Hyacinthe [Hyacinthe Cordonnier], *Recherches philosophiques, sur la nécessité de s'assurer soi-même de la vérité* (London [i.e., Paris], 1743), 9–10.

nally, those geographers who, detailing known regions with care on their maps, do not at all fear leaving empty spaces in place of unknown lands."[32]

Evaded here is what this radical step into the unknown entails. The blind know their way in the fog only because they have traveled the same route in advance. In unknown territory, the blind step, however small, is fraught with risk. D'Alembert's prisoner must in fact risk injury, because any movement of exploration in this dark cell is a radically uncertain leap. Precisely because of this condition, however, it is hardly surprising that this prisoner seeks to follow the glow of light, however feeble, that enters the cell. The terror of being lost in any forbidding dark space forces the mind to move forward and escape; fear is what induces us to follow these phantom lights, in the hope that they may guide us out of the constricted obscurity. As Holbach noted, "solitude, the obscurity of the forest, the silence and shadows of the night . . . are for every man . . . objects of terror."[33] And there, "lost in the forest in the middle of the night, I have only a small lamp to guide me," the light of reason, as Diderot once noted.[34]

D'Alembert considerably complicates this predicament in a remarkable passage of his earlier "Preliminary Discourse" to the *Encyclopédie*. Having followed there the twisting paths of human inquiry, its logical and historical developments, he gives the reader a pause. D'Alembert then notes that in the disorienting obscurity of this intellectual topography, truth itself may very well imitate, in a strange but significant way, the deceptive flash of light that has been linked with error.

> Let us stop here a moment and glance over the territory we have just covered. We will note two boundaries within which almost all of the certain knowledge accorded to our natural intelligence [*lumière naturelle*] is, so to speak, concentrated. . . . Between these two limits [i.e., the knowledge of self and certain mathematical truths] is an immense distance where the Supreme Intelligence seems to have wanted to deceive [*se jouer*] human curiosity, as much by the innumerable clouds it has spread there as by some flashes of light that seem to burst out at intervals to attract us. One might compare the universe to certain works of a sublime obscurity whose authors occasionally bend down within reach of those who read them, seeking to persuade them that they understand nearly all. We are indeed fortunate [*heureux*] if we enter this labyrinth and do not leave the true road [*véritable route*]! Otherwise, the

32. D'Alembert, *Essai*, 1: 152.
33. Holbach, *Système de la nature* (1771), 5.
34. Denis Diderot, *Pensées philosophiques*, no. 9, in *Oeuvres complètes*, ed. J. Assézat and M. Tourneux, 20 vols. (Paris, 1897–1913), 1: 159.

flashes of light intended to lead us there would often serve only to lead us farther from it [*nous en écarter davantage*].[35]

In d'Alembert's allegorical wilderness, the flash of light that deceives the traveler is not fundamentally different from the flash of insight that leads us to the truth. What d'Alembert implies here is that without a clear indication of the final destination of truth, and without a comprehensive map of this space, the mind can never be assured of where the proper road lies, can never be sure that the illumination is genuine.

For d'Alembert, then, the "wandering of the mind" that leads to so many intellectual difficulties can be induced by both the false light of error and the authentic flash of truth. A complex connection is made here, then, between the "errant" paths of an exploring mind and the destination that is truth. Looking at his later work, the *Essai sur les éléments de philosophie*, we see d'Alembert once again describing the difficult and often dangerous philosophical adventure with key spatial metaphors. "One can see Metaphysics as a large country, of which a small part is fertile and well known, but surrounded on all sides by vast deserts, where one finds at intervals only some jerry-built shelters, ready to tumble down on those who seek refuge there." In this wilderness, insight is problematic. Searching for truth, can we ever know which path will lead to a new perspective and a fertile zone of inquiry? At this troubling point, d'Alembert emphasizes the critical importance of error in this topography. The errancy of previous epistemological travelers is precisely what allows the mind to identify the promising new trail. Here the search for truth and the inevitable aberrations of the mind are intimately linked. As d'Alembert would explicitly point out, the history of error in philosophy has a crucial epistemological function. The genealogy of errors, he said,

> by showing us the paths [*chemins*] that have diverged [*écarté*] from the true, . . . facilitates our search for the true path [*sentier*] that leads there. It seems that nature has tried to multiply the obstacles in this area. The mistaken mind [*esprit faux*] deviates by preferring a simple road to difficult and tortuous ways; the just mind sometimes deceives itself by taking, as it must, the way that seems to it the most natural. Error, in a certain sense, must therefore necessarily precede truth; but error itself must then become instructive, by saving those who follow us from fruitless steps. The deceptive roads that have seduced and confused so many great men would have

35. D'Alembert, *Discours préliminaire de l'Encyclopédie* (Paris, 1965), 36–37.

steered us, like them, away from the true; it was necessary for them to explore so that we might know the reefs.[36]

The way to truth is not a linear or even particularly methodical path; it does not extend predictably through the topography of knowledge. Instead, error is a constant and ever-present reality. In the metaphorical space, truth is really an endlessly deferred destination that is always obscured in the moment of actual exploration.

This is why d'Alembert, in a famous passage from the "Preliminary Discourse" to the *Encyclopédie,* described human knowledge as "a sort of labyrinth, a tortuous road that the intellect enters without quite knowing what direction to take." The *Encyclopédie* was conceived as a massive knowledge machine that would organize this labyrinthine space and act as a guide for any future exploration of unknown territories. "It is a kind of world map that is to show the main countries, their positions and mutual dependence, the straight path there is from one to another, a path often interrupted by a thousand obstacles, which can be known in each country only by the inhabitants or explorers, and which can be shown only in highly detailed individual maps."[37]

D'Alembert was not the only one in Enlightenment France who recognized that the aberrations and even failures of philosophical exploration were a necessary preparation for insight into truth. A number of prominent intellectuals sketched a similar historical structure. Turgot's famous discourses given at the Sorbonne in 1750, for example, emphasized the same point. "It is not error that prevents the progresses of truth." The true evil was really laxity and inactivity. Turgot would in fact conclude "that men have had to pass through a thousand errors before arriving at the truth."[38] Condorcet, protégé of both Turgot and d'Alembert, often remarked on the relationship between error and truth in the history of human thought. Condorcet's remarkable testament, his *Esquisse d'un tableau historique des progrès de l'esprit humain,* written while he was in hiding during the Terror, revealed that errors were an essential aspect of the history of progress. "Like the truths that perfect and enlighten [the human mind], they [errors] are the necessary result of its activity." Those

36. D'Alembert, *Essai,* 1: 125.
37. D'Alembert, *Discours préliminaire,* 125, 60. On this imagery in the *Encyclopédie,* see my "Cartographic Aberrations: Epistemology and Order in the Encyclopedic Map," in *Using the "Encyclopédie": Ways of Knowing, Ways of Reading,* ed. Daniel Brewer and Julie C. Hayes (Oxford, forthcoming).
38. Anne-Robert-Jacques Turgot, *Pensées et fragments . . . sur les progrès et la décadence des sciences et des arts,* in *Oeuvres de Turgot,* ed. Eugène Daine and Hyppolyte Dussard, 2 vols. (Paris, 1844), 2: 655.

errors that once were truths were important because they stimulated further explorations.[39] Without the initial error, the inquiry that *identifies* the error (and thus points to truth) would never have been possible. Even the *Encyclopédie* article on philosophy includes the following citation from Fontenelle, a tribute to the *erreur féconde:* "We are not at all permitted to arrive all of a sudden at any reasonable conclusion on any subject whatsoever; first we are required to wander for a long time, and pass through diverse kinds of errors."[40]

Diderot would draw together a number of these topographical images in his own description of philosophical inquiry in the *Pensées sur l'interprétation de la nature.* There he described the "experimental" mind as, literally, blindfolded. It stumbles onto something interesting only while wandering in an erratic fashion. Following behind, the "rational" mind diligently collects these precious materials and tries to fashion some kind of "torch" from them. As Diderot suggests, however, this supposed torch is really less useful than the blind and erring movement of the experimental philosopher. This figure may not know where he is going, and one cannot predict his direction, but the important thing is that he works without rest, he is constantly on the move. The rational one, Diderot says, is always weighing possibilities and pronouncing judgments, an activity that in the end halts all progress forward.[41] The aberration that is the blind search must precede the formation of any "truth." The philosophe here has a split personality, whose success is predicated on the unresolvable tension between radical errancy and systematic truth.

LOST IN THE LABYRINTH

Of course, the epistemological space that we have been tracing, a space that for some thinkers revealed the positive potential of intellectual aberration, is one that could be interpreted in less than optimistic terms. One sophisticated example is a long work on errors and superstitions by the obscure but in many ways typical Enlightenment figure Jean-Louis Castilhon.[42] Interrogating these same spatial metaphors of

39. Condorcet, *Esquisse d'un tableau historique des progrès de l'esprit humain,* ed. Alain Pons (Paris, 1986), 87.

40. *Encyclopédie,* s.v. "philosophie," 12: 511.

41. Denis Diderot, *Pensées sur l'interprétation de la nature,* no. 23, in *Oeuvres complètes,* ed. Herbert Dieckmann et al. (Paris, 1975–95), 9: 43.

42. Castilhon (1720–ca. 1793) was not a marginal figure. A lawyer, he edited journals and dictionary projects with such prominent intellectuals as Joncourt and Robinet. He wrote nine books and was a member of the Académie des jeux floraux.

knowledge, Castilhon focuses specifically on the status of intellectual aberration. In his long and intriguing theoretical preface, Castilhon notes that his work will not simply expose a string of particular errors. "I thought it necessary," he writes, "to go back to their source, and I admit with some ingenuousness that I was not able to arrive there myself without weariness." This "vast land of errors" can be reached only by an "arduous, arid, tiring road." Castilhon then describes this topography of error. Again we find the human mind described as a traveler, and Castilhon exploits all the anxieties associated with the early modern voyage. "How cruel and painful is the situation of a Traveler who has imprudently wandered into a forest where he knows neither the winding paths nor the detours nor the exits!"[43] Unlike Descartes's methodical traveler who, in the *Discourse on Method*, simply walks in a straight line until he emerges from the depths of the forest,[44] Castilhon's is confronted with all the fears of being lost in the dark.

Here, in the absolute obscurity of the wilderness, the traveler is easily misled by the sudden flashes of light, the *feux follets* that seem to indicate torches in the distance. (Note that in English these lights are known as "will-o'-the-wisps," a wisp being "lit hay"—a torch, in other words.) Unfortunately for our traveler, though, this "perfidious phosphorus leads him to the edge of a precipice," where he soon loses his step and plunges into the abyss. Castilhon then asks: Who could deny that the human mind resembles this unfortunate traveler?

> Strangers, isolated and lost [*égarés*] in a world and in the midst of a host of objects we do not know, we drag ourselves along painfully in this shadowy labyrinth [*dédale*], in this world full of prejudices and errors. Guided by some meteors, we move forward into uncertainty, all the while believing that we are following the luminous road that leads to truth.[45]

This "luminous" road turns out to be a deceptive path. Each hesitant step leads us closer to the abyss, and we eventually fall into the endless depths of extravagant systems, elaborate superstitions, and ridiculous errors, a place from which it becomes impossible to extricate ourselves, because the human mind refuses to recognize its essential limitations. Cast into this dark forest, this "shadowy labyrinth," the mind ignores the limited sphere of its "natural enlightenment" (*lumière naturelle*), de-

43. Jean-Louis Castilhon, *Essai sur les erreurs et les superstitions anciennes et modernes*, new ed., 2 vols. (Frankfurt, 1766), 1: 9–10.

44. René Descartes, *Discours de la méthode*, in *Oeuvres philosophiques*, ed. Ferdinand Alquié, 2 vols. (Paris, 1963), 2: 595.

45. Castilhon, *Essai*, 1: 10.

scribed by Castilhon as a kind of feeble glow illuminating only what immediately surrounds our being. Instead, the mind invents a vast array of speculations. We believe that we have reached ever greater heights "the more we err in the shadowy spaces, in the immense deserts of intellectual beings."[46]

There is no easy solution to this predicament, according to Castilhon. He does suggest that we reject, in a radical Cartesian move, all received knowledge, knowledge that infects our natural reason from the moment we begin to learn. But a move toward some kind of disciplined empiricism is not going to follow this purification of the mind. The essential errancy of the human mind will not be eliminated simply by the destruction of some of the concrete aberrations of human thought. The mind, Castilhon tells us, is chronically weak, constantly prone to the infection of error and superstition. Unlike other authors who also unmask a wide array of human failings, Castilhon seeks out the "general, universal, *inextinguishable* source of our wanderings and our prejudices." And he claims to find the source of this more radical errancy in an original moment of alienation, caused by some global disorder occasioned by some catastrophic event. "Tranquil and without fear before this tragedy," humans were subsequently isolated and filled with terror, susceptible to "numerous deviations."[47] Again, one cannot trace back and eradicate the individual error. Inevitable errancy must be worked through if the mind is going to move forward in the pursuit of truth. In other words, Castilhon acknowledges the potential usefulness of error. The error of a superstition (his example here is Islam) might very well provide a source of cohesion for nations divided by violence and conflict. In this way, the poison becomes the remedy; the error provides the potential conditions for a future truth.[48]

Still, we seem to confront, again, a basic question at this point: How can we distinguish the inevitable error from the appearance of truth, given that any "truth" may, from another perspective, turn out to be yet another error? Because of its radical errancy, the mind has lost sight of its origin and its destination, and therefore cannot identify the one single path to truth. Turgot described the problem this way: "When man has wanted to double back on himself, he has found himself in a labyrinth that he had entered with eyes blindfolded. He can no longer recover the trace of his steps."[49] Condillac, the emblematic sensationalist philoso-

46. Ibid., 4.
47. Ibid., 35, 38–44, 73.
48. For example, ibid., 2: 86–87, 95.
49. Turgot, *Plan du second discours*, in *Oeuvres*, 2: 645.

pher of the French Enlightenment, described the situation in similar terms. In his *Traité des systèmes*, an indictment of speculative metaphysics, he explained that the mind is like a man who has come out of a "deep sleep, finding himself in the middle of a labyrinth." In this deceptive space, "where a thousand detours are marked out just to lead us into error," the way to truth does not immediately reveal itself. In fact, with hindsight, we might see that the least promising path turns out to be the road to success. The first efforts of those who traced this labyrinth are critical, Condillac says, and he condemns those who either delude themselves into thinking they have emerged from the labyrinth when they have not, or who try to trace the complete map of this maze before engaging in any concrete exploration.[50]

Despite appearances, this was not a retreat into a simplistic empirical method of trial and error. In Condillac's most influential text, his *Essai sur les origines des connaissances humaines* of 1746, which became a kind of textbook of epistemology in France and elsewhere, we see clearly that in the Enlightenment space of knowledge, this original moment of deviation is critically important. In the introductory section of this work, we find again the topographical imagery we have repeatedly encountered. For the philosopher to make progress in the search for truth, Condillac says, he must chart all the mistakes of previous adventurers who have sailed into the unknown. "The experience of the philosopher, like that of the pilot, is the knowledge of the reefs where others have run aground." Because there are no maps of new territory, the only compass guiding the philosopher, Condillac says, is the survey of failed, errant voyages— a nautical version of d'Alembert's epistemology of error. But Condillac probes the problem more deeply here. He notes that the specific mistakes of past explorers are less important than the paths that led to them. The very nature of errancy, and not the mere presence of the mistake, is what interests Condillac. And identifying just the immediate causes of particular errors is not enough:

> It would be necessary even to trace back from one cause to another, and come to the first; since there is one that must be the same for all those who stray, and that is like a common starting point for all the paths leading to error. Perhaps then, alongside this point, one could see another that opens the sole path that leads to truth.[51]

50. Etienne Bonnot de Condillac, *Traité des systèmes*, in *Oeuvres philosophiques*, ed. Georges Le Roy, 3 vols. (Paris, 1948), 1: 127.
51. Condillac, *Essai sur les origines des connaissances humaines*, in *Oeuvres philosophiques*, 1: 4a.

There is, for Condillac, an original error, the ancestor of all intellectual aberrations. But was it really possible to trace back every concrete error to some original turn from truth?

The *Encyclopédie* article on error makes this project seem rather problematic. Here the congenital weakness of the mind is emphasized, as it was in Castilhon's text. The entry on error claims that, like a man of "feeble temperament" who gets over one particular illness only to fall into another, the human mind never manages to separate itself from its numerous errors; it only exchanges them for new ones. Eliminating error would require us to ignore the specific details of the pathology—the symptoms, as it were—and "go back to their source and dry it up." But the source of intellectual illness is difficult to eradicate, given that it is located in the very historical development of the individual mind, which has, in a sense, been trained for error. The original deviation is traced to an unmasterable past; traced, that is, to the imprecise formation of ideas in infancy, the slow development of reason, and the often haphazard connections made between signs and ideas as language is gradually learned. The instability that results from this imprecision provides the occasion of error. The passions seize on the "vague principle," "metaphorical expression," or "equivocal term" in order to divert the mind away from its proper path.[52]

Following a cross-reference from the article on error to the article on "evidence," we encounter the same critique of imprecision and the same ambivalence regarding any solution to the problematic straying of the mind. The source of error is traced to the use of artificial ideas, those abstractions that organize the bewildering complexity of experience and memory. Yet it is admitted that we must use these intellectual tools, because the mind is so limited in its capacity. But the error of the general idea is hardly a correctable mistake, since it does not in fact refer to anything outside its own structure. Error becomes here a kind of infection of the mind, haunting its very operation, and is not a discrete mistake of some sort.[53] Error is uncomfortably linked with "delirium," the literal aberration from the straight line of the "furrow." Error is nothing but the pathological wandering of reason, like madness itself.[54] Yet the mind seems incapable of ever constructing

52. *Encyclopédie*, s.v. "erreur," 5: 910.
53. Ibid., s.v. "évidence," 6: 150.
54. Ibid., s.v. "délire," 4: 785, and "folie," 7: 44. In the article on delirium it is noted that *délire* is derived from the Latin phrase *aberrare de lira*, or deviation from the "furrow." On this conceptual link, see Michel Foucault, *Madness and Civilization: A History of Insanity in the Age of Reason*, trans. Richard Howard (New York, 1965), 99–100.

that perfectly straight path, the linear furrow that signifies control of the landscape.

There was no guarantee that any particular path in this epistemological labyrinth would lead to the truth, no guarantee that a flash of light would not lead us in the wrong direction. So it is not surprising that we find in many Enlightenment texts the dream of rising above the landscape in order to see everything in perfect clarity. "It is glorious to consider from the height of a craggy mountaintop the errors and wanderings of feeble mortals. . . . It is from the peak of this mountain that one learns why *truth*, daughter of the sky, becomes withered under the weight of the chains of superstition."[55] "Enter into the winding paths and tortuous undulations of the streets of an immense city: it appears to you an inextricable labyrinth. You come across only difficulties, obscurities." Climb a tower, however, and see this labyrinth as the birds see it, and this uncertainty "ceases." Human minds, however, inevitably "err among uncertainties." [56] Many thinkers, then, often defined this lofty, fantastic perspective as divine insight. As d'Alembert, for example, once noted, for the supreme intelligence the "immense labyrinth" that is the space of human inquiry is completely "without mystery," since this being can "comprehend all the detours in one glance."[57] Rousseau offered this formulation: "The supreme intelligence has no need of reason . . . it is purely intuitive, it sees equally everything that is and everything that can be; all truths are for it only a single idea, as all places a single point, and all times a single moment."[58] However, condemned to wander in the obscure topography (the complex city, the dark forest, the disorienting labyrinth), the limited intellect could not, of course, simply rise above the terrain.

ERROR AND THE CONJECTURAL LEAP

Yet if we look closely, some Enlightenment texts do reveal that our minds were not really limited to this almost blind exploration, aided only by the highly problematic glow of a potentially aberrant human reason. In certain versions of the Enlightenment epistemological topography, the leap into dark unknown spaces was not in fact a leap across an *absolute* discontinuity. For example, d'Alembert once suggested, in what

55. *Encyclopédie*, s.v. "vérité métaphysique," 17: 71.

56. François Louis d'Escherney, *Les lacunes de la philosophie* (Amsterdam and Paris, 1783), xliv–xlv.

57. D'Alembert, *Essai*, 1: 25.

58. Jean-Jacques Rousseau, *Émile, ou De l'éducation*, in *Oeuvres complètes*, ed. Bernard Gagnebin and Marcel Raymond, 5 vols. (Paris, 1964–95), 4: 593.

was really a rather unusual move, that the logic of demonstration—the science of certainty, in other words—was often less useful in the search for truth than what he called the art of conjecture—a word that implies, quite literally, throwing oneself into the unknown.[59] D'Alembert's subsequent explanation of this suggestion is extremely provocative. He notes that by all means the mind should train itself in logic, which he calls in this same text the "torch" that guides us in the epistemological labyrinth. But d'Alembert will add that this training is useful not because logic will help us find the truth but rather because logical rigor will teach the mind how to *recognize* truth, only after it appears. There is no "logic" of discovery here. But d'Alembert goes even further. He cautions the reader that the habit of overly rigorous thought can sometimes blind the intellect with its dazzling certainty, actually preventing the discovery and recognition of less obvious and less visible forms of truth. Contrary to Foucault, then, it is not just the "unreason of madness" that leads to "dazzled reason" in this period.[60] D'Alembert writes that

> some ordinary eyes, too accustomed to the force of intense light, no longer distinguish the gradations of weak illumination, and see only thick shadows where others still sense some brightness. The mind that recognizes the truth only when it is directly struck by it is well beneath the one that can not only recognize it close up but still have an intimation of it [*le pressentir*] and make it out in the distance from some fleeting features [*caractères fugitifs*].[61]

The image here is very suggestive. D'Alembert implies that in the epistemological terrain, the truth may hover dimly in the distance, providing clues for the intellect as it moves along the darkened path.

Even more suggestive, however, is d'Alembert's description of the "fugitive" traces of truth, especially when juxtaposed with Condillac's own allusive definition of the "fugitive" (in a *Dictionnaire des synonymes* he wrote for one of his students) as "one who, having been forced to flee his country, errs here and there."[62] We might tentatively say at this point that in the Enlightenment space of knowledge truth itself is a fugitive, because it is something that cannot really appear in the limited and obscure confines of human experience. But at the same time, truth may leave its traces in this world, some fleeting impressions. As Condillac noted, again in his *Dictionnaire*, "to err" means to wander without any

59. The Latin root of "conjecture" is *jacere*, to throw.
60. Foucault, *Madness and Civilization*, 108.
61. D'Alembert, *Essai*, 1: 154.
62. Condillac, *Dictionnaire des synonymes*, in *Oeuvres philosophiques*, vol. 3, s.v. "errant," "errer," "erres."

certain route, but he also intriguingly says it can mean "to leave tracks," in French *donner des erres*. These tracks, *des erres*, are traces of a journey that is itself errant and unpredictable—the word *erres*, like *errant*, emerges from two etymological roots: *iterare* (to journey) and *errare* (to stray). What is crucial here is the implication that truth, incapable of fully presenting itself in this complex terrain, makes only fleeting appearances. Pascal once said: "This is not at all the land of truth. It errs unknown among men."[63] But in the metaphorical spaces of the Enlightenment, truth in its erring journey leaves some tracks, however ambiguous they may be.[64] As Condillac wrote, *erres* are mere impressions of something that is no longer present in any form, unlike the vestiges of something, which are physically tangible and can be reconstructed.[65] If truth leaves tracks, then, following them accurately is a real difficulty, since the trace may very well be a deceptive form. The search for truth is like a hunt, which takes place in a dark, labyrinthine space where uncertain clues, fleeting impressions, and flashes of light may point to truth but may also lead the mind astray and into the abyss. The wandering that characterizes the errancy of human thought may well turn out to be either productive or dangerous. There could never be one straight path to a truth that has, in the end, no specific location. The essence of truth ultimately escapes the concrete boundaries of human temporal and spatial experience, the boundaries that define the epistemological terrain for Enlightenment thought, even though truth haunts this space with its phantom appearances.

This rather elusive metaphorical structure, one that links truth and error in an unexpectedly intimate way, seems to contradict the Enlightenment ideal of methodical and patient investigation, aided by the pure techniques of mathematical analysis. Indeed, Condorcet, in his reception speech at the Académie française in 1782, depicted the eighteenth century as one "where the method of discovering truth had been reduced to an art, and so to speak, to a formula; where reason has finally recognized the road it must follow, and seized the thread that will prevent it from going astray [*s'égarer*]." The human race would no longer witness those alternations of "obscurity and light."[66] The Enlightenment thread of Theseus in the epistemological labyrinth was the Newtonian method. But

63. Blaise Pascal, *Pensées*, ed. Philippe Sellier (Paris, 1976), no. 78, p. 55.
64. Note that by the nineteenth century, the verb *errer* can mean "to appear in a fugitive fashion." See *Grand Larousse*, s.v. "errer."
65. Condillac, *Dictionnaire*, s.v. "vestiges."
66. Condorcet, "Reception Speech at the Académie Française," in Keith M. Baker's edition, "Condorcet's Notes for a Revised Edition of his Reception Speech to the Académie Française," *Studies on Voltaire and the Eighteenth Century* 169 (1977): 17–18.

Condorcet would add this critical qualification in a note later appended to the text. "These methods," he wrote, "do not replace [*suppléent*] the genius, but they direct him, they make him more independent of chance. The genius, if he is not guided by a method, owes to chance not the force necessary to follow the road that can lead him to truth, but often of having recognized this road." The method, as we have already seen, comes *after* discovery.[67] Only the genius himself had the prescient qualities necessary for tracking truth in its errant course. "He soars beyond the eagle's flight toward a luminous truth."[68] The genius takes enormous risks, since he leaves the known territory without any real guide. "There are unknown truths, like countries, where we can find the proper road only after having tried all the others. It is therefore necessary for some to run the risk of straying, in order to show the right path to others."[69] "Errors are the share of those who begin," according to Condillac. "If we had preceded those who strayed, we would have strayed like them."[70]

This necessary breaching of the borders of knowledge leads Condillac to argue that the mind must, if it is to make any progress, "hazard judgments on things it has not sufficiently examined." This structure is the essence of an Enlightenment conjectural epistemology. Yet the leap that characterizes the moment of conjecture was not entirely random, even if it was not guided by past discoveries or a certain methodical path. These conjectural forays "can be false, but they also can be true. They are in fact often true, since [the mind] has this discernment which *touches* truth before having seized it."[71] Condillac will conclude that despite the fact that conjecture has a degree of certainty "the farthest from evidence," it is always the necessary first step that allows the mind to collect evidence. Evidence is the proof for something we already believe to be true. Conjecture, then, is the risky move that initiates any journey into obscure lands. "It is by means of [conjectures] that all the sciences have begun, because we obscurely sense [*entrevoyons*, a kind of seeing between the lines] the truth before we see it, and evidence often comes only after tentative efforts [*le tâtonnement*]."[72] Like d'Alembert, Condillac is suggesting here that the mind follows dim, distorted visions of its destination. The obscurity introduces the risk of errancy; but the vision also holds out the promise of progressive movement. What is important, in this con-

---

67. Ibid., 37n.
68. *Encyclopédie*, s.v. "génie," 7: 583.
69. Ibid., s.v. "hypothèse," 8: 417.
70. Condillac, *Cours d'études VI: Extraits du cours d'histoire*, in *Oeuvres philosophiques*, 2: 23a.
71. Condillac, *Traité des sensations*, ibid., 1: 317b.
72. Condillac, *Cours d'études IV: De l'art de raisonner*, ibid., 1: 680b.

text, is that the mind move forward and seek out this truth that calls us, however ambiguously.

We find in the *Encyclopédie* entry on "genius" this important declaration: "In philosophical productions, the true or the false are not at all the distinctive characteristics of *genius*."[73] In another article, we read this plea for the aberrations of the mind: "It is by permitting divergences [*écarts*] that genius gives birth to sublime things. Let us allow reason to bring its torch to bear at random and sometimes without success on all the objects of our desire, if we want to put the genius within reach of discovering some unknown road."[74] Genuine progress is, in a rather surprising way, prepared by the very aberrations of an unpredictable and often unsuccessful intellect. "The genius . . . does not know regular progress," as one author noted in a text on the pathologies of the mind; "he puts together the most distant things and reunites the most contrary."[75]

In the topography of knowledge traced by Enlightenment epistemological texts, the aberration that is error assumes a new role in the discovery and exploration of new zones of inquiry. In the absence of truth, which is the very destination of understanding, the wandering that is error cannot be so distinguished from a straight line. In fact, the wandering of the mind that frees it from established knowledge leaves it open to the new insight, the ephemeral appearance of truth.

At this point we must leave the metaphorical depiction of this epistemological problem and look more closely at how error was, in more particular contexts, defined and identified, in order to see how specific errors might be connected with concrete forms of knowledge. Psychological models of knowledge, which we will examine next, define error as "mistaken judgment." What kind of truth can be found in acknowledged aberrations of the intellectual faculties?

73. *Encyclopédie*, s.v. "génie," 7: 583.
74. Ibid., s.v. "goût," 7: 767.
75. Antoine le Camus, *Médicine de l'esprit* (Paris, 1753), 138.

CHAPTER 3

Improper Couplings: Language, Judgment, and Epistemological Desire

As Ernst Cassirer observed in *The Philosophy of the Enlightenment*, epistemology was central for eighteenth-century thought. The intense examination of nature in the late seventeenth century generated critical reflection on the origin and limits of human knowledge. In fact, it was held in the eighteenth century that, as Locke had pointed out, before we can know anything about the world, we have to know something about the nature of our own experience of that world. This was not an easy task; as Cassirer says, "exact insight into the specific character of the human understanding cannot otherwise be obtained than by tracing the whole course of its development from its first elements to its higher forms."[1] Enlightenment psychology was not merely descriptive; it aimed to be the anatomist of the mind, explaining where these various abilities came from and how they worked. For the Enlightenment philosophes, particularly in France, these "first elements" of the mind were understood to be the basic simple sensations, sensations that were brought together, taken apart, and transformed by the mind to form various ideas. Locke was so important for eighteenth-century thinkers not only because he introduced this sensationalist doctrine so powerfully but because he advocated a scientific approach to the mind. Instead of lapsing into vague metaphysical fancies, Locke wanted to investigate the mind with basic observation and a minimum of speculation. If Descartes, Malebranche, and Spinoza all wanted to argue that our ideas are what connect us to some transcendent reality (and thus could be a valid

1. Ernst Cassirer, *The Philosophy of the Enlightenment*, trans. Fritz C. A. Koelln and James P. Pettegrove (Princeton, 1951), 93.

source of knowledge in that context), Enlightenment philosophers took their cue from Locke and sought the origin of ideas in our own experience, by patiently following the causal chains that led back to the foundational starting point of thought: sensations themselves. "I believe," wrote the Marquis d'Argens, "that one could just as easily prove existence by saying *I sense, therefore I am,* as by saying *I think, therefore I am.*"[2]

Sensationalism had a profound effect on the conceptualization of error in the eighteenth century. Error had been understood as a kind of failure: if our ideas were somehow divinely inspired, then mistakes of judgment and false propositions must be the result of human inadequacy, although philosophers such as Spinoza would be trapped by the difficulty of explaining why a higher faculty such as reason could err at all, given its origin. Descartes tried to solve this problem by arguing that although our ideas can be perfectly clear, our will often takes these ideas too far and eventually strays from the truth. However, once the divine character of reason and of our ideas gave way to a more secular understanding of mental operations in the Enlightenment, error was redefined. No longer failure, error was explained in terms of the interconnection of our ideas and sensations. This made error at once less mysterious and more controllable, at least in theory, for there was really no reason why our ideas might not be more precisely ordered with discipline and education. Especially in the first half of the eighteenth century, then, Enlightenment philosophy was concerned with what was called the association of ideas.

This sensationalist psychology did over the course of the eighteenth century develop into a very sophisticated framework, but as psychology became more complex, the epistemological questions, the very starting point of these investigations, became more diffuse and less tractable. As more and more emphasis was placed on the inner dynamics of mental operations rooted in sensory data, the less obvious it was that the human mind could ever really know anything objective about the external world. The mind, in this Enlightenment line of thought, was understood to be a kind of intellectual machine, manipulating sensations but cut off from any direct knowledge, whether of God or of nature. French philosophers, such as Maupertuis and Condillac, are not surprisingly best known as thinkers who tried to systematize this radical approach to psychology and epistemology: everything mental was reduced to a series of modifications of sense. The emblematic figure of Enlightenment epistemology is the statue-man made famous by Condillac in his *Traité des sensations,* who rises to (intellectual) life from a single sensation—the smell of a rose. Sensationalist theory achieves genetic psychological insight at

2. Marquis d'Argens, *La philosophie du bon sens* (Paris, 1746), 178.

the expense of epistemological certainty, or so it might seem. Cassirer, for one, argued that the Enlightenment tradition of thought falters on exactly this problem of knowledge, pointing to Maupertuis, who once noted that any judgment about the *world* can be reinterpreted as a statement about our own *ideas*. According to Cassirer, the "judgment" in Enlightenment thought can in fact be defined *only* in terms of self-enclosed propositions about perceptions and the signs we use to identify them.

Error, at least in one sense, disappears as an epistemological problem and reappears as a psychological category, a matter of internal semiotic coherence. It was not possible to make the leap from internal (subjective) impression to knowledge of some objective existence. This would explain both the turn to radical subjective idealism, as in the case of Berkeley (or even Condillac, according to Cassirer), and the move to Hume's brand of skepticism. In France the sensationalist tradition reaches its endpoint in the late eighteenth-century science of *idéologie*, a school inspired by Condillac's analytic sensationalism. *Idéologie* was, it might be said, a conceptual dead end, epistemologically, because it was such a rigorously self-referential system, purged of anything extrinsic, anything that might constitute actual knowledge. Antoine Destutt de Tracy, a leading *idéologue*, was caught in this epistemological circle. In the end he could not even identify error at all, since all we really knew were our own thoughts, which obeyed their own logic of association.[3] The epistemological problem would be solved then only outside the parameters of a classical Enlightenment psychology. Cassirer, for example, would locate this solution in an eighteenth-century German line of thought, one influenced by Leibniz (through the texts of Christian Wolff), a tradition that redefined the truth of the universal in terms of individual experience and thus prepared the way for the Kantian notion of a transcendental (and not merely propositional) logic.[4]

This narrative of Enlightenment epistemology, however, hardly accounts for some of the surprising, even strange, observations on error we have traced in the first chapter. Both d'Alembert and Condillac, mainstream and influential philosophes in the sensationalist tradition, hinted at some deeper connection between our limited minds and the greater truths of nature. How was the mind connected with this greater reality if it was limited to ideas based on concrete sensory impressions that could never be objectively analyzed or verified in any way? The answer lies

3. Antoine Destutt de Tracy, *Elémens d'idéologie III: Logique* (Paris, an XII [1805]). On Tracy see Emmet Kennedy, *A Philosophe in the Age of Revolution: Destutt de Tracy and the Origins of "Ideology"* (Philadelphia, 1978).

4. Cassirer, *Philosophy of the Enlightenment*, 117–33.

along a path not well traveled in intellectual history. But to understand better this juxtaposition of transcendental approaches to error and scientific sensationalist psychology, we can begin by looking again at the precise character of this sensationalist doctrine. While it is traditional to begin with Locke before discussing Condillac's "purification" of the Lockean structure of the mind, it might be useful to look first at Hobbes's sensationalist theory as expounded in *Leviathan*, since Locke was answering (and raising) some important questions with respect to Hobbes. We can then see whether it is possible to bring together the paradigmatic and seemingly reductive Enlightenment psychology of Condillac with the almost mystical epistemology hinted at in so many speculations on truth, error, and discovery in this period.

ERROR AND THE SIGNS OF DESIRE IN HOBBES'S *LEVIATHAN*

While materialism and even sensationalist doctrines have been around in some form since antiquity, the modern version of these ideas emerged in the seventeenth century, when new scientific frames of thought coincided with a serious questioning of religious, ethical, and political structures. Hobbes is the exemplary figure of this historical juxtaposition, someone who adopted radically new "mechanical" philosophies and applied them rigorously to human problems that had traditionally been understood on a somewhat higher plane. In his late and highly influential work *Leviathan*, Hobbes developed an argument about political order by first outlining the radical relativity of human perception. Hobbes did not assume anything about the mind's operation. He simply began with the act of reading his own mind as a way of understanding human behavior.

The first result of that reading of thoughts was this declaration: "The Originall of them all, is that which we call SENSE; (For there is no conception in a mans mind, which hath not at first, totally, or by parts, been begotten upon the organs of Sense.)"[5] This was the foundation of Hobbes's whole argument on humanity and political order. We did not even need to know the natural causes of sense, since we were effectively bound by our own experience. What was needed was a rigorous exposition of our mental life as it derives from this foundational origin. Now it would seem that from the start Hobbes is at an impasse, for how can we move from the immediacy (and passivity) of sense impressions to the higher faculties of reason and decision? Hobbes takes us out of the radical im-

5. Thomas Hobbes, *Leviathan*, ed. Richard Tuck (Cambridge, 1991), 13. Further page references are in the text.

mediacy of sense by introducing what he calls "imagination," which is nothing but "decaying sense," the lingering persistence of something no longer present. Once thought is freed from immediacy, all sorts of connections can take now place between sensations. Sometimes, as Hobbes notes, thoughts "wander" with no guide (though even in these cases Hobbes hints that "secret" connections between these thoughts may be uncovered), but our train of thought is usually ordered in some way. He describes mental life as a constant process of investigation. "In summe, the Discourse of the Mind, when it is governed by designe, is nothing but *Seeking* . . . a hunting out of the causes, of some effect, present or past; or of the effects, of some present or past cause" (21–22). The mind is running around, attempting to recover or discover the traces of some intended object. Thought follows certain paths because, Hobbes says, of the bodily impulses of "appetite" and "aversion." As he writes: "The Thoughts, are to the Desires, as Scouts, and Spies, to range abroad, and find the way to the things Desired" (53).

The introduction of speech, or mental signs of experience, greatly increases the efficiency of these often chaotic searches, Hobbes points out, because signs register thoughts for ease of organization. Signs also mark the very introduction of truth and falsity in mental life, for Hobbes, because the sign fixes meaning for the first time. There is no such thing as truth until the mind constructs a definition of it. "For *True* and *False* are attributes of speech, not of Things. And where Speech is not, there is neither *Truth* nor *Falshood*." But Hobbes also immediately remarks: "*Errour* there may be, as when wee expect that which shall not be; or suspect what has been; but in neither case can a man be charged with Untruth" (27–28). The error is not, as one might expect, "untruth," but rather a consequence of a more basic human uncertainty. The error is not itself logically inconsistent: it is a reasonable (i.e., coherent) conjecture that just turns out to be wrong in the future. There is no way of avoiding this kind of error in advance (33–34). With precise words marking our experiences, "senseless falsehood" will be avoided, but the consequences deduced from these mental constructions do not always match reality. So reason, for Hobbes, is nothing more than a function of this mental processing of signs, a reckoning, or series of additions and subtractions, of the consequences of agreed-upon general terms for certain experiences. With organized thinking, we can better face the uncertain situation. Here we must, as Hobbes says, *conjecture*, throw ourselves into the unknown, and although everyone, even the most prudent, is subject to error, at least we come prepared by previous encounters with the world.

What is normally called "error" Hobbes defines as absurdity, or "senseless speech." Hobbes realizes we can never avoid the error of conjecture, but we can definitely avoid wandering aimlessly in our own muddled thinking. He states clearly: "The Light of humane minds is Perspicuous Words, but by exact definitions first snuffed, and purged from ambiguity. . . . And on the contrary, Metaphors, and senseless and ambiguous words, are like *ignes fatui* [foolish fires]; and reasoning upon them, is wandering amongst absurdities" (36). It is not the case that the "light" of discourse will lead us to truth, though. The goal of this science of reason is not epistemological insight. For Hobbes, human beings seek to satisfy appetites or desires, in particular the desire to live. Reason is part of the process of attaining what the passions want. Reason *calculates* possible effects of actions, it guides those scouts of desire who race each other into the future when various passions conflict in their aims. The human being is a kind of machine that constantly seeks out objects of desire while avoiding pain or death, and experience is organized to that end, either to deduce *certain* consequences or at least to face new situations with some idea of probable outcomes. "No Discourse whatsoever, can End in absolute knowledge of Fact, past, or to come. For, as for the knowledge of Fact, it is originally, Sense; and ever after, Memory. And for the knowledge of Consequence, which I have said before is called Science, it is not Absolute, but Conditionall. No man can know by Discourse, that this, or that, is, has been, or will be" (47).

The difficulty with Hobbes's own deductive argument is that it cannot deal adequately with the problem of human will, given his own sensationalist account. Hobbes can define will in this system only as "the last Appetite, or Aversion, immediately adhaering to the action, or the omission thereof" (41). "Free" will is for Hobbes one of these *ignes fatui*, a kind of absurdity, mere senseless speech. And yet Hobbes's whole picture of the operations of the mind hinges on his discussion of speech, the introduction of arbitrary signs that allow the mind to begin coordinating experience and memory effectively, and that introduce the very possibility of conjecture (futurality). One must have will, in the radical sense, to introduce something new like this to experience. How is it possible to deduce the origin of language from sensations? This mysterious beginning of language, and the subsequent rise of reason, was a recurring, if unresolved, question for Enlightenment philosophers interested in the workings of the human mind. Linked with this difficulty was the problem of the self: Hobbes's vision of our being was of a sensing creature acting out various relationships of desire. There was no place, indeed no need, for a unified seat of consciousness. Yet the intervention of language and the abstract thought that comes with it pointed to the existence of just such a willing spiritual entity.

IN THE TWILIGHT OF PROBABILITY: ERROR AND INSIGHT IN
LOCKE'S *ESSAY CONCERNING HUMAN UNDERSTANDING*

Locke's *Essay*—which would become the touchstone for Enlightenment reflection on human psychology—seems to take its inspiration from Hobbes, in that Locke is concerned with the sensory origin of ideas and its implications for understanding "understanding" itself. Locke "confessed" in Book II of the *Essay* "that external and internal Sensation, are the only passages that I can find, of Knowledge, to the Understanding."[6] But the *Essay* put much more emphasis on the problem of language and consciousness. Locke followed his confession with an image that suggested that some identity was in fact *experiencing* these sensory impressions. He described sensations as "the Windows by which light is let into this *dark Room*. For, methinks, the *Understanding* is not much unlike a Closet wholly shut from light, with only some little openings left, to let in external visible Resemblances, or *Ideas* of things without" (162–63).

So while Locke could deny that there were any innate ideas, his conception of self-identity allowed him to affirm the possibility that new ideas might be generated not by sense alone but by mental reflection, ideas that "the Mind gets by reflecting on its own Operations within it self" (105). Locke envisions a unifying consciousness as the self that experiences and organizes sensations. This implied center of activity, often metaphorically described as a kind of internal "eye," allows Locke to avoid the logical paradox Hobbes encountered in his effort to reduce all thought to sensations; that is, the problem of explaining the emergence of the arbitrary sign. Locke allows the self to intervene in experience. As he notes, in the section of the *Essay* devoted to language, signs allow the mind to express itself to others, for invisible ideas need external signs to be understood. "Thus we may conceive how *Words,* which were by Nature so well adapted to that purpose, come to be made use of by Men, as *the Signs of* their *Ideas;* not by any natural connexion . . . for then there would be but one Language amongst all Men; but by a volontary Imposition, whereby such a Word is made arbitrarily the Mark of such an *Idea*" (405).

In fact, these words make possible the higher operations of thought, for the "complex idea," an association of discrete sensations (or "simple ideas"), can be fixed only by an arbitrary sign that holds these parts together in the mind. This general idea is a pure mental construction, and

6. John Locke, *An Essay Concerning Human Understanding,* ed. Peter H. Nidditch (Oxford, 1975), 162. Further page references are in the text.

does not represent anything objectively real. Despite repeated attempts to distinguish the "mode" (the artificial idea) from "substance" (a natural kind), Locke never is able to articulate what it is that makes a collection of ideas more than arbitrary. The mixed mode is defined as "perfectly arbitrary" and substances as "not perfectly so," but the "pattern" that supposedly defines this latter form is never available (428). In fact, Locke repeatedly emphasizes that not only do we arbitrarily create boundaries when we fix substances, nature herself hardly ever stays within any boundaries. The almost obsessive attention paid to monstrous births and changelings in his text reveals Locke's anxieties about establishing any kind of stable "pattern" that would ground our purely mental associations. Even the substance most intimately familiar to us ("Man") is highly problematic: "It having been more than once doubted, whether the *foetus* born of a Woman were a *Man*, even so far, as that it hath been debated, whether it were, or were not to be nourished and baptized" (416).

Locke's reformulation of the sensationalist model (the division between mind and the materials of knowledge, ideas) creates then a new difficulty, one that was basically irrelevant for Hobbes: the problem of epistemology. As long as an idea was not absurd (that is, contradictory), it was not really possible to ascertain what was "chimerical" and what was "real"—that is, in "conformity with the real Being," as Locke puts it (372–73).[7] For Hobbes, it was not so important to know the truth of the external world from the evidence of the senses, since, at least in *Leviathan*, he described the human mind as resolutely pragmatic; what mattered was that desires were attained and life was preserved. Reason was a tool of desire, and not a path to higher knowledge. With a well-made language, the Hobbesian man interacted with the world that provoked sensations in the probabilistic mode of trial and error. Locke's reintroduction of consciousness inevitably made epistemology more critical. For Hobbes, truth and falsity were in speech, and error was contingent uncertainty—hardly a conceptual difficulty. For Locke, it was not enough to say that knowledge was a function of linguistic relationships only. He wanted to show, in other words, that this "knowledge of our own *Ideas,* goes a little farther than bare imagination" (563). After describing the mind's ability to take apart and combine ideas and affix names to ideas, Locke tries to argue that what constitutes knowledge is

7. Locke admits that only simple ideas are real in this way, and that complex ideas have only a mental reality—their existence is a function of internal consistency. Cf. Leibniz, *New Essays on Human Understanding,* trans. and ed. Peter Remnant and Jonathan Bennett (Cambridge, 1981), 265.

the agreement or disagreement of ideas. The mind perceives, intuitively, a genuine inner relationship between two ideas. However, while Locke can give examples of intuitive perception of *disagreement* (black is not white), he never comes up with a clear example of intuitive agreement.

Still, knowledge for Locke is that process of discovering connections, and not simply the manipulation of experience, as it was for Hobbes. Locke rejected the idea that reason was simply "deduction," or the calculation of certain consequences of given ideas, as Hobbes had argued. If this were the case, Locke said, reason could never make new discoveries, could not project us toward truth. "*Syllogism*, at best, is but the Art of fencing with the little Knowledge we have, without making any Addition to it" (679). But rather than *identify* the power of discovery, as we would hope, Locke continues his discussion of reason with a catalogue of failure: reason falters because of the failure of ideas, the obscurity of ideas, failure to perceive ideas, false principles taken as true, the ambiguity of words and signs. Locke cannot, in the end, really say how reason ever succeeds. Remarkably, he actually says that some things the mind perceives only through intuition: and this intuitive knowledge is, he notes, "beyond all Doubt, and needs no Probation, nor can have any; this being the highest of all Humane Certainty." And, as Locke tells us,

> in the Discovery of, and Assent to these Truths, there is no use of the discursive Faculty, *no need of Reasoning*, but they are known by a superior, and higher degree of Evidence. And such, if I may guess at Things unknown, I am apt to think, that Angels have now, and the Spirits of just Men made perfect, shall have, in a future State, of Thousands of Things, which now, either wholly escape our Apprehensions, or which, our short-sighted Reason having got some faint Glimpse of, we, in the Dark, grope after. (683)

Locke admits that the mind has this kind of inspiration only in flashes, "some Sparks of bright Knowledge." The movement of knowledge is in the end a kind of divine intervention, quite literally. "When we find out an *Idea*, by whose Intervention we discover the Connexion of two others, this is a Revelation from God to us, by the Voice of Reason. For we then come to know a Truth that we did not know before" (598). Yet without this divine inspiration, we can make discoveries with a more limited form of reason. This diminished kind of insight, though, takes us back to Hobbes. Locke explains that, with our reason, we can really only compare ideas and make judgments about their relation: "*Judgement*, is the thinking or taking two *Ideas* to agree, or disagree, by the intervention of one or more *Ideas*, whose certain Agreement, or Disagreement with them it does not perceive, but hath observed to be frequent and usual" (685).

The only measure here of the judgment is conditional frequency; the "truth" is at best a kind of Hobbesian probability.

Perhaps it is fitting then that Locke for all intents and purposes ends the argument of the *Essay* with a discussion not of truth but of error. (A short chapter on the division of the sciences ends the book proper.) And what is error? The initial definition is not so helpful. "Knowledge," wrote Locke, "being to be had only of visible and certain Truth, *Errour* is not a Fault of our Knowledge, but a Mistake of our Judgment giving Assent to that, which is not true" (706). The key here is the phrase "not true." For in the end, Locke catalogues error not as a relation to truth but as a premature claim to truth. For Locke, error is a mistaken judgment. Without the divine inspiration of intuitive knowledge, the mind was prone to lose its way among the plurality of ideas and make inaccurate connections among them. Error is simply "wrong assent." However, the only kind of mistake that we can identify is the one that is a result of badly associated ideas. The correction of error would for the most part be entirely negative; that is, it would be a critical dismantling of judgments, rather than a comparison of "idea" with "reality." Error, Locke explains, results from "latent fallacy," the evasion of known probabilities, wrong measures of probability, or the uncritical acceptance of common opinions (715–19). Locke ends this section, rather optimistically it seems, with this assertion: *"There is not so many Men in Errours, and wrong Opinions, as is commonly supposed."* However, Locke is not saying anything very comforting, since he adds this: "Not that I think they embrace the Truth; but indeed, because, concerning those Doctrines they keep such a stir about, they have no Thought, no Opinion at all" (719).

ENLIGHTENMENT ERRORS OF JUDGMENT

The Lockean idea of error as mistake would constantly reappear within the French philosophical tradition throughout the eighteenth century. Error was understood to be a fault in the network of inferences drawn from our own ideas; the form of our ideas did not match the truth of the world. As one philosopher wrote early in the century, "a man, who forms an idea, is mistaken only from the moment he assumes that this idea represents an object it does not represent; in this sense his error consists not in the formation of this idea but in a bad application."[8] It is rare *not* to find in French Enlightenment texts discussing the limitations of human knowledge a recurrent image (made famous by Malebranche,

8. Jean Pierre de Crousaz, *La logique, ou Système des réflexions, qui peuvent contribuer à la netteté & l'étendue de nos connaissances*, 2d ed., rev., 3 vols. (Amsterdam, 1729), 1: 20.

among others) of a square tower that looks from a distance to be round. That was the model of human error: although there was no particular aberration in the sensations—the raw information itself—there was a misplaced step in the series of mental operations that tried to reconstruct this information into an image of an exterior space.[9] "Thus error is not in the sensation, but in the conjecture."[10] As another philosopher explained: "If a painter has not succeeded in representing what he wanted to represent, that is an error on his part; there is none at all on mine to see in the image that it presents to me the traits of proportion and regularity."[11] The Enlightenment critique of error was, it seems, conducted within a boldly "positivist" framework: it was possible to "correct" error with rigorous mental discipline, and, more obviously, as new evidence appeared (we move closer to the tower and see how we erred). There was no such thing as false sensations; they were either agreeable or disagreeable, as Hobbes had said.[12] A false sensation would be a nonexistent one.[13] A similar formulation later in the period claimed that the "error of our judgments can never come from simple, clear, distinct ideas. . . . Error, then, exists only in the judgments we make that what we see truly exists outside."[14]

The seemingly positivist model of error that lurks at the surface of these rationalist texts presented its own particularly difficult problem for Enlightenment thought. If error consisted in the process of mistaken judgments, it would be necessary first to define the suspect mental decision with strict parameters before error could be corrected. The mind, however, was obviously trapped within its own space and the essence of reality was not immediately visible as a mark of comparison. Unlike the painter, we cannot see the object of our mental images. Error would in fact hardly be possible if truth were always clearly visible. Error is the essential *risk* of a reasoning process that had to work its way out from the simple ideas of perception that, in and of themselves, conveyed no real knowledge without comparison and judgment, without, that is, the in-

9. This conclusion would follow from Locke's, that "our *Ideas* are *not capable* any of them *of being false*, till the Mind passes some Judgment on them; that is, affirms or denies something of them": *Essay*, 385. Of course, physiological damage, as some eighteenth-century figures noted, made even the basic sensation suspect. See L. de La Caze, *Idée de l'homme physique et moral, pour servir d'introduction à un traité de médecine* (1775), new ed. (Paris, an VII [1797]), 415; and M.J. Fr. Dufour, *Essai sur les opérations de l'entendement et sur les maladies qui les dérangent* (Paris, 1770), xv.

10. Antoine Le Camus, *Médicine de l'esprit* (Paris, 1753), 39.

11. Abbé Lecren, *Principes de certitude, ou Essai sur la logique* (Paris, 1763), 12.

12. Le Camus, *Médicine de l'esprit*, 40.

13. Lecren, *Principes*, 15.

14. Dufour, *Essai*, 325.

tervention of reason.[15] And once reason intervened, with the construction of complex ideas, it was difficult to disentangle epistemological error. "It is still even more difficult to avoid error in the judgment founded on composed, complex, confused ideas . . . because it is very difficult, not to say impossible, to attain evidence through their means."[16] In this context, Enlightenment "epistemology" was largely negative. The example of the tower is again instructive. There is nothing inconceivable about the preliminary judgment. It is a "true" judgment, in that all the ideas are in their proper place. It just turns out we lack important information. And of course no judgment is final, since our experience is obviously so fragmentary and incomplete. "A true proposition," then, rather than represent reality, "must link ideas that agree and separate those that do not agree." These are internal relations. Agreement is ambiguous. At best, the mind can eliminate any quality "opposed" to another. Consistency is the mark of "truth," even though this truth may turn out to be error when new, and disruptive ideas are acquired.[17] Error is now less an epistemological category than a function of psychological order.

If this were really the case, it should follow that all opinions concerning the actual state of things were fundamentally flawed and ought to be abandoned, as one young French philosopher in Berlin pointed out.

> Our principles, our practices, our senses can be more or less perfect than we think; we will not know how to judge them, because we lack, if I dare speak thus, some scale [*tarif*]. We would need to have a perfect model, according to which we could determine the degree of perfection or imperfection of our principles, practices, and senses, by the greater or lesser conformity there would be between it and us.[18]

For Louis de Beausobre, this stark situation meant that any speculation about what is outside our experience was just madness. Any search for metaphysical foundations was like the quest for the philosopher's stone. New opinions were only new errors. Nature is a "closed book" for the human mind. All we know is our own experience. "But will experience,"

15. See Le Camus, *Médecine de l'esprit*, 71, on how reason introduces error, even though reason is always necessary to navigate the multiplicity of our ideas.

16. Dufour, *Essai*, 326.

17. Lecren, *Principes*, 55–56.

18. Louis de Beausobre, *Le pyrrhonisme raisonable* (Berlin, 1755), 40–41. This is the second edition of *Le pyrrhonisme du sage* (Berlin [i.e., Paris], 1754). Louis's father was Isaac de Beausobre, who wrote the often cited *Histoire critique de Manichée et du manichéisme,* 2 vols. (Amsterdam, 1734–39).

Beausobre asks, "be a torch that leads us to truth? What a guide, that consumes itself without throwing any light."[19] This ephemeral experience, moreover, must travel so many paths between objects and our mind that it inevitably becomes disfigured in the process.

Beausobre doubts that signs are an answer to this epistemological predicament. Words, he says, just mask the radical diversity of our individual experiences. He concludes: "Il est de l'homme d'errer." "The one who suspends his judgment is the most enlightened [*éclairé*]. Everything we affirm, founded on what we prove, is an error." The problem of judgment is resolved by avoiding it altogether. Beausobre rather provocatively suggests that, as "a sage has said . . . to recognize [errors] would require a calculus of aberration."[20]

Diderot, the "sage" to whom Beausobre referred, wanted to find a way to navigate error without relying on the overly theological idea that truth would be found only through speculation of the purest sort. Diderot's interest in the discontinuities and diversities that emerged from the observation of humanity and nature led him to suggest that we give up the search for pure, unmediated knowledge and work our way through the disorganized, complex, and unpredictable world that we actually live in, a world that is more immediately available to us.

> One of the truths that has been heralded these days with the most courage and force . . . is that the territory of mathematicians is an intellectual world, where what we take for rigorous truths completely lose this honor [*avantage*] when they are brought into our world. It has been concluded from this that it was up to experimental philosophy to correct the calculations of geometry, and this consequence has been acknowledged even by geometers. But to what end correct the geometric calculation by experiment? Is it not simpler to be contented with the result of the latter? From this we see that mathematics, particularly transcendent, leads to nothing precise without experiment; that it is a kind of general metaphysics where bodies are stripped of their individual qualities, and that, at the very least, it would remain to create a great work that one could call *The Application of Experience to Geometry*, or *Treatise of the Aberration of Measures*.[21]

However, the search for such a mathematical law of errors that might reveal truth by calculating the system of aberrations was, in the eighteenth

---

19. Ibid., 44–46, 68–69, 82–83, 139, 178.
20. Ibid., 213, 184–85, 215.
21. Denis Diderot, *Pensées sur l'interpretation de la nature*, in *Oeuvres complètes*, ed. Herbert Dieckmann et al. (Paris, 1975–95), 9: 28–29.

century, still in its formative stages.[22] Yet this idea of working through a condition of error to find truth was not unfamiliar in the eighteenth century. Leibniz, for one, believed that it was possible to penetrate the aberrations of error and see the truth embedded there. Leibniz thought that "intelligible properties," like those anamorphic images, distorted and confused to the naked eye, that were revealed as orderly when looked at through an appropriate mirror or from a certain perspective, might be revealed in otherwise distorted and errant ideas.[23]

Without an epistemological version of this anamorphic transformation, however, the human mind would seem to be condemned to failure. The problem, of course, was that only the creator of the image knew the key to its distortions. We had no way of breaking out of our (always potentially) errant condition. "All our ideas are imperfect, *partial* and incomplete; they always leave something to be discovered in an object; they reveal it, as it were, only by fragments. . . . Perfect ideas, total and complete, are a prerogative of the infinitely perfect Being."[24] For the mainstream of Enlightenment thought, the best protection against error (and here error is really defined, as it was by Locke, as an unfounded *claim* to truth) lies in the means used for maintaining our internal order; that is, the signs of language. Though Locke believed that this infant science of signs was a crucial part of understanding human understanding, he was not altogether optimistic about this endeavor to rid ourselves of error. In his analysis of the relation between language and error, Locke recognized that human reasoning was always going to be somewhat imperfect. Words, established as necessary instruments of reason, were also a source of "obscurity and disorder." Perhaps there was no clearly "visible certain truth." The will of God itself, Locke claimed, would become "liable to doubt and uncertainty" as it expressed itself in human language (488, 490). And even if these signs were perfected, there was no guarantee that we were any closer to epistemological certainty with respect to the external world.

French philosophy supposedly founders once Condillac and his followers decide to focus their attention on the perfection of signs and the ordering of ideas, while effectively abandoning the problem of errant judgment. The critique of error, for these late Enlightenment philo-

22. See Zeno Swijtink's article on error theory in *Reader's Guide to the History of Science*, ed. Arne Hessenbruch (London, 2000).
23. Leibniz, *New Essays on Human Understanding*, 258. On the tradition of anamorphic art, see Jurgis Baltrušaitis's fascinating study *Aberrations: An Essay on the Legend of Form*, trans. Richard Miller (Cambridge, Mass., 1989).
24. Jean-Baptiste Cochet, *La clef des sciences & des beaux arts, ou La logique* (Paris, 1750), 36.

sophes, was more a critical deconstruction than an effort to acquire fundamental truths. As the *Encyclopédie* article on error noted, many things we take to be true are in fact just the result of an improper association of signs and ideas. Without proper discipline, we may act on all kinds of "truths" that turn out to be merely artificial (and often misleading) constructions of the mind. As Locke argued in the *Essay,* everyone was a bit "mad," because everyone possessed strange associations of ideas that were not at all the products of careful reasoning. If the truth of a proper connection was somewhat elusive, with attention it was possible to eliminate outright impropriety (394–95). Locke found that often we think ideas are necessarily connected when in fact the connection is merely a product of habit, education, or accident. Leibniz, commenting on this section of Locke's *Essay* in his own *New Essays on Human Understanding,* offered these examples:

> M. Descartes when he was young was fond of a person with a squint, and throughout his life he could not help being drawn to people with that affliction. Another great philosopher, Mr Hobbes, could not (they say) remain alone in the dark without being terrified by visions of ghosts; he did not believe in ghosts, but the impression of them had stayed with him from children's stories. . . . And it is one of the commonest examples of a non-natural association which can generate error—this associating of words with things despite the presence of an ambiguity.[25]

It was useful to examine, then, the ways we associate ideas so as to avoid this kind of error. Improperly "coupled" ideas are, Locke says, "the foundation of the greatest, I had almost said, of all the Errors in the World"(401). So Locke invited philosophers to limit themselves to analyzing and controlling the association of ideas, to limit their intellectual desires and to avoid fantastic metaphysical theory; "our Faculties are not fitted to penetrate into the internal Fabrick and real Essences of Bodies" (646).

We usually see French Enlightenment philosophy as a response to this invitation. Error would be attacked not as a failed relation to metaphysical or transcendent truth but as an unjustified claim to truth. Epistemological accuracy was now a secondary concern. Error, as the *Encyclopédie* article on the topic explained, was located not so much in the moment of the mistaken judgment as in the mental indiscipline that led to the illusion of truth. Precisely ordered ideas would prohibit these kinds of speculative claims, and, if not lead to truth, at least guide us to something. But to what exactly? This article on error, which has always been cred-

---

25. Leibniz, *New Essays on Human Understanding,* 270–71.

ited to J. H. S. Formey, offers little explanation. But in fact the central sections have been lifted intact from Condillac's *Essai sur l'origine des connaissances humaine.*[26] This textbook of Enlightened analytic philosophy has usually been interpreted as a refined version of this modest Lockean epistemology, one that focuses on the human production of knowledge and the proper association of ideas, rather than on building a metaphysical picture of universal reality. And yet Locke raised the fundamental problem of identifying proper and improper connection of ideas without ever resolving it adequately. Given Condillac's tantalizing thoughts on the relationship between error, *erres,* and "fugitive" truth, traced in the first chapter, this foundational text, along with Condillac's other work, calls for a much closer examination.

ERROR AND IDENTITY IN CONDILLAC

If Condillac was perhaps the most influential philosopher of the late eighteenth century, his place in the history of thought is somewhat less exalted. Condillac supposedly wanted to reduce all thought to its original base in sensation, and while that project appealed to many scientific minds in this period (sensationalism was seen to be a kind of Newtonian physics of the mind), the limitations of that approach soon became obvious, and sensationalism became the emblem of a cold, rational Enlightenment that could not comprehend the inner realities of human life: the self, the soul, the creative energy of the mind, everything the Romantics would value in the nineteenth century.[27] There is no question that Condillac did perceive his project in this framework. He believed that he could purge the Lockean system of unnecessary elements and reduce all human mental operations to transformations and associations of sensations. So in the *Essai* Condillac denied Locke's claim for reflection, and while he seemed to acknowledge "will" in the human mind, nowhere in the *Essai* is it systematically studied. However, the cri-

26. See Richard Schwab and Walter Rex, *Inventory of Diderot's "Encyclopédie," Studies on Voltaire and the Eighteenth Century* 85 (1972): 397. The editors of the *Encyclopédie* do refer the reader to Condillac, but note that the "article was taken from the papers of M. Formey," who sold his own encyclopedia material to Diderot and d'Alembert rather than try to compete with their project. See E. Marcu, "Un encyclopédiste oublié: Formey," *Revue de l'histoire littéraire de la langue française* 53 (1953): 303. At any rate, most of the article is copied from pt. 2, sec. 2, chap. 1 of Condillac's *Essai:* "De la première cause de nos erreurs et de l'origine de la vérité."

27. A sympathetic reevaluation of Condillac and sensationalism still repeats this critique: John C. O'Neal, *The Authority of Experience: Sensationist Theory in the French Enlightenment* (University Park, Pa., 1996), esp. 59.

tiques of Condillac's Enlightenment sensationalism take for granted an unproblematic foundation—the seemingly simple "sensation." Yet as we will see, Condillac was doing something quite extraordinary in his analysis of sensation. Indebted more to Leibniz than to Locke in many ways, Condillac was trying to establish intricate, and by no means mechanical, relations among basic sensory experience, an increasingly complex range of mental operations, the identity of the self, and, most important, an elusive universal or divine reality.

Condillac believed that philosophy could not aim at the truth without first analyzing all the previous errors (and their causes) that marked the history of thought. As Locke before him had advised, we have first to know how and what we know before making any claims about ourselves or the world at large. So the first study is the human mind (*l'esprit humain*). Like the pilot, the philosopher must look at all the shipwrecks and figure out what led to them, and that would take him back to the first cause of error, the very nature of our vessel and the way it interacts with its environment. At this point, the philosopher might see that "unique path" that leads to truth.[28] So epistemology is a function of psychology. Condillac is asking: What kind of being are we that allows us to follow the path of truth? For it is clear, from his speculations on discovery and conjecture, that he suspected that the human mind did have a special relationship with truth, however ephemeral it might be. Conjecture "touches" truth in a way; it allows us to identify the possibility of error or the promise of truth. Condillac's epistemological psychology is an attempt to elucidate these relations. His method is, like Locke's, historical, but it is not merely descriptive. He wants to begin at the beginning (the initial impressions of the senses) in order to identify the production of knowledge and the moment of error. In fact, by isolating the mind from ideas, and by isolating ideas from themselves by making them "simple" and "discrete," Locke was never able to reestablish proper relations between ideas, and between ideas and the mind. The border between error and truth is blurred. Condillac, by pushing Locke's story of knowledge farther into the past, wants to demonstrate the intimate connections between mind and ideas at the origin. He thus seeks to explain not the "production" of human understanding but instead a radical separation and a narrative of reconnection. In the process, Condillac locates knowledge, in a strange way, precisely in error, for the recovery of self that is narrated in the *Essai* is described as essentially incomplete

---

28. Etienne Bonnot de Condillac, *Essai sur l'origine des connaissances humaines,* in *Oeuvres philosophiques,* ed. Georges Le Roy, 3 vols. (Paris, 1948), 1: 4a. Further page references are in the text.

and fragmentary. The "operations" of the mind are failed techniques of (psychological) redemption.

So Condillac begins his *Essai* by rejecting any *direct* attempt to transcend the particularity and limitation of our immediate experience. Given that any truth remains invisible and must be the object of some kind of quest, Condillac denies the legitimacy of a search for knowledge that begins with the destination; that is, descriptions of God, systems of ontology, conjectures about spiritual reality. For Condillac, this "philosophical" quest traces out relations that begin with our own particular existence. In the *Essai,* what is being introduced is a metaphysics of *limitation* that Condillac opposes to a more traditional search for hidden essences that ground the structure of reality. This new metaphysics "adapts its researches to the feebleness of the human mind, and as little worried about what might escape it as it is eager for what it can seize, it stays within the limits [*bornes*] marked out for it" (3a). At first glance this distinction reveals what seems to be an epistemological modesty rooted in a rational empiricist tradition. Yet this idea of mental "feebleness" is elusive. The marking of the boundary of human knowledge is not such a simple task. For Condillac, the feebleness of the human mind is not really defined as an inability to penetrate objective reality and directly perceive the "hidden essences" behind the surfaces of appearances, the starting point of a pyrhonnist position. His sensationalist method, it turns out, is not just a systematic analysis of our limited experience drawn from the physical senses.

For Condillac, human inadequacy, which structures the very organization of the *Essai* and defines the central relationship between truth and error, is traced to an even more radical disjuncture within the heart of our being—traced, that is, to the very spatial and temporal modes of human existence. Knowledge, Condillac will show, is not a "product" of individual sensations and their relation. It is more accurate to say that the separation *from* knowledge is defined in terms of a *lapse* into the world of sensation; Condillac is going to describe the very foundation of "Enlightenment psychology" as a highly problematic zone. Our experience is, he will tell us, an essentially errant *disruption* of some preexisting existential continuity. Condillac situates human knowledge between the truth of total interconnection and the absolute immediacy of a self-enclosed world of experience, and the name for this intermediate zone is really error.

The first section of the *Essai* establishes that sensations are the *materials* of knowledge, and not knowledge itself. So the foundational moment of Condillac's history is the distinction between thought and its materials.

Without describing thought, without giving it any concrete determination, Condillac notes that thinking begins with a negation: sensation is a kind of agitation of the mind, but perception *is not* this agitation. Perception is not produced by sensation, it is occasioned by the concrete sensory impression. Similarly with consciousness, which Condillac defines as the difference between perception and the awareness of the perception. Having perception awakens the experience of knowing one is perceiving. And once perception is "self-aware," it is possible, Condillac goes on to say, that the mind can begin to organize perception, for if it is aware of having perception, it can be aware of having one perception instead of another. This discrimination is named "attention." Again: attention is not produced by perception, but rather is made possible by the experience of perception. And given the focus of attention on particular perceptions, the mind begins to create what Condillac calls a "bond" or *liaison* between perceptions that succeed one another. At some moment, a perception is repeated, and this occasions a sense of self, for in the repetition is marked continuity. Here the mind recognizes that despite the variety and succession of perceptions, there is a constant identity of self that grounds the very space of perceptual attention. This is called "reminiscence," and the word here is significant. Condillac implies that the mind *remembers itself* at the moment of repetition. Self is not a product of this narrative of perception, but rather the underlying potential revealed only after the concrete experiences that make its appearance possible (10b–11a).

This narrative, then, begins at the end, for the story of mental progress depends on the identity of the self that is in question. If Condillac tries to explain how Locke's internal "eye" could ever arise, he seems to have just deferred or displaced this identity. Yet Condillac does in the end explicitly address this critical question. In the section of the *Essai* on abstraction Condillac goes beyond the basic problem of general terms to provide a complex explanation for this "fallen" self. Here he says the limitation and weakness of the human mind that ground the new metaphysics are not located in the alienation of mind from an external reality. The fundamental limitation of the mind in fact is what produces the very split between ideas and mental operation, the division that Locke and so many others assumed from the start. The self, according to Condillac, cannot be considered a transcendent subject that moves through time, experiencing individual sensory data received from external sensors; the self as an identity lapses *into* time in order to perceive anything at all. Condillac writes that our first "ideas" are basic ones: sights, sounds, movement.

Now all these ideas [i.e., sensations, simple ideas] present a true reality, since they are strictly speaking only our own being variously [*différemment*] modified. Our mind, being too limited to reflect *at the same time* on all the modifications that can belong to it, is forced to *distinguish* them in order to take them *one after the other*. (50a; my italics)

Condillac suggests here that because the mind can deal with only so many "modifications," it wrenches itself apart to accommodate any excess. It violently "abstracts" itself from its modifications, and in the process creates what appear now to be independent entities: ideas. Since ideas were at one time simply "being" (a "true reality"), the *trace* of reality still lingers in them; that is why the mind takes them to be real.[29] What Condillac provides here is a theory of self and knowledge predicated on the structure of error. The mind fails to control its own reality, so it creates a fictional reality of ideas that it must at the same time pretend to be real. The narrative of self that begins the *Essai* is really a narrative of recognition, but it is the recognition of radical error; hence the emphasis, at this point of the text, on negation. The mind, through a series of confrontations with experience, realizes that it is *not* that experience, while recognizing that its own identity is strangely absent when it is separated from the realm of concrete experience.

Condillac wrote about this problem in another context, in an early anonymous dissertation on Leibnizian monads. He explained there that our sense of self is necessarily vague at any one point of time. We perceive ourselves in succession, in the midst of multiple, particular experiences, and it is only by peeling away the concrete determinations of this original identity, Condillac says, that we can hope to find again the ground that structures their appearance. The difficulty is that when we take our modifications separately, we see that there is no one particular sensation that we could not strip away. "Consequently, we strip ourselves successively of one and the other sensation, and we seek to consider our *nous* by making an abstraction of all that can belong to it." What is left over from what Condillac calls a "violent abstraction" is not so much a real idea or acquaintance with something tangible as a "name that we give to something we do not know at all."[30] Identity, in Condillac's text, is not a fixed structure defining relations; identity inhabits an endless series of differences and differentiations. It does not follow, however, that the self is simply an artificial construction.

29. Condillac plays on the temporal and spatial connotations of the verb *différer* in his *Dictionnaire des synonymes*, in *Oeuvres philosophiques*, 3: 210a.

30. Condillac, *Les monades*, ed. L. L. Bongie, *Studies on Voltaire and the Eighteenth Century* 187 (1980): 145.

In the *Essai,* Condillac thus affirms that the subject of thought must be *one* but at the same time avoids any detailed discussion of what that unity must be. What is clear, he says, is that the "thinking being" cannot be a collection of parts, a "multitude." The relation between parts can be only an external one. Condillac acknowledges the possible objection that this "property of thought" itself is unified, although "possessed" by a whole made up of parts, analogous to the way the property of keeping time does not rest in any one part of a watch but only in the totality of this structure. Condillac, however, dismisses this analogy; significantly, he objects that the property of keeping time is particularly suited to a composed subject precisely because time is successive and measurable. A true unity, he writes, cannot be decomposed into discrete parts; it is altogether something different (7b). As he will say later in the *Essai,* our experiences seem to belong to something, "affecting, despite their variety and succession, a being who is constantly the same *nous*" (14a). This apparent paradox is explained by the original fall of the self into an artificial but inescapable division. This original fall is the essential "contradiction" that marks for Condillac both the origin and limitation of human knowledge. Because we cannot reflect simultaneously on all our self-modifications, we *abstract* ourselves from these variations and consider these modifications as external, outside our essential being. In the process we begin to lose the intimate reality both of these modifications and of our *moi,* which is alienated in this fragmented and temporally dislocated experience. For Condillac, the self is lost in time. It is not pieced together out of discrete experiences, nor is it a transcendent entity that exists outside of its basic determinations, its "modifications"; it is expressed in fragmented form and thus loses its own identity at any one particular moment. Condillac's unified soul, the *point de réunion* for ideas, was not a contradictory, orthodox addition to his radical analysis of thought as a fractured network of sensations.[31]

This lapse into temporal forms has its spatial counterpart for Condillac. Our inability to comprehend at one time the total relational network that modifies our own being requires us to dissect our experience into

31. Resistance to this idea of fragmented identity results in some misreadings of Condillac's work. Isabel Knight can see only an essential contradiction in Condillac's juxtaposition of discrete sensations and a unified "soul." Condillac atomizes the self into a "collection of sensations," she writes, then simply restores its identity "by *fiat.*" Her argument is that at some level Condillac resisted his own radical philosophy of mind, and thus annexed this "collection of sensations" to an orthodox, immaterial soul, without ever defending the move. For Knight, he "tacks on" a conservative theological idea to a philosophy "uncongenial to it": *The Geometric Spirit: The Abbé de Condillac and the French Enlightenment* (New Haven, 1968), 97–98.

discrete sensations and consider the objects presented to us as individual entities. In order to perceive anything at all, we abstract the world into parts. "The notion of extension, stripped of all its difficulties and taken from the clearest side, is just the idea of many beings that *appear to us* the ones *outside* the others" (9b, my italics; Condillac voices a similar formulation in *Les monades*, 169). Differentiation of spatial relations is an errant but necessary mode of understanding. As Condillac explains in the *Traité des systèmes*, the different forms of things conceal their essence in its original purity, yet these same forms reveal this essence in a fragmentary manner, just as the pure shape of something is never wholly present in any one particular "object" but still can be perceived in its successive determinations. We cannot fix this perfect shape in one specific place, but it is possible to abstract it from many places.[32]

If space and time are the results of an essential fragmentation of our being, a lapse into the particular that is marked by discrete sensations of discrete objects, then the search for knowledge cannot be accomplished through the reconstruction of the whole by means of these discrete parts.[33] The path to truth, for Condillac, is the path back to this original identity (of self, mind, and experience of reality). The human mind must seek to regain an identity that exists now radically outside this successive and differentiated existence that defines human understanding.[34] For Paul de Man, one of the few commentators to focus on this particular aspect of Condillac's text, this essential fragmentation is, however, evidence in Condillac's work that there is in fact no identity outside of what is *constructed* by a self-constituting subject. Abstraction, de Man argues, is not an effort at regaining something lost in a fallen condition, but the "only way [the subject] can constitute its own existence, its own ground." Therefore, de Man writes, for Condillac "being and identity are the *result* of a resemblance which is not in things but *posited* by an act of the mind which, as such, can only be verbal."[35]

32. Condillac, *Traité des systèmes*, in *Oeuvres philosophiques*, 1: 171.

33. On this point, see Erik Ryding, "La notion du moi chez Condillac," *Theoria* 21 (1955): 129.

34. Rousseau's social contract is the obvious analogy here: the general will is a perfect unity at the origin, yet can be expressed only through the imperfect, fragmented individual citizens. Yet these citizens are not a multitude or aggregation of independent entities. The common bond defines these individuals as fragments of something higher, transforming them into participants in the general will. The general will may always be right, but there is no one privileged location for its appearance; it is always mediated by the potentially errant individual. See *Du contrat social*, bk. II, chap. 3, "Si la volonté générale peut errer."

35. Paul de Man, "The Epistemology of Metaphor," *Critical Inquiry* 5 (1978): 24–25; my italics.

However, Condillac's explicit concern with the problem of error does, I think, lead him to the idea that the very recognition of failure that he has unfolded in his history of the self gives us insight into an identity that must *precede* the very experience of fragmentation. The process of following transformations and differentiations is not, to be sure, a cumulative one. Error is not the difference between identity and disorder, but rather is a name for the border between them. This kind of error is not something that can be easily eliminated.[36] Error, for Condillac, is suspended between identity and fragmentation, order and disorder, and is really a function of the mind's original weakness. This ambiguous and complex relationship between error and identity, which runs through Condillac's sensational narrative, must be clarified.

The simple idea, the abstracted modification, exists in itself, indivisible, immune to any misrepresentation, a "true reality," as Condillac puts it. Two simple ideas cannot be compared, they merely succeed one another. But to remain in this state of pure succession, where ideas are never connected, only experienced in their simplicity, is to be an imbecile, writes Condillac in the *Essai*. This person "would be without imagination and memory. . . . He would be incapable of reflection." However, the basic inadequacy of the human intellect means that it is impossible to make sense of all these ideas taken together in all their complexity. An individual who randomly connected all ideas with one another could not escape total confusion, and would be mad. Some middle ground must therefore be found that allows us to escape mere succession and recover some remnant of our original identity, yet avoid the bewildering continuity of ideas (18b).

The construction of general ideas, abstractions, is the way the mind frees itself to traverse its temporally marked and spatially fragmented mode of perception. The sign binds itself with the simple idea and frees it up from its immediate and fixed position. The sign also frees mental attention from the "dependence" on those objects that immediately act upon it. With the appearance of the sign, the mind is able to begin making connections across the temporal boundaries of successive sensations. But here error intervenes. Abstractions isolate and separate ideas from their concrete surroundings and force them into relations with other similarly isolated ideas, excised from other locations. The abstraction, as Condillac conceives it, is a mark both of man's unique ability to tran-

---

36. See Ryding, "La notion du moi," 130. Compare James Stam's argument that the "natural sequence of things" was, for Condillac, a *corrective* against error. See his "Condillac's Epistemolinguistic Question," in *Psychology of Language and Thought: Essays on the Theory and History of Psycholinguistics,* ed. R. W. Rieber (New York, 1980).

scend his immediacy and of his failure to regain in a complete form the identity of his total existence. The rise of the abstraction frees man to trace out the multiple forms of his experience (and the world), yet through this very process opens up the possibility of error. For the abstraction is possible only when an idea is excised (*retranchée*) from its context and juxtaposed with other ideas. The simple idea is never errant, and has no confusion or obscurity, but the general idea introduces error by taking things from certain aspects only, subtracting from or adding something to what was originally there (111b).[37] In fact, these ideas are always "defective" because the mind can never fully integrate all aspects of its perception (50a). Abstractions, then, are never reconstructive. The abstraction does not mimic a specific entity in time or space, but serves to establish relations among ideas that from the beginning are the result of a radical fragmentation of identity. In other words, abstractions are not dangerous because they "violate" pure sensations; they are dangerous because in seeking the higher order of existence that has been lost in our lapse into space and time, abstractions always fail to integrate all possible forms and relations within our experience and outside ourselves. Nonetheless, they allow us to distinguish our ideas (our self-modifications) in a manner that goes beyond mere succession (50).[38]

The problem of mapping the paths to knowledge is therefore not the collection and organization of discrete parts encountered along the way. Knowledge consists in retracing *rapports* between ideas, relations that have been in a sense lost because of a radical intellectual inadequacy. The composition and recomposition of ideas is the search for *rapports*, an effort at discovering resemblances obscured by differentiations and deferrals. A *rapport* is, in Condillac's terms, a mark of identity, not a bridge

37. Rousseau takes up this idea in the "Profession de foi du vicaire savoyard." Sensation cannot penetrate the reality of objects: the "passive being" lacks the force to "bend back" (*replier*) objects upon one another. The active faculty of judgment disrupts "objects" in an effort to discover relations. This activity introduces error, "since the operation that compares is faulty, and because my understanding which judges relations mixes its errors with the truth of the sensations that only reveal the objects": *Emile, ou De l'éducation*, in *Oeuvres complètes*, ed. Bernard Gagnebin and Marcel Raymond, 5 vols. (Paris, 1964–95), 4: 571–73.

38. Knight can see in Condillac's discussion of error only a basic inconsistency, since she sees the problem only in terms of a basic inside/outside structure, where ideas are wholly "subjective" or alternatively representational of some outer "reality." Thus Knight argues that Condillac "failed to face squarely the problem of reality created by the subjectivist epistemology": *Geometric Spirit*, 35. It is possible, though, that both "inside" and "outside" for Condillac were modeled on a radical fragmentation of something that existed without these spatial restrictions. This fragmentation was destabilizing but at the same time it allowed for the interpenetration of psychological and "essential" forms, since they were united at some higher level.

across a divide. As he noted in the *Dictionnaire des synonymes*, the word *rapport* (from *rapporter*) properly means the carrying of something back to the place from which it had been sent. The *rapport*, in other words, is a "relation" of something to itself. Even in normal, figurative use, a *rapport* signifies a resemblance or an analogy; that is, some characteristic "having been carried one place has been carried back to another" by the mind. Condillac points out that *rapport*, in the sense of a "report," means quite literally the repetition of something that has already taken place somewhere else, at another time. A "relation," then, is a mark of common participation in some higher order: two things related are two versions of one thing in different spatial or temporal locations.

Therefore it is hardly surprising that the very foundation of Condillac's psychology is an organic one. Attention, the basic differentiating force, is a matter not of will but of affinity, he writes. "Things attract our attention from the side where they have the most affinity [*rapport*] with our temperament, our passions, and our condition" (14b). The *rapports* between ourselves and the objects that act on us create ideas, and these ideas form *liaisons* among themselves that serve to manifest the various faculties of memory, reflection, and so on. For Condillac, the fundamental relations he describes here are never external ones; that is, these relations do not link independent units or entities into larger forms. As a special form of *rapport*, the *liaison* also serves to integrate differentiated entities that are already part of something higher than both of them. Condillac never describes the "links" (*liens*) between ideas, for a link only "serves to hold many things together," and is essentially negative: it can only temporarily impede the forces of separation. The *liaison*, on the other hand, "forms part of the things united [*liées*], and it forms a single body, a single whole."[39] These organic relations that are the products of mental activity are consequently not arbitrary, Condillac explains. In his scheme, analogy becomes a powerful and prolific tool, since the network of relations is infinite, yet these relations are never imposed or invented. Contrary to many linguistic formulations, the sign is never arbitrary for Condillac, even if it is often conventional and "unnatural."[40] Each word supposes a reason for its adoption, although the process of analogy on which language is built might take many forms.[41] The human intellectual quest, then, is the discovery (unconcealing) of *rapports* through the combination of ideas, by means of abstractions.

39. Condillac, *Dictionnaire des synonymes*, 358b.
40. See Sylvain Auroux, "Empirisme et théorie linguistique chez Condillac," in *Condillac et les problèmes du langage*, ed. Jean Sgard (Geneva and Paris, 1982), 181.
41. Condillac, *La logique*, in *Oeuvres philosophiques*, 2: 419a.

For Condillac desire is the organizing force for this analogical quest, the energy driving the composition and recomposition of ideas. It is important to note, however, that desire is not merely a primitive energy that is in its pure form nothing more than restlessness. As Condillac describes it, desire arises from need, and need is structured as a repetition of what has already taken place. Desire "is the direction of our faculties toward the objects of which we are deprived."[42] If the *rapport* is defined as the movement of something from one place to another and back again, then need signifies a lack, an anticipation of the movement back toward the place (our own being) where the object of desire *once was*. "To be deprived of a thing you judge necessary for yourself produces uneasiness or disquiet in you."[43] To have a desire, Condillac wrote, is to know of a better condition.[44] It is impossible to desire something that is not already known, and thus the organizing of ideas according to need is an effort to regain something that has been lost. Only the precision of our signs will allow this organizing force to search out with accuracy those objects that will complete our lack. The "equivocal term" or "metaphoric expression" confuses the destination of desire, causing it to seek out inappropriate objects with tenuous connections to our essential self. Truth and error, however, cannot be reduced to a structure of biological need. Condillac goes on to say that the very necessity of this "quest for resemblance" to complete our endless variety of needs is the *fundamental* lack that structures our existence in the world, our fundamental separation from our own self-identity and the identity of the experienced universe. Desire is itself, Condillac writes, the "most pressing of our needs"; desire *has become necessary* to the soul [*lui est devenue nécessaire*]."[45] "Desire" is a lack that results from our alienation from totality, an alienation that conditions our lapse into a sensationalist mode of being. Again, Condillac structures alienation as a loss. Yet this means

42. Condillac, *Dictionnaire des synonymes*, 200–201.
43. Condillac, *Cours d'études*, in *Oeuvres philosophiques*, 1: 25.
44. Condillac, *Traité des sensations*, in *Oeuvres philosophiques*, 1: 232b. Rousseau also wrote that "one can desire or fear things only on the basis of the ideas one has of them": *Discours sur l'origine de l'inégalité*, in *Oeuvres complètes*, 3: 143.
45. Condillac, *Traité des animaux*, in *Oeuvres philosophiques*, 1: 372b. On this aspect of Condillac's philosophy, Cassirer writes: "In order to understand the latent energy behind all the metamorphoses of the mind, which does not permit it to retain any form but drives it on to ever new shapes and operations, one must assume in the mind an original moving force": *Philosophy of the Enlightenment*, 103. This "original force" of desire is linked to the original identity of being. It seems to me that Condillac's theory of desire does not at all lead to the conclusion that his "associationism enslaved belief to fantasy and self-interest" or "wishful thinking," as Lorraine Daston argues in her *Classical Probability in the Enlightenment* (Princeton, 1988), 370, 210.

that the *rapports* that we articulate and follow are not merely contingent: they may (but do not necessarily) constitute a rediscovery of this previously known identity we lack (and desire). This lack is the fundamental origin of any search for knowledge. Our errant journey is itself evidence of the truth we seek. Condillac here steps away from the traditional epistemological concern with judgment; that is, with establishing the accuracy of any particular representation of external reality. He is essentially redefining our internal mental life, that constant modification of being, *and* our being in the world, as similarly fragmented aspects of one universal totality. There is in Condillac's work an ambiguous relation between the internal and external; there is no simple mapping of the relationship between these worlds because the border space is destabilized in his account.

For Condillac, then, the nature of analogical relationships precludes any clear path to truth. All analogies necessarily allow for movement in different directions: this errancy is a condition of the transformative nature of *rapports*. A lack of discipline in the formation of these analogies, however, would send this energy of desire in completely inappropriate directions. The errant analogy will lead to truth, for Condillac, only if the path is a truly natural one. Identifying the path of natural relations is the central problem. Condillac's solution, Sylvain Auroux writes, was not a referential but a genetic one. Identity was in fact just the continuity of a transformative process. Yet Auroux goes on to claim that for Condillac this transformative process was, in the end, strictly linguistic. Deprived of any representative content, knowledge could be controlled only through the system of a well-made language.[46] However, if error is the risk of an analogical adventure that is possible only because of the very difference of forms (linguistic or otherwise), then, if we follow Auroux, Condillac's philosophy of control would appear to be condemned to "frivolity," an endless substitution of forms that may not "err," but still the chain of substitutions never goes anywhere, either.

This is how Derrida reads Condillac's semiological epistemology. Derrida criticizes Condillac's effort to maintain the concept of identity in the midst of difference: "As we have noted, the degree, the gradual difference ruins the identical proposition by dislocating the *is*. But at the same time the degree makes the identical proposition possible by giving it a synthetic value which advances knowledge and prohibits frivolity." Derrida denies that such a "synthesis" can have any ontological significance. Metaphysics is just the tracing of a temporal chain of gradual differences

46. Sylvain Auroux, "Condillac, ou La vertu des signes," introduction to Condillac, *La langue des calculs*, ed. Anne-Marie Chouillet (Lille, 1981), xvii–xviii, xxiv.

that always tends to frivolity, since both the sign and the idea always escape each other yet exist only in a mutually determining relation.[47] Derrida (and Auroux) do not want to consider the possibility that Condillac has a conception of an order that structures these two realms without ever appearing in its own form.[48]

As Condillac describes, although the comprehensive truth of universal totality inevitably escapes us, we can still map out these paths of analogy, the "identical" truths that are manifested in different forms in time and space. The analogous *rapport* marks both continuity and the intervention of the new. The continuity is not found in the two elements; rather, in the difference the identity is revealed. In his later work, Condillac emphasized that truth was found only in identical propositions. The model for truth was the strict set of identities mapped in mathematical calculus. As he explained in the *Langue des calculs:*

> Let us recall that we can go only from the known to the unknown. Now how can we go from one to the other? It is because the unknown is present [*se trouver*] in the known, and it is there only because it is the same thing. We can therefore pass from what we know to what we do not know only because what we do not know is the same thing as what we know.[49]

On first reading, it is true, it would seem that truth is really only tautology, and thus entirely frivolous. But Condillac takes great pains to make clear that identity in this context does not mean "exactly the same." As he explains, "*Six is six* is a proposition identical and frivolous at the same time," and thus there can never be any need to form it: "It would lead us nowhere." Meaningful identity requires that two things are different *forms* of the same thing. And therefore *three and three make six* is an identity that is not at all frivolous. As should be clear, Condillac does not believe that identity (understood now as the *ground* of all appearances) can be made visible, but the variant forms of its expression can be traced and mapped in an endless series of analogical relations. This is metaphysics. So identity does not signify the equality of two separate things, but rather one totality expressed in two forms or places. "In effect, ob-

---

47. Jacques Derrida, *The Archeology of the Frivolous: Reading Condillac*, trans. John P. Leavey (Lincoln, Neb., 1980), 132. See also Nicolas Rousseau, *Connaissance et langage chez Condillac* (Geneva, 1986), esp. 396–97.

48. Auroux does say that in his early work Condillac assumed that "nature" was the teleological foundation for this path of resemblance, but that his own philosophy of language led him to the more radical position of the *Langue des calculs*, where the well-made language is the only criterion for the validity of knowledge. See Sylvain Auroux, "Condillac," in *Dictionnaire des philosophes*, ed. Denis Huisman (Paris, 1984), 1: 587–92.

49. Condillac, *La langue des calculs*, 431b.

jects must present themselves to created intelligences according to the *rapports* they have with them."[50]

In essence, the universe is always taking on new appearances, depending on the modes of understanding, the specific nature of interaction. "In this way [the universe] multiplies itself in some way. It is a Proteus, which takes an infinity of forms."[51] The variety of perceptions and the faculties founded on them also express a Protean self: "Senses, memory, imagination, understanding are only a Proteus that passes through different transformations."[52] Truth, then, is in the identification of forms (our own and "objective" ones), and not the equation of independently existing entities. As the *Encyclopédie* puts it, "*identity* does not suppose two different things, [as] there would no longer be *identity;* it supposes only two aspects of one same object."[53] The very possibility, in Condillac's scheme, of a relationship of self, sense, and world indicates the possibility of their common participation in a higher form of being. No one relation is sufficient to outline the form of this identity, yet when the various versions are identified and the incoherent (false) relation is eliminated, some sense of this reality will reveal itself.

The human mind progresses, then, by constantly seeking new directions and new ideas so that it can discover yet another dimension of the Protean universe. The intervention of misplaced links is an inevitable danger since we are abandoned in the midst of a differentiated and fragmented world, and it is not always easy to discern the analogical paths. A degree of error is ever present because the "infinity of forms" can never stabilize and be perfectly integrated into one whole. The incommensurable cannot be eliminated in the name of a totalizing truth in this epistemological framework. Since unity is not available to measure the gap between organic resemblance and mistaken juxtaposition, it is difficult to distinguish missteps from errant progress. Without this master truth, it is difficult to regain the perfect identity of expressions. It is often necessary to make many detours to arrive at one truth, Condillac said,[54] though God, outside of time and space, "has no need for [general ideas]; his infinite knowledge comprehends all individuals, and it is no more

50. Ibid., 431b–32a.
51. Condillac, *Les monades,* 196. Cf. Condillac, *Traité des systèmes,* in *Oeuvres philosophiques,* 1: 171a.
52. Condillac to Gabriel Cramer, June 10, 1750, in L. L. Bongie, "A New Condillac Letter and the Genesis of the *Traité des sensations," Journal of the History of Philosophy* 16 (1978): 94. This "Protean logic" in Condillac is sketched out in Bongie's introduction to Condillac, *Les monades,* 89–107.
53. *Encyclopédie,* s.v. "identité."
54. Condillac, *Cours d'études VI: Histoire moderne,* in *Oeuvres philosophiques,* 2: 221b.

difficult for him to think of everything at once than to think of one by it-self."[55] Our knowledge is in fact a product of error, but error of a certain kind. The knowledge we gain is true but partial.

> A thinking being would not form propositions if it had all knowledge with-out having acquired it, and if its view could seize at one time and distinctly all the ideas and all the relations [*rapports*] of that which is. This is God: each truth is for him like two plus two equals four, he sees all [truths] in one only, and nothing is more frivolous to his eyes than this science with which we in-flate our pride, however good it is to convince us of our feebleness.[56]

Our knowledge is supplementary and therefore somewhat imperfect. But the error of knowledge is between this unitary truth and mere disor-dered experience; it is error on the way to truth. In any case, Condillac's self works through an errant condition of limited knowledge by patient and sometimes tentative forays into the unknown. These searches are never totally speculative, because they build on previous relations through the mode of analogy, but the analogy is always the introduction of something new that projects the previous knowledge into a new zone. The conjecture has this function. It "can blaze [*frayer*] a path to new knowledge [*connaissances*]."[57] "Let us not allow ourselves, above all in the beginning, to fall back often on the same ideas; and let us try to speak each time in a different manner."[58]

As Condillac wrote to his friend Gabriel Cramer, the mathematician, in 1749, "It is true, Monsieur, that all the properties of an object are only the essence of it seen in different respects [*envisagée sous divers égards*]."[59] Unity is revealed partially in the sequence of *rapports* we identify. The key difficulty, of course, is locating the identity, identifying the continu-ity between forms. Condillac believed that we can begin to articulate identity by mapping out resemblances, even if we fail to seize it in one visible form. This articulation was not simply a product of linguistic analogy, but neither was it a representative analysis of some fixed exter-

---

55. Condillac, *Essai*, 49b.

56. Condillac, *Cours d'études IV: De l'art de raisonner,* in *Oeuvres philosophiques,* 1: 748b. Rousseau repeats this image: "The supreme intelligence has no need to reason; for it there are neither premises nor conclusions, there are not even propositions; it is purely intuitive, it sees equally everything that is and everything that can be, all truths are for it only a single idea, as all places a single point, and all times a single moment. Human power acts through means, divine power acts by itself": *Emile,* 4: 593.

57. Ibid., 1: 682b.

58. Condillac, *Langue des calculs,* 450a.

59. Condillac, *Lettres inédites à Gabriel Cramer,* ed. Georges Le Roy (Paris, 1953), 73. Cf. *Langue des calculs,* 454b.

nal nature. The path of relations could be natural even as the very existence of this path precluded a total understanding of the nature that was revealed to the mind. For Condillac, we dimly sense the truth, and this meant that we must seek it out in the immediate relations of our own being and mind. Trying to elaborate that image is a mistake. The metaphor of the path illuminates this conception of knowledge. As Condillac once noted, the genius does not gain direct access to truth: "What is a genius, then? A simple mind [*esprit*] who finds what no one has been able to find before him. Nature, who puts us on the path of discoveries, seems to watch over him so that he never deviates from it."[60]

Error cannot therefore be measured against the truth of the voyage's destination. If truth were available, the only problem would be the need to overcome the obstacles that separate us from this goal. Condillac never introduces this kind of structure in his writing. The constant image in all his works is that of the path, whether the *chemin de la vérité* or the *chemin des découvertes*. And, as he later explained in the *Dictionnaire des synonymes*, there is a crucial distinction between the *chemin* and what he calls the *route* (road): "The *route* is a path considered in relation to the place where it leads. . . . The *chemin* is more related to the means one employs."[61] A *route* crosses a space to reach a destination, and there is no need to attend to the countryside. A *chemin*, on the other hand, follows the contour of the land and may lead somewhere, but only after it has traversed the natural geography. The *route*, etymologically, signifies a rupture (from the Latin *rumpere*), a break of continuity, whereas the *chemin* follows the accidents of the terrain. This wayward path is sometimes obscured, and therefore it is always possible to lose the way, but these errant steps that can never march straight to the truth gradually reveal the complex topography of knowledge. The mind, for Condillac, redeems its fragmented state by embarking on an errant adventure through the tropical wilds of analogy. The self is not adrift in a chaos of atomized objects and sensations; rather, it is a fragmented, monadological entity working through error with the limited tools of reason.[62]

60. Condillac, *Langue des calculs,* 470b.
61. Condillac, *Dictionnaire des synonymes,* 121a.
62. As Cassirer writes, the atom "is a unit which, so to speak, resists multiplicity and retains indivisibility despite every attempt to resolve it into subdivisions. The monad, on the other hand, knows no such opposition; for with the monad there is no alternative between unity and multiplicity, but only their inner reciprocity and necessary correlation. . . . It is a whole which is not the sum of its parts but which constantly unfolds into multiple aspects. . . . [E]very individual substance is not only a fragment of the universe, it is the universe itself seen from a particular viewpoint": *Philosophy of the Enlightenment,* 31–32. See Condillac, *Les monades,* esp. pt. 2, chap. 9, "De la première monade ou de Dieu."

Reading Condillac from this perspective of loss and rediscovery opens up a theological dimension to Enlightenment psychology and the epistemology of error. This framework is not dogmatic, but arises from the very analysis of human identity itself.[63] It is, in other words, a secular theology of the mind, and the radical fracture of mind constitutes a philosophical original sin for Condillac. The origin of error that leads to shipwreck is, in the end, an inevitable condition, and the "sole road" that leads to truth turns out to be, if not mythical, at least errant, fragmented, obscure.

This framework allows us to follow the problem of error and aberration into an entirely different realm of Enlightenment thought, the realm of the political. With Condillac, we saw that reason, systematic thought, and logic all were means to be employed in the pursuit of a mysterious truth that constantly escapes our limited sphere of existence as fragmented individuals in time and space. Politically, late Enlightenment thought struggles with an analogous problem: how to rediscover the original identity of a community among fragmented, even antagonistic individuals. How was it possible to prepare insight into the sublime unity that defines the very possibility of community even as it escapes our direct observation?

63. It seems less than certain to me that Condillac's "religious assertions are always extraneous and often absurd," that "the most striking thing about [his] religious references is their irrelevance to everything in his philosophy," or that there was a "sharp separation between his religious claims and his philosophy." This is what Knight argues, in *Geometric Spirit*, 297, 141, 143.

CHAPTER 4

Cutting through Doubt: Condorcet and the Political Decision

In the *Encyclopédie*, a decision was defined briefly but significantly as a "resolution taken on some question that was controversial or in doubt."[1] The decision was made in a state of uncertainty and thus constituted a risk, and although this risk might be characterized in a variety of ways, depending on how the situation was understood, it would seem that the very conditions that made a decision necessary—namely, doubt or controversy—are what make the decision itself problematic: by definition it can have no precedent. Any problem that cannot be solved in its own terms or within the parameters of established norms requires an intrusion of some kind from the outside,[2] which is exactly what the etymology of the verb *décider* implies. The Latin root *caedere* means, appropriately, "to cut off, to slice, to separate, to cut into pieces."[3] The decision can be seen as a violent intervention into a situation that in and of itself cannot be "decided." Within a community, then, a decision carries with it the potential for destruction. The problem of the decision is the problem of cutting through dissension while preserving the essential identity of the original whole.

For any Enlightenment analysis of the political decision, it was necessary to explain how, in the midst of difference and dispute, the commu-

---

1. *Encyclopédie, ou Dictionnaire raisonné des sciences, des arts et des métiers . . .* , ed. Denis Diderot and Jean d'Alembert, 17 vols. (Paris, 1751), s.v. "décision."

2. "Every decision is like surgery. It is an intervention into a system and therefore carries with it the risk of shock": Peter F. Drucker, *The Effective Executive* (New York, 1967), 155.

3. *Le grand Robert de la langue française*, 2d ed. (1985), and *Grand Larousse de la langue française* (1972), s.v. "décider."

nity would stay together, rallying behind a decision that clearly went against the express wishes or interests of some segments of that community. For Rousseau, as for many other eighteenth-century writers, the basic question of agreement was solved by the idea of the social contract, an original unanimous decision to give up the individual right to make decisions precisely so that the social body would not fall apart at the first crisis. Still, the question remained as to how the decision could best be made within constituted political communities. In other words, there was still the problem of making sure the decision that reintroduced order would be a *legitimate* one. Condorcet, perhaps the first systematic theorist of decision in the eighteenth century, used a "scientific" approach. He saw that the decision was not always correct simply because it was made by an authorized figure or political body. Error always threatened political decisions. Condorcet did not, however, try to analyze decisions themselves in scientific terms. What he attempted to do was analyze the *probability* of decisions so that the community, which was by definition split on a particular issue, would stand behind the decision that was made. Condorcet's approach was grounded in a complex intellectual context; he was drawing on rather new Enlightenment ideas concerning the nature of probability, the nature of the social community, the rational nature of the individual, and the relationship between historical progress and truth. But it is difficult, I think, even to understand the real problem Condorcet was addressing if Rousseau's deeply complex confrontation with the nature of political decision is ignored. So before unfolding Condorcet's own complex intellectual environment, I will begin with a discussion of the *Social Contract* and the role error plays in Rousseau's conceptualization of decision and legitimacy.

DECISION AND ERROR IN ROUSSEAU

In the *Social Contract* Rousseau realized that the decision operated on the boundary between identity and fragmentation. His attempt to describe political association as the original agreement to give all rights up to the nation as a whole was one way of preserving order in the community despite internal disagreement. And yet, for Rousseau, it was clear that the "general will" was not simply a transcendent authority that could somehow arbitrate particular disputes in the name of order, like the Hobbesian sovereign. To remain general, wrote Rousseau, the general will cannot be directed toward any particular entity or interest. It cannot even decide between public and private interests when consensus is lacking, since "it loses its natural rectitude when it is directed toward any individual and specific object."[4] Once the general will sides with any one interest, Rousseau said, it becomes merely particular, a concrete position that is therefore, he noted significantly, "subject to error."

The decision, then, is not for Rousseau a process of some kind that merely weighs the merits of specific alternatives. This is why the general will cannot be found simply by summing up individual voices: the general will lies instead in "the common interest that unites" these individuals before any disagreement arises. The deciding force of the general will cuts through the errant particulars to reintroduce this original commonality. The general will emerges from the collective subject of decision. For this reason, Rousseau noted, a political decision is not at all analogous to a judicial one:

> The admirable agreement of interest and harmony that gives to communal deliberations an equitable character one sees fade away in the discussion of any particular action [*affaire*], for want of a common interest that would unite and identify the ruling of the judge with that of the litigant [*partie*]. (374)

The part must already form part of a whole for the genuinely political decision to be effective. Rousseau's difficulty, then, is to formulate a method whereby the decision of the sovereign authority can be identified with *conflicting* positions. For only then will the losing party accept the decision as final.

One of Rousseau's important arguments, therefore, was that the general will must articulate laws that always remain general; that is, make laws that apply to all equally and do not designate a particular group within the nation. The specificity of each particular law, then, cannot reside in its application to a defined part of the social order. A law, Rousseau explained, "if it forms a relation, it is between the entire body from one point of view and the entire body from another point of view, without any division of the whole" (379). And so when genuine—that is, legitimate—disagreements arise in the political sphere, they are not a function of competing particular interests to be "decided," but rather the manifestation of alternate *perspectives* of the whole. The general will must decide on *these* perspectives, Rousseau indicates, on the basis of the common interest uniting them. The difficulty, for the individual citizens

---

4. Jean-Jacques Rousseau, *Du contract social; ou, Principes du droit politique*, in *Oeuvres complètes*, ed. Bernard Gagnebin and Marcel Raymond, 5 vols. (Paris, 1964–95), 3: 373. Further page references (including references to the earlier "Geneva manuscript" version of this work) are in the text.

searching for this kind of decision, is knowing when to have faith that the ultimate decision really "unites and identifies" the alternatives. The "common interest" cannot appear unproblematically, or rather, if it did there would be no problem of decision in the first place.

So did Rousseau give any solutions to this epistemologico-political quandary? In the short chapter that precedes this discussion of law, headed "Whether the General Will Can Err," Rousseau quotes the Marquis d'Argenson, who commented that the "harmony between two interests is created by opposition to that of a third." Here, in this rather marginal comment, Rousseau hints that the very problem of individual aberration points the way to political truth. Rousseau goes on to say that

> the harmony of all interests forms itself by opposition to that of each. If there were no different interests at all, we would hardly be conscious of the common interest, which would never meet with any obstacle: everything would go by itself, and politics would cease to be an art. (371n)

The general and the particular (whole/part) do not reduce to one another. The general will is that perfect identity, an unrealized unity, that *integrates* the individual wills of the citizens despite their tangible resistance to this force. The individual, for Rousseau, both expresses the general will and acts as its barrier. That is why, in this chapter, Rousseau can write that "the general will is always right [*droite*] and always tends to the public good, but it does not follow that the deliberations of the people always have the same accuracy [*rectitude*]." If the general will cannot err, the individuals who must occasion its concrete appearance often do. Each error is a deviation from the pure will of the general interest. Therefore, the wills of individuals cannot just be added up to find the decision. Instead, as Rousseau explained in a notoriously cryptic passage, we might "strip away" differences from these individual expressions, strip away the deviant error, so that in the end we would be left with the general will. This echoes Condillac's idea that the mysterious identity of the self would emerge once all its "modifications" were stripped away, and looks back to Rousseau's own suggestion, in the *Second Discourse,* that "natural man" could be discovered if all the modifications and errant "mutations" of social existence were removed. Of course, only with this original form is it possible to identify the errant deviation.

The problem is that the unity of the original contractual identity is never fully visible: the individuals are fractured images of this collective self that exists outside of history. Citizens are alienated from their collective will, and must seek to prepare its appearance: "Let us assume they are always subject to the general will, how would this will be able to manifest itself on all occasions?" (309). Rousseau declares that the law is the "organ" of this common will, "this celestial voice that dictates to each citizen the precepts of public reason" (310). The difficulty, of course, is that the law presupposes exactly what it serves to bring to the inevitably errant individual: the identity of the nation. This is why Rousseau introduces the Legislator, a political Christ figure who is intimately a part of the community yet outside of the nation spatially and temporally. Without an outside intervention, the people would never become what they must be, unless there were a reversal of cause and effect. Nonetheless, citizens must still strive to find that "celestial voice" which would legitimize their legal structures. The mission of the Legislator is proved by his ultimate success, but this original foundational act must be preserved and repeated by the succeeding generations of citizenry, just as Christ's appearance on earth does not relieve subsequent generations of their religious duties.

The duty of the citizen, for Rousseau, is therefore the constant effort to "abstract himself" from his errant individuality and find the common voice of the general will that resides within him. Voting is not an expression of opinion but a search for the general will. "The general will is in each individual an act of the understanding that reasons in the silence of the passions" (286; here Rousseau is quoting from Diderot). Of course, the individual always risks error, since, as Rousseau asks, "where is the man who could thus separate himself from himself?" The faculty of generalizing his ideas is one that develops slowly, and when it comes time to "consult" the general will on any one particular problem, a disjuncture often arises, indeed must arise, since to remain general this will has to preserve its abstractness. The individual tries to navigate the particular passions of his own being and the collective interest that speaks from the *voix intérieure*. "What will he do to guarantee himself from error? Will he listen to the inner voice?" (287). We all try to reach the general will that is in each of us, and, as Rousseau does point out, it is possible that the individual error can be ultimately measured against the majority vote: "When an opinion contrary to mine prevails, it only proves that I was mistaken" (441). Immediately, however, Rousseau acknowledges that the true measure of error, the general will, is not always to be found in the majority decision, and we seem to be left once again with the fundamental problem of errancy in a fragmented world where truth refuses to make itself fully known.

DECISION AND TRUTH: CONDORCET'S POLITICS OF COMMON
REASON

Condorcet's mathematically oriented political writings have
often been interpreted as an attempt to create what might be called a science of decision making, a science that would rationalize the forms and
functions of government processes and consequently eliminate the very
difficulties Rousseau described in the *Social Contract*. But while it is true
that Condorcet believed that the social sciences could be as rigorous as
any other empirical science, this interpretation of Condorcet's rationalist
method in politics is hard to reconcile with the nature of what may be
called authentic decisions, which inevitably mark the appearance of
something that is essentially novel because they are made in conditions
of crisis.[5] As Rousseau wrote, politics is necessary only because conflict
arises. A true science of the decision would in fact be a science that strove
to eliminate the very problem of decisions, by establishing rational and
comprehensive norms for action that would eliminate the unexpected
situation. Politics would become the mechanical application of established principles, not the decisive response to critical disruptions. If we
want to see Condorcet as a representative of Enlightenment rationalism,
we have to say that he was making an attempt to control through mathematical analysis not decisions themselves but the situation of uncertainty that made them necessary in the first place. Condorcet might be
seen as advocating a progressive reduction of the inherently arbitrary
character of political decisions by means of probability analysis; that is,
through a widening of the cognitive context of political action under-
taken in situations of uncertainty. Social and political problems would be
submitted to the predictable application of reason rather than the spontaneous and unpredictable irruption of will.[6]

This rationalization of politics through the mechanization of decision
making could be seen as a step toward the elimination of politics altogether. This is exactly what Carl Schmitt was arguing when, following
Jean Bodin, he claimed that the authentic decision was the very essence
of political action. For Schmitt, the sovereign could be defined only as
"he who decides on the exception," an emergency situation that intrinsically defies all reconciliation because it lies outside the accepted legal

5. As Peter Drucker has written: "In all matters of true uncertainty . . . one needs 'creative' solutions which create a new situation": *Effective Executive*, 152.
6. For the argument that eighteenth-century probability theory, with its application to
political decision making, was founded on the model of the rational individual rather
than social identity, see Lorraine Daston, *Classical Probability in the Enlightenment* (Princeton, 1988).

and institutional norms. Decisions in fact *create* the norms that inevitably follow from them. The legitimacy of a decision is not so much derived from its content (which is necessarily new and unprecedented) but instead is founded on the competence of those who make it, those who best articulate the sovereign voice.[7] Those endless discussions that characterized modern liberal democracies served only to evade decisions and deny definitive disputes, which was, for Schmitt, the very denial of politics.[8] More profoundly, Schmitt criticized the Enlightenment precisely because it could not accommodate and in fact rejected the very category of the exception, because it was theoretically incompatible with rationalism, where only the normal can be of scientific interest. "The exception confounds the unity and order of the rationalist scheme."[9] As we have seen, Horkheimer and Adorno made a similar point when they wrote that Enlightenment is "totalitarian" because it can recognize only what can be grasped in unity: "Its ideal is the system from which all and everything follows." The different is made equal by reducing everything to position and arrangement, to abstract quantities. Enlightenment "excises the incommensurable," those exceptions to the rule, in its effort to submit the world to calculation.[10] In the course of what Reinhart Koselleck called this "all-encompassing" Enlightenment criticism, "the true is separated from the false, the genuine from the spurious, the beautiful from the ugly, the right from the wrong."[11]

It would not be hard to identify Condorcet, who tried to submit the social world to mathematical calculation, and in fact all of human endeavor to a decimal system of classification, as an expression of these totalitarian tendencies in Enlightenment thought.[12] Indeed, Koselleck declared that Condorcet's (supposed) suicide in 1794 while in prison

7. Carl Schmitt, *Political Theology: Four Chapters on the Concept of Sovereignty* (1922) rev. ed., trans. George Schwab (Cambridge, 1985), 5–15, 32–33.

8. "The essence of liberalism is negotiation, a cautious half-measure, in the hope that the definitive dispute, the decisive bloody battle, can be transformed into a parliamentary debate and permit the decision to be suspended forever in an everlasting discussion": ibid., 63.

9. Ibid., 13–14, 37.

10. Max Horkheimer and Theodor Adorno, *Dialectic of Enlightenment* (1944), trans. John Cumming (London, 1973), 6–7, 12.

11. Reinhart Koselleck, *Critique and Crisis: Enlightenment and the Pathogenesis of Modern Society* (Oxford, 1988), 103, 116.

12. Keith M. Baker, "An Unpublished Essay of Condorcet on Technical Methods of Classification," *Annals of Science* 18 (1962): 99–123. Baker argues, for example, in his indispensable analysis of Condorcet's intellectual terrain, that Condorcet's classificatory methods "revealed and fulfilled" the dictates of Foucault's classical *episteme*. See his *Condorcet: From Natural Philosophy to Social Mathematics* (Chicago, 1975), 125.

during the Terror was an act of hypocrisy: he was a victim only of his own naive, rationalist effort to eradicate the fundamental "differences and contrasts" that animated society. This effort was a critical negation that inevitably led to the terrorist ideology of "correcting an intrusive reality."[13] In a similar vein, Schmitt derided Condorcet's identification of law with truth, the idea that "everything concrete is only a case for the application of a general law."[14] Moreover, he criticized the Enlightenment myth of collective will; to accept Condorcet's "enlightened radicalism," wrote Schmitt, one would have to believe that "human society will transform itself into a monstrous club," and that "truth will automatically emerge through voting."[15] Condorcet, the failed revolutionary, was emblematic of the failure of the Enlightenment to confront difference.[16]

And yet we need to examine more closely Condorcet's repeated attempts to clarify the nature of the political decision. It seems clear that he was never really interested in a science of "decision making" (a term that appears nowhere in Condorcet's writings, given even the most lenient translations) that would rationalize the specific *content* of political acts. It is misleading to assume from the start that Condorcet and like-minded philosophes "believed that social life could be submitted to the same rationalist method which had been used to discover rules governing inanimate objects."[17] As even Schmitt's analysis would suggest, Condorcet approached the decision not as a problem of production, of making something according to fixed rules, but as a search for something; namely, truth. The political process was therefore a particular way of accessing some kind of elusive collective identity, the common reason that would provide the foundation for general laws and legitimize the concrete expressions of human will.

What is clear throughout Condorcet's work on politics was that this process was anything but automatic; divided individuals who harbored both passions and interests at once resisted and participated in what Condorcet called "collective reason." This collective identity was a non-

13. Koselleck, *Critique and Crisis,* 120–22, 167; cf. François Furet, "Terror," in *A Critical Dictionary of the French Revolution,* ed. Furet and Mona Ozouf, trans. Arthur Goldhammer (Cambridge, Mass., 1989), 137–50.

14. Carl Schmitt, *The Crisis of Parliamentary Democracy* (1923), trans. Ellen Kennedy (Cambridge, Mass., 1985), 44–46.

15. Schmitt, *Political Theology,* 122. Alexandre Koyré also noted that Condorcet's constitutional proposals would in effect transform France into a "permanent debating club." See "Condorcet," *Revue de métaphysique et de morale* 53, no. 2 (April 1948): 166–89.

16. See Baker's plausible analysis of Condorcet's career as a series of political "failures" in his "Condorcet," in Furet and Ozouf, *Critical Dictionary,* 204–12.

17. Gary Kates, *The "Cercle Social," the Girondins, and the French Revolution* (Princeton, 1985), 265.

specific principle of political action, and as Rousseau realized, the abstracted identity could not be reached through normal methods of analysis. This was something that Condorcet did not attempt to avoid in his own work. In this context, the problem of error turns out to be an ambiguous concept that uneasily linked his understanding of the decision with his ideas on human reason and social progress. It is within this complex of ideas that the relationship of Enlightenment, error, and identity will again reveal itself.

DECISION AND AUTHORITY

Condorcet was adamant that the political arena was not a battlefield where decisions were reached only after the struggle of opposed forces. In a prerevolutionary work he noted that the whole concept of a balance of powers implied that each combatant in the dispute had some legitimacy, or alternatively that the only problem was one of stability.[18] A balance of powers, he maintained as late as 1793, only signaled the existence of a "ruthless" war within society.[19] For these reasons, Condorcet rejected a marketplace model for political decisions, for it assumed that the interests within society could really be opposed, something he would not accept.[20] The political decision was not founded on conflict and did not just express a particular victorious will, enlightened or otherwise.[21] And so Condorcet rejected expedient decision making in favor of a method that "sees the future in the present, and considers the entire system of the social order in each particular law."[22] Condorcet was to emphasize throughout his career that decisions should be based on the real interest that unites people in a society. The crucial problem was how to produce such a decision, how to identify this interest. Must the political nation be transformed into some kind of unwieldy, "monstrous club" that would institute a multileveled version of direct democracy?

In fact, Condorcet's discussions of political procedure were hardly idealistic. While he outlined an almost abstract rapprochement between

18. M.-J.-A.-N. Caritat, marquis de Condorcet, *Lettres d'un bourgeois de New-Haven à un citoyen de Virginie sur l'inutilité de partager le pouvoir législatif entre plusieurs corps* (1788), in *Oeuvres de Condorcet*, ed. A. Condorcet-O'Connor and François Arago, 12 vols. (Paris, 1847–49), 9: 1–93.

19. Condorcet, *Réflexions sur la révolution de 1688, et sur celle du 10 août 1792* (1792), in *Oeuvres*, 12: 408.

20. Condorcet, *Que toutes les classes de la société n'ont qu'un même intérêt* (1793), in *Oeuvres*, 12: 646.

21. Condorcet, *Lettres d'un bourgeois de New-Haven*, 58.

22. Condorcet, *A monsieur *** sur la société de 1789* (1790), in *Oeuvres*, 10: 70–71.

members of society, Condorcet actually feared the concrete assembly of people for political purposes. In an early revolutionary writing on the form that elections should take, he described enthusiastically an Italian academy that conducted all its important business without ever being assembled.[23] This is an idea that occurred frequently in Condorcet's pre-revolutionary political essays. In a work on provincial assemblies, for example, he outlined all the potential dangers of excessive discussion within these bodies, especially during elections, before finally suggesting that the assembly itself be suppressed if it was at all possible. Discussions, he wrote, "can create divisions." Deliberation did not simply delay or suspend the decision-making process; it was in fact "one of the principal causes of error, feebleness, [and] incoherence of decisions." Discussion created an opportunity for "momentary passions that could lead the assembly astray" and subvert its true desires.[24] Condorcet therefore believed that assemblies should be made up of decisive individuals: "Prefer those who have a firm point of view [*opinion décidée*] to those who invent conciliatory schemes," he advised the members of the Third Estate in 1789.[25]

This fear of public discussion and rejection of political compromise seems to contradict a broadly liberal interpretation of Condorcet's politics. Clearly he did not think that any political decision could be the result of reasonable discussion about a specific problem. The decision for Condorcet was to be a "manifestation" of truth,[26] which allowed no compromise. Politics was to be a procedure for discovering the one decision that on any one occasion conformed to truth and justice. This did not, however, entail some kind of simplistic vision of a scientific politics, an enlightened communal effort to calculate *technically* the best decision given a certain set of conditions. Although he often suggested such an analogy, Condorcet was not advocating an elite body of social engineers to solve social questions. Condorcet was interested in the science of the political decision, the problem of matching the expressions of political bodies with the genuine appearance of some transcendent truth. This was a complex and anything but technical problem. As Condorcet saw, the case of the political decision was bound up with the special nature of social truths and the specific difficulties involved in discovering them.

23. Condorcet, *Sur la forme des élections* (1789), in his *Sur les élections et autres textes* (Paris, 1986), 456.
24. Condorcet, *Essai sur la constitution et les fonctions des assemblées provinciales*, in *Oeuvres*, 8: 208, 211. On this point, see also Rousseau, "Economie politique," in *Oeuvres complètes*, 3: 246.
25. Condorcet, *Lettres d'un gentilhomme à messieurs du Tiers-État* (1789), in *Oeuvres*, 9: 258
26. Condorcet, *Aux citoyens français, sur la nouvelle constitution* (1793), in *Oeuvres*, 12: 654.

As he noted in his reception speech at the Académie française in 1782, the building up of scientifically valid principles from observed facts (the cornerstone of the Baconian method) was complicated in the moral sciences by the elusive and problematic character of social truth. We found the facts of the social order difficult to discern, having, as he comments, only "bribed or prejudiced judges," since we as observers formed the very object of inquiry.[27] The decision could not be based simply on the facts, because the facts themselves had to be "decided" by the corrupt judges who always had an interest in the outcome of the decision. The social and the individual were linked by wayward paths, a relation distorted by passions, deviated by interests. Thus the moral sciences, which Condorcet claimed would eventually equal the physical sciences in exactness, were fundamentally different in one important aspect.

In an unpublished note intended for the revised edition of this speech (which never appeared), Condorcet comments on a passage where he compares the moral and physical sciences, observing that those who wield authority would always fear the advances of moral science and the subsequent rationalization of the political sphere. "Almost nothing would remain arbitrary," he claims, because all particular questions would be "decided" in advance by the principles established by a science of the political. Returning to the text of the speech, however, we find that these moral principles, the arbiters of social order, would hardly be self-evident, given the nature of social truth; in fact, writes Condorcet, "we should not be surprised if the principles on which [the moral sciences] are established need to compel, so to speak, our minds to receive them."[28] This is a curious yet significant image, for it helps explain why Condorcet almost paradoxically advocated the formation of a communal decision that was expressed only after the individual members of the body involved in the decision were isolated so far as possible, insulated from seductive and disruptive discussion. The individual had to be protected not only from the possibility of persuasion but also from the very fact of her individuality, the inherent resistance to the common good offered by individual interests and passions. The susceptibility to wayward influences was not just a problem of the collective body. An individual could be deceived by others only because she could deceive herself.

This helps explain why Condorcet would later claim that the enlightened individual must seek to surpass his individuality, to gain access to

27. Condorcet, *Discours prononcé dans l'Académie française à la réception de M. le marquis de Condorcet* (1782), in Keith M. Baker, "Condorcet's Notes for a Revised Edition of His Reception Speech to the Académie française," *Studies on Voltaire and the Eighteenth Century* 169 (1977): 19.

28. Ibid., 43n, 19.

a truth that was in a sense *revealed* to the mind in the tranquillity of meditation.[29] Interests, passions, habits of "unreason," as well as the influence of other people, all could make an individual stray from the truth. Political associations, then, exacerbated all the difficulties that were inherent even in the individual search for enlightenment. Error, Condorcet claimed, lurked even in the philosopher's silent study, and so what must be its effect, he asked, "when it is a matter of deciding oneself in an instant, and in the middle of the tumult of an assembly?"[30] It is significant that Condorcet here uses the term *se décider*. He implies that this communal decision was really founded on a multiplicity of individual decisions, and not the expression of reasonable opinions that could somehow be tallied up to produce a composite general decision. The decision was not a consensus arrived at through mathematical analysis of diverse particular interests or opinions. The individual had to decide the question before him. The individual searched for truth on behalf of the political assembly; he did not articulate the wishes of his constituents or express his own opinion, Condorcet would argue. In fact, even at this individual level the decision is described as coming from the outside, constituting an intervention of sorts. To decide on a proposition is, as Condorcet explained in his important treatise on probability and politics, another way of saying that one sees that it "conforms" to a truth outside the confines of an individual's reason.[31] The individual, in isolation, tries to access a decision that is in essence *already made* by what Condorcet called a common reason, completely purged of any particular bias because it is the faculty of a collective subject.

So genuine social action, Condorcet explained, required that the individual obey not her own reason but the *raison collective* of the body of citizens, which is clearly distinguished from the arbitrary *will* of the majority; a collection of people must distinguish what they want from what is reasonable and just.[32] But where exactly was this reason located? Condorcet, in his 1782 reception speech, did write rather cryptically that "the voice of reason will make itself heard to enlightened men,"[33] but the problem, of course, was creating the right conditions for such a revelatory experience, since the very situation that required a decision (the ex-

29. Condorcet, *Dissertation philosophique et politique, ou Réflexions sur cette question: S'il est utile aux hommes d'être trompés?* (1790), in *Oeuvres*, 5: 380.

30. Condorcet, *Sur les assemblées provinciales*, 583.

31. Condorcet, "Discours préliminaire" to *Essai sur l'application de l'analyse à la probabilité des décisions rendues à la pluralité des voix* (Paris, 1785), in *Sur les élections*, 101.

32. Condorcet, *De la nature des pouvoirs politiques dans une nation libre* (1792), in *Oeuvres*, 10: 589–90.

33. Condorcet, *Discours prononcé dans l'Académie française*, 20.

istence of competing alternatives) would arise only because the truth remained hidden in some way. Condorcet had to explain how we could ever be sure that we had in fact crossed the divide between individual opinion and collective reason. This was the subject of his prerevolutionary and revolutionary political works.

ERROR, DECISION, AND PROBABILITY

What Condorcet was trying to do in his infamous massive book on majority decisions—the *Essay on the Application of Analysis to the Probability of Decisions Given by the Majority of Voices*—was to provide some kind of reassurance that a particular collective decision did in all probability conform to the truth. This dense and almost impenetrable mathematical text, prefaced by a less daunting but no less complex "preliminary discourse," might in fact be read as an elaborate footnote to Rousseau's brief discussion of voting in the *Social Contract*, where he famously pointed out that a single voter may well express the genuine general will of the community. Condorcet was, it seemed, trying to systematize the decisions of the general will (something Rousseau consciously avoided), despite the lack of any representational model that could somehow measure the adequacy of these collective decisions. Condorcet's decision theory has, in fact, been repeatedly criticized precisely on these grounds: no amount of calculation could really prove that any one decision was more or less truthful than another unless it was taken as given that individuals were likely to make correct decisions, which was a rather circular argument.[34] However, this critique of Condorcet's seemingly naive belief in the "inherent calculability" of human decision making[35] is based on a fundamental misunderstanding of the

34. See L. E. Maistrov, *Probability Theory: A Historical Sketch,* trans. and ed. Samuel Kotz (New York, 1974), esp. 129–35. He writes, for example, that "it should be noted that the whole direction of this memoir by Condorcet is unfounded. Not having a clear idea concerning the realm of applicability of probability theory and searching for possible applications, Condorcet stumbled onto the wrong path." Decisions, tribunals, and so on, according to Maistrov, are "beyond the scope of probability theory" (135).

35. Ivo Schneider, "Laplace and Thereafter: The Status of the Probability Calculus in the Nineteenth Century," in *The Probabilistic Revolution,* vol. 1: *Ideas in History,* ed. Lorenz Krüger, Lorraine Daston, and Michael Heidelberger (Cambridge, Mass., 1987), 198–99. In the same volume, see Lorraine Daston, "Rational Individuals versus Social Laws: From Probability to Statistics," 295–304, where Condorcet's individualistic and "prescriptive" conception of moral science, founded on the universality of human reason, is contrasted with nineteenth-century "social" approaches to human organization. Daston argues that the experience of the French Revolution revealed the inadequacy of this belief in a single "rationality."

status of the decision in his thought. It was not so clear that Condorcet believed he could mathematize the *content* of political decisions, understood as the expressions of a collective identity.

The *Essai* was really concerned with two logically distinct problems concerning the nature of the collective decision. On one level, Condorcet was trying to formalize how decisions made their appearance in assembled bodies; in other words, how voting procedures accessed what was in essence a particular decision waiting to be drawn out of a collection of individuals, a decision that was "made" yet unarticulated. But at another level, Condorcet was concerned with whether or not this particular decision itself accessed a truth that would alone legitimize it. Thus there were two structures of appearance governing the expression of decisions, each providing different opportunities for error and deviation. The *Essai* aimed at systematizing these structures to ensure that a decision would, to the greatest degree, appear in the end as itself. The various probabilities involved in any collective decision thus revolved around these two main problems: the probability of an assembly giving a true or false decision (which in this case means whether or not the assembly will stray from itself) and, subsequently, the probability that this decision, once it has been rendered, strays from the truth. The confusing terminology means that there can be a "true" decision that does not in the end conform to the truth.[36]

Condorcet's greatest achievements, in terms of modern voting theory,[37] fall in the first category of problems, which concerns the way voting methods access decisions that lurk within the assembled body in a kind of potential state. The cyclical majority problem is perhaps the most cited. Condorcet pointed out that in any election with three candidates, for example, the majority vote did not necessarily represent the real voice of the assembly, since the two most popular candidates would compete for votes without some system of ranking, perhaps allowing a third candidate to win unfairly.[38] Discussing problems such as these, Condorcet was concerned with how voting procedures could best access the true decision, or rather the real voice that often failed to express itself

36. Condorcet, "Discours préliminaire," 25.
37. Some of Condorcet's work on elections and voting is still current. For example, a 1990 issue of the journal *Mathématiques, informatique et sciences humaines* (no. 111) was devoted to the topic "Condorcet et les élections." Earlier works on the mathematics of Condorcet's decision theory include Duncan Black, *The Theory of Committees and Elections* (Cambridge, 1958), and Gilles-Gaston Granger, *La mathématique sociale du marquis de Condorcet* (Paris, 1956).
38. Condorcet, "Discours préliminaire," 60–69. See also Condorcet, *Sur les assemblées provinciales*, 194–95, 559–78.

in simple majority counts. He traced mathematically the often devious path from individual votes to collective decisions by positing hypothetical arrays of these votes, then extrapolating the consequences of different voting methods and the effects of various other factors, such as collusion.[39]

But Condorcet warned against mistaking the probability of having a true decision with the probability that such a decision conformed to the truth. This is not as confusing as it may seem, once we carefully distinguish the two paths of access involved in any effort at producing a collective decision. Condorcet gives us an example: the jury trial. The first probability would involve the relationship between the votes of the jury members and the eventual verdict. The probability of a true decision would be the chance that a guilty man (or, more accurately, someone the jury really believes is guilty) will be condemned. The second probability is that a condemned man is really guilty (that is, the verdict matches the truth). Thus the first difficulty is to make sure that the procedure for accessing the common decision of the body of jurors will produce a condemnation. This decision, once rendered, can then be measured, at least theoretically, against the truth.[40]

But when we move from a judicial to a political context, any analysis of the probability that a particular decision conforms to the truth becomes quite problematic. While it seems clear that there is an objective relationship between a criminal act and the guilt of an accused (despite the mediation of evidence and the uncertainties it involves), it seems impossible to calculate with any accuracy the probability that a law is "true" or a certain candidate the "best" when there is no objective measure of success in these situations.[41] Condorcet is acutely aware of the difficulty involved here, but he evades the crucial implication at this point in the text. He can come up with only the rather weak suggestion that "enlightened committees" study the past decisions of an assembly in order to assess the probability of future ones, while admitting that this probability itself would be only a "median" one, without any real empirical foundation.[42]

Not surprisingly, Condorcet's calculations are far more effective

39. Condorcet, *Essai sur l'application de l'analyse*, pts. 1–4.

40. Condorcet, "Discours préliminaire," 26.

41. See Black, *Theory of Committees*, 163. Black goes on to say that "the phrase 'the probability of the correctness of a voter's opinion' seems to be without definite meaning" (ibid.). Nonetheless, Black does extract a theory of elections from Condorcet's work, but this theory is confined only to voting methods and does not confront the political metaphysics of late Enlightenment thought.

42. Condorcet, "Discours préliminaire," 80–90.

when he is analyzing the forms and procedures that allow a decision to appear than when he is trying to assess the probability of individual or collective voices matching the truth that they seek to reveal. And yet for Condorcet this last problem was by far the most important. The form given to an assembly could never guarantee that the content of its decisions would be a manifestation of truth.[43] Only the enlightenment of individual members of the assembled body could give that assurance.

But the question of enlightenment in this particular setting was a complicated one. For Condorcet, enlightenment was not the mere accumulation of knowledge. As he would later write in the prospectus to the revolutionary *Journal d'instruction social* in 1793, "the goal of this journal is not to give opinions, but to bring about the formation of one. . . . It is not a political catechism that we want to teach."[44] Enlightenment was understood in this context to be that special ability to access the "common reason," that is, the whole community's desire for the general utility that prevailed over individual members of society on all questions of social import, uniting what might seem to be conflicting passions and interests. Clearly, this common reason would not be fulfilled simply by a count of individual opinions. The individual had to submit to what everyone, not himself alone, deemed reasonable. "In effect, every man has the right to conduct himself according to his own reason; but when he enters into a society, he agrees to subject to the common reason those activities that for everyone must be well regulated, according to the same principles."[45] Of course, society expressed itself only *through* the individuals, and thus it was necessary for each citizen somehow to free himself from his restricted self-identity. The only way that this breakthrough to the collective identity could be achieved, the only way an individual could reach for the common reason, was through a denial of the self, by "making an abstraction of his own judgment" in the moment of a decision, as Condorcet put it. The "majority" is formed by these multiple attempts to abstract away particular traits or interests, when everyone "to maintain equality" denies his or her own personal judgment.[46] The collectivity of this process increases the probability that the common reason will emerge, whereas corruption could infect a single leader or small elite, however well intentioned, with only one instance of failure. Politics thus becomes for Condorcet a collective exercise in intellectual asceticism.

43. Ibid., 169; cf. Condorcet, *Sur les assemblées provinciales*, 118.

44. Condorcet, *Que toutes les classes*, 613.

45. Condorcet, "Discours préliminaire," 102.

46. Condorcet, *Des conventions nationales, discours dont l'assemblée fédérative des amis de la vérité a voté l'impression le 1ᵉʳ avril 1791*, in *Oeuvres*, 10: 194.

Man "must learn to impose silence on his passions" in order to interrogate himself properly, free from all prejudice.[47] This is of course exactly what Rousseau had argued earlier.

Both Rousseau and Condorcet were faced with the same problem: how to recognize this common identity, which was by its very nature elusive. In a concrete political context, this problem was very urgent. Unanimity was always going to be impossible, since the actual division of the social body into individuals and groups guaranteed some conflict. The general will or the common reason would always be imperfectly expressed in political acts. If the general will can never err, the individuals who try to give it voice often do; unfortunately, there is no guide that would define these errors—the signs of social corruption often appear too late, as Rousseau warned.[48] Condorcet described the problem of consent in exactly the same terms, noting that when every citizen

> submits himself to a law that is contrary to his own opinion, he must say to himself: "It is not a matter of myself alone, but of everyone; I must not behave according to what I believe to be reasonable, but according to what everyone, in making as I do an abstraction of their own opinion, must see as corresponding to reason and to the truth."[49]

The only problem was *recognizing* the truth, hearing *la voix intérieure* that spoke to enlightened citizens. For as Rousseau wrote in a fragment, "moral signs are uncertain, difficult to submit to calculation,"[50] a sentiment that is also behind Condorcet's warning that truth in the moral sciences can have only bribed and prejudiced judges. If the general will were self-evident, everything would "go by itself, and politics would cease to be an art." Thus there could never be an exact formula for producing consensus. The potential for error was ever present. Despite his continued faith in majority decisions, Condorcet knew that assemblies, like individuals, could often veer from the truth in acts of self-deception.[51]

I think it was for this reason that Condorcet never tried to submit the process of self-abstraction to mathematical control in the same way he did voting *procedures*. Instead, he focused on improving the access to

---

47. Condorcet, *Fragment de l'histoire de la Xe époque*, in *Oeuvres*, 6: 517.
48. Rousseau, *Contract social*, 441.
49. Condorcet, "Discours préliminaire," 102.
50. Rousseau, *Contract social*, 309.
51. Condorcet, *Sur la forme des élections*, 473. See as well Condorcet's *Esquisse d'un tableau historique des progrès de l'esprit humain; suivi de Fragment sur l'Atlantide*, ed. Alain Pons (Paris, 1988), 217.

truth by creating the right conditions for its appearance. Condorcet realized that political decisions would always be imperfect, yet he struggled to preserve the essential unity of all social action.[52] Unanimity was politically unrealistic,[53] but a fragmented unity was what bound individuals together in society at all, or rather, individuals were fragments of a unity that defined the existence of a social relation. In the same way that probabilistic thinking in the Enlightenment did not mask a fundamental skepticism, the imperfections of the social order did not prove, as Condorcet said, that individuals submitted to an arbitrary order only for personal security.[54] Common reason was not just a name for some kind of mathematical remainder, something left over once individual passions, interests, and errors were accounted for. In some real manner, social identity (in the form of a common "moral rule of justice") generally found its way into individual actions, Condorcet believed.[55]

ERROR AND THE PROGRESSES OF THE HUMAN MIND

The immediate concern for Condorcet, especially during the Revolution, was that the very elusiveness of common reason would heighten the danger of lapsing into an artificial order of some kind, one that would prevent the appearance of true decisions and stifle the progress of the human race with a mere illusion of social cohesion. Like Condillac's simple ideas, individual citizens could often form illegitimate relations that would lead to a collective error along the lines of a poorly constructed general idea. Cabals, passions, enthusiasms of the moment, all could link individuals in ways that made them stray from the truth.[56] In a way, this was hardly surprising, since the appearances of truth, according to Condorcet, were always provisional, always evolving, and always in motion, impossible to secure in one place. "The friends of truth are those who search for it, and not those who boast of having found it."[57] Enlightenment was not the fixation of knowledge; for

52. See Condorcet, *Instruction sur l'exercice du droit de souveraineté* (1792), in *Oeuvres*, 10: 533–34.
53. "From the moment men felt the need to live under common rules, and had the will to do it, they have seen that these rules could not be the expression of a unanimous will": Condorcet, *Des conventions nationales*, 193.
54. Condorcet, *Que toutes les classes*, 646–47; *Des conventions nationales*, 194; "Discours préliminaire," 90.
55. Condorcet, *Dissertation philosophique et politique*, 352.
56. Condorcet, *De la nature des pouvoirs politiques*, 612.
57. Condorcet, *Des conventions nationales*, 191.

Condorcet (as for Kant) enlightenment was a critical ability that could attack rigid order and be receptive to the new and unprecedented idea. For Condorcet, the goal of education was not "to consecrate established opinions, but, on the contrary, to submit them to the free examination of successive generations."[58] Condorcet distinguished between respect for the laws and a "stupid enthusiasm" for them, a "political superstition that interrupts the progress of reason."[59]

In fact, error was often the direct result of man's misguided desire to regard the constant as true. The mind usually feared innovation, and had a "natural aversion" to novelty.[60] The "attachment to established things" was often a barrier to perfection, especially in political situations.[61] The decision often creates a new situation, so decisions would often be unpopular. Contradiction and disruption were therefore necessary to provoke the mind into a search for new truths and new solutions to problems: the old order had to be shaken so that the novelty of the decision might be accepted. For this reason, Condorcet knew that error was not simply a gap between the true and the false that would be steadily closed over time; while it might signal the very collapse of inquiry, it could stimulate discovery. Essentially, there were two modes of human error, according to Condorcet: the illegitimate relation or mistake that complacency made habitual and the more basic condition of uncertainty that fueled our desire for knowledge. We could search for truth precisely because we were separated from it, which meant that this search was always forward looking. Education did not transmit fixed truth; rather, it allowed the "doors to error" to be closed, so that truth "will settle down [*s'établira*] without pain" into the minds of people when the opportunity arises.[62] The elimination of mistakes did not automatically produce truth but prepared individuals to receive it.

For Condorcet, accessing this truth was possible only when order was in some sense disrupted. In the political arena, this was the function of public discussion: the provocation of ideas and the clash of critical opinion. Discussion could never resolve issues, and thus played no role in decision making itself, yet it was necessary to indicate the possible paths to truth. Discussion, in other words, revealed the inevitable differences, ex-

---

58. Condorcet, *Sur l'instruction publique* (1791–92), in *Ecrits sur l'instruction publique*, ed. Charles Coutel and Catherine Kintzler, 2 vols. (Paris, 1988), 1: 60–69, 102.

59. Condorcet, *Aux amis de la liberté sur les moyens d'en assurer la durée* (1790), in *Oeuvres*, 10: 180.

60. Condorcet, "Discours préliminaire," 100; *Esquisse*, 102.

61. Condorcet, *Des conventions nationales*, 199.

62. Condorcet, *Dissertation philosophique et politique*, 381.

ceptions, and conflicts that had to be "decided."[63] The proper preparation for the decision included the creation of dissension and disagreement. No decision was of course necessary if there was total consensus. What Condorcet was concerned with was a false consensus founded on complacency and fear of the future. He emphasized that in both politics and scientific practice rigid and dogmatic formulations would prevent anything novel from appearing, and hence prevent progress. Progress was, for Condorcet, unpredictable in its precise course, even if it was inevitable. The "new combinations" of ideas that were the foundation of human development were by definition without precedent.[64] Progress was not, therefore, the linear unfolding of established order. In fact, Condorcet encouraged the "speculative truth" as a way to diversify the human experience, opening it up to the limits of what nature would allow.[65] There would never be a political catechism because the evolution of political order was closely linked to the progress of the human mind.

But for Condorcet, progress was indefinite—the termination of human history did not structure its evolution. Progress was the result of human reason constantly pushing the frontiers of knowledge, both within humanity itself and outside in nature. The stages of human development that Condorcet outlined in his last and most famous work, the *Sketch of a Historical Picture of the Progress of the Human Mind,* were hardly logical and inexorable ones. Society would be perfected not through the laws of history but through the crossing of the horizon of human limitation. As Keith Baker has noted, "Condorcet's conception of social science was not historical" and was in a sense antihistorical.[66] In fact, he criticized those philosophers who tried to totalize human activity, whether across history or within the structure of society.

> Some, like More and Hobbes, deduced the framework of an entire system of social order from a few general principles, imitating Plato, and presented the model that practice should ceaselessly approach. Others, like Machiavelli, sought in a thorough examination of the facts of history rules according to which one could pretend to master the future.[67]

63. Condorcet, *Sur les assemblées provinciales,* 213; see also Condorcet, *Dissertation philosophique et politique,* 380: "[The sovereign] must allow opinions to be discussed publicly; otherwise, it will be impossible for him to know on which side truth may exist." Peter Drucker isolates this feature of the true decision: decisions are not made by acclimation. "They are made well only if based on the clash of conflicting views, the choice between different judgments": *Effective Executive,* 148.

64. Condorcet, *Esquisse,* 79.

65. Condorcet, *Ecrits sur l'instruction publique,* 1: 42.

66. Baker, *Condorcet,* 344.

67. Condorcet, *Esquisse,* 200–201.

Progress, Condorcet suggested, implied the future appearance of completely new problems that could not even be foreseen in the present, problems that would arise from intended or accidental juxtaposition and true discovery, the continual interplay of reason and contingency. The more knowledge we acquire, wrote Condorcet, the more "we will see that there remains research to be done of which the idea has not even presented itself."[68] This is the mark of the modern idea of progress, according to Hans Blumenberg: when Galileo first began to reckon with the "unknown problems" that had yet to be revealed in the course of research, progress could no longer be seen as a linear and eschatological movement toward a singular goal. Progress was "recognizable as consisting in the production of problems by the solution of problems," and science became the prediction of the unpredictable.[69]

The appearance of new problems, and with them new opportunities for authentic progress, is occasioned by the inevitable appearance of what Condorcet calls obstacles. The removal of the unnecessary impediments that the human race burdens itself with—tyranny, corruption, and so on—will free up the pursuit of truth but will never eliminate the basic, tension-filled relationship between truth and error: "In politics as for all the sciences, error and truth ... are mutually linked and bound together."[70] Freed from its chains, reason

> can no longer be hindered except by these obstacles that are inevitably renewed with each new advance [*progrès*], because they have as their necessary ground the very makeup of our intelligence; that is, the relation established by nature between our ways of discovering truth and the resistance with which it opposes our efforts.[71]

But Condorcet does not merely acknowledge the inherent relationship between obstacles and the progressive search for truth, he exploits this fundamental condition in his descriptions of scientific and political method. In Condorcet's vision, order and knowledge were not something that could be perfected slowly and gradually over time; they had to be continually disrupted and recreated anew.

---

68. Condorcet, *Elémens du calcul des probabilités et son application aux jeux de hasard, à la loterie et au jugement des hommes ... avec un discours sur les avantages des mathématiques sociales* (1805), in *Sur les élections*, 521. See also Condorcet, *Discours prononcé dans l'Académie française*, 18–19.

69. Hans Blumenberg, "On a Lineage of the Idea of Progress," *Social Research* 41 (1974): 27.

70. Condorcet, *Vie de Turgot* (1786), in *Oeuvres*, 5: 220.

71. Condorcet, *Esquisse*, 213–14.

We can see, then, that Condorcet's somewhat extreme plans for elaborate and comprehensive systems of classification expressed a very real desire to *experiment* with ideas in order to discover unexpected combinations and relations. Classification was not some totalitarian domination of nature but an attempt to expand the limitations of human perception. "It is the feebleness of the human mind, the need to save time and energy, that obliges us to divide, limit, and classify the sciences."[72] The method of classification Condorcet described was not an effort at fixing data in one system of order. He hoped to reduce all objects of knowledge into diversified groups of variable characteristics, where each individual modification of these characteristics could be assigned a numerical value, and thus easily manipulated and compared with a wide variety of conditions and other variables.[73] The vast tables of information were essentially a means of creating *disorder* among data that were, according to Condorcet, too rigidly organized in traditional classifications.[74]

Condorcet wanted to facilitate discovery, not objectify knowledge, and discovery required conflict and disruption. This is precisely why he stressed the crucial significance of the free mobility of ideas. In the *Esquisse* Condorcet describes the invention of printing as revolutionary not so much because it could spread information as because it could bring together disparate ideas from wide-ranging sources, and thus disrupt dogmatic formulations with the constant and free circulation of opinion. "Every new error is opposed as soon as it arises, and often attacked even before it has been spread; it has no time at all to take root in the mind."[75] The free circulation of ideas also loosened up the search for knowledge. For Condorcet, truth was never static: "No system of truths is sterile." Invention and discovery were both "sublime and comforting," while blind enthusiasm for fixed truths would only degrade these truths into prejudices.[76] Progress continually prepared the way for the birth of truth. Like any birth, however, the appearance of a new truth was at once violent and disruptive. Condorcet's vast outline of human progress in the *Esquisse* is filled with conflict—it describes the history of the human mind as a dialectical struggle, in which truth often degenerates into error and error sometimes spawns truth in an endless cycle of crisis and achievement.[77] Condorcet writes that these struggles between truth and

72. Condorcet, *Elémens du calcul*, 622.

73. Baker, "Unpublished Essay," 110–12.

74. Condorcet, *Elémens du calcul*, 506–21.

75. Condorcet, *Esquisse*, 187–212.

76. Condorcet, *Discours prononcé dans l'Académie française*, 18–19; *Fragment de l'histoire de la Xe époque*, 577–78.

77. On this point, see Baker, *Condorcet*, 358–59, and Coutel's introduction to Condorcet's *Ecrits sur l'instruction publique*, 1: 2.

error signal not a "degeneration of the human species but a necessary crisis in its gradual march toward absolute perfection."[78] In an earlier work, he wrote that man will for a long time be the "plaything of error, before coming to the fixed point where truth lies." He describes this movement as the swing of a pendulum; human progress will always oscillate between one direction and the next.[79]

In fact, the relationship between truth and error was even more intimate. The progresses of the human mind are possible, Condorcet says, only because of a fundamental separation from truth that plunges us into uncertainty while simultaneously instilling in us a desire to overcome this inadequacy. The history of errors is therefore an integral part of the history of progress, as he explains in the introduction to the *Esquisse*: "Like the truths that perfect and enlighten [the human mind], they are the necessary result of its activity, of this ever-present discrepancy between what it might know, what it has the desire to know, and what it believes it needs to know."[80] Curiosity fuels the search for truth, which always remains beyond the grasp of the individual, precisely because every discovery opens up new possibilities, new frontiers of knowledge.

This idea was hardly uncommon in eighteenth-century philosophy. Condorcet's mentor, Turgot, described this phenomenon of curiosity in similar terms in his own memoir on the progress of the human mind (an obvious model for Condorcet's final work).

> Always restless, incapable of finding repose anywhere but in truth, always excited by the image of this truth, which she imagines touching and which flees beyond her, human curiosity increases the number of questions and disputes, and always makes it necessary to analyze facts and ideas in an increasingly exact and more thorough manner.[81]

For this reason, conflict and error are the very pathway to a truth that eternally recedes into the future. "It is not error that prevents the progresses of truth. It is laxity, stubbornness, habit [*esprit de routine*], everything that encourages inaction."[82] Turgot wrote that the human mind must always move on to new ideas, new objects of inquiry.

But as Blumenberg has argued, this description of human curiosity also implied a special relationship with the past: in Enlightenment dis-

78. Condorcet, *Esquisse*, 102–3.

79. Condorcet, *Réflexions sur la jurisprudence criminelle* (1775), in *Oeuvres*, 7: 3.

80. Condorcet, *Esquisse*, 87.

81. Anne-Robert-Jacques Turgot, *Second discours, sur les progrès de l'esprit humain . . .* (1750), in *Oeuvres de Turgot*, ed. Eugène Daine and Hippolyte Dussard, 2 vols. (Paris, 1844), 2: 601.

82. Turgot, *Pensées et fragments . . . sur les progrès et la décadence des sciences et des arts*, in *Oeuvres*, 2: 672.

cussions of the history of knowledge, curiosity and originary inadequacy were often linked. "Curiosity is the constitutional condition of a being that is no longer able to see its original connections, that collides with its de facto locatedness in space and time."[83] Quoting Maupertuis's *Essai de cosmologie*, Blumenberg focuses attention on the same problem Condorcet dealt with in the *Esquisse*, but in the context of the past:

> When I consider the narrow limits within which our knowledge is confined, the extreme desire that we have for knowledge, and our incapacity to instruct ourselves, I could be tempted to believe that this disproportion, which exists today between our knowledge and our curiosity, could be the result of a corresponding disordering [event].[84]

History and progress are linked to the errant condition of man, who was separated from his original connections, both social and natural. For Turgot, this "disordering event" was the biblical flood, which wrenched man away from his natural, harmonious environment and from himself, dispersing the human race around the globe and diversifying language and culture. The social unity of the original community was divided.[85] For Rousseau, the original state of man was, as Blumenberg has written, "characterized by the idyllic absence of tension." The individual lived completely within the present, and satisfied his needs wholly within the "zone of the accessible." Curiosity, and with it the progressive movement of culture, is impossible in this environment; Rousseau must posit a "mythical act of aberration" for this moment to occur.[86] But once man has moved into this condition, there can be no return to complacency and total stasis. Progress is endemic, for we cannot ignore the desire for a knowledge that always flees ahead of us.

The condition of complete rest signifies either the mythical beginning or end of history, as Condorcet's image of the pendulum implies, and as such this condition is unattainable. Man can neither ignore his desires nor pretend they have been satisfied. Thus for Condorcet the only real difference between truth and error is in the end the difference between motion and rigidity, that is, between discovery or stagnation. Returning to the *Esquisse*, we can see why a truth can be transformed into an error once it solidifies, becomes a mere habit and no longer excites the mind, whereas errors such as those of Descartes can lead to truth simply be-

83. Hans Blumenberg, *The Legitimacy of the Modern Age*, trans. Robert M. Wallace (Cambridge, Mass., 1983), pt. 3, chap. 10; quote is from 415.
84. Quoted ibid., 416.
85. Turgot, *Second discours*, 598–600.
86. Blumenberg, *Legitimacy of the Modern Age*, 416–17.

cause their "very audacity" agitates minds, and forces them to take new directions.[87] Error had to be overcome and eliminated whenever possible, but it was the errant condition of humanity that kept individuals restless and inquiring, striving to touch a truth that was always beyond them. The condition of error situated man between absolute perfection (which was, according to Condorcet, eternally distant) and a static self-sufficiency that limited him to his own immediate needs. Political action was the effort to create order in this mediate position, and thus even if individual political decisions could be purged, mathematically, of any obviously arbitrary elements, the essence of the decision was always going to be that fundamental gap between the individual and the collective, between the errant self and the common reason that it sought to regain.

While it is true that Condorcet relentlessly looked to the future of mankind and condemned the past as the history of subjection, he could not avoid the problem of origin. And Condorcet describes the origin of political institutions, the very origin of the problem of the decision, as the breakdown of identity. In the *Esquisse* he explains how society is formed by the "identity of interests" between individuals, their mutual desire to help each other, and their common affection for society itself. Resolution was, Condorcet suggests, spontaneous and unanimous. Authority was introduced only to execute this common resolution. Every decision was made by all those who were affected by its outcome. The problem of the decision arises when this identity of interests inexplicably breaks down and dissension is introduced within the social body of the tribe. "The quarrels that arose in the heart of a single society disturbed its harmony, and could have destroyed it; it was thus natural to agree that the decision would be entrusted to those who by their age and personal qualities inspired the most confidence."[88] Here the decision has been loosened from its moorings, dissociated from the immediate identity of social interests that are no longer self-evident. The problem of consent is no longer knowledge and participation but probability—the leader is competent to decide because he is most likely to make the best decisions. Here the dangers of authority arise, because confidence can always be gained by deception or subverted by fear, as Condorcet never failed to demonstrate. And so from this point on, the history of human society would be the almost paradoxical one of regaining social identity through the progress and indefinite perfection of the errant individual.

87. Condorcet, *Esquisse*, 211.
88. Ibid., 92–93.

CHAPTER 5

"The General Will Cannot Err":
Representation and Truth in Early
Revolutionary Political Thought

The line of thought traced so far brings together an epistemology of error with an ontology of aberration. The very errancy of knowledge, our failure to penetrate the totality of truth, was, in the eighteenth century, linked to a condition of limitation defined in terms of imperfection. Both epistemologically and ontologically, however, the *relationship* between the failure of the aberration and the goal that is truth proved to be crucial, for it was thought that the errant path progresses only because the goal we seek is actually present in some form within the errant distortions that are the particular fragments of our existence. The error conceals truth but is not merely the opposite of truth; error reveals in the form of a trace, or distortion, some characteristics of truth. The exalted figures of Enlightenment thought are those who can break through the present structures of knowledge and gain new insight into truth, however fleeting and imperfect that insight may be.

As Rousseau and Condorcet demonstrate, this structure of thought had a political variant in the eighteenth century. The identity of the community, a reality transcending the particularity of the individuals making it up, was, for these two prominent intellectuals of the French Enlightenment, the only force that legitimized political decision and action. Epistemologically, the goal of politics was to find the community's original voice, the "general will," or, in Condorcet's terms, the "common reason" of the collective identity. What complicated the epistemological task, as we saw, was the premise that this voice of identity does not have one privileged point of expression. It is, in its essence, intangible, even mute. The only way this collective voice speaks is though the individual members in specific contexts. But as both Rousseau and Condorcet explained, the individual is inevitably aberrant. The collective voice, then, is understood to be mediated through errant particularity. The individual citizen acts at once as barrier and vehicle of the collective identity. Given this situation, the goal of politics would be to purify this expression, to correct the multiple forms of aberration. Rousseau, of course, always failed to offer one simple method (and most likely never intended to do so), and in fact despaired at the prospect of a legitimate polity in a large and complex nation like France. In Rousseau's work, the general will remains very mysterious, and the relationship between the collective and the individual in the space of the self was fraught with tension and conflict. Condorcet, on the other hand, saw that a certain relation to "reason" might be the solution to the political challenge of unity: the task, he said, was to create a space for knowledge, a clearing in the midst of conflict that would help prepare individuals to manifest reason, while eradicating as much as possible the inevitable interferences of errant individuality.

But as we move into the revolutionary period we encounter not simply political conflict but an excess of extreme violence, a spectacle of death and war that haunted Europeans throughout the nineteenth century. This radical failure appears to undermine any Enlightenment attempt to preserve the subtle interplay of error and truth. The example of Condorcet is revealing. Not only did he fail, after much effort as an elected representative, to establish a rational space of politics in the Revolution, he would eventually end up in hiding during the Terror, trying to avoid execution for the "crime" of wanting to establish a rational constitution and administration. Before his capture and subsequent death in prison, Condorcet was, as we noted, writing a book that ignored all these failures and disappointments, as he looked beyond the harsh specificity of his own revolutionary experience to celebrate the great power of history on the broadest scale imaginable. Reason, he implied in his famous posthumous work, the *Sketch of the Historical Progress of the Human Mind,* would eventually triumph over the momentary aberration that was the Terror; enlightenment, he believed, would ultimately prevail over the current darkness of death and unreason. In a way, Condorcet's recourse to reason's historical inevitability in this text absolved him of any need to articulate a specific way of working through such extreme "error" to truth. But in the wake of Terror, civil war, and violence in France, this question would be repeatedly asked. What exactly was the source of this deadly aberration and how might it be contained?

THE REVOLUTION AS POLITICAL PATHOLOGY

Although the French Revolution stands as one of the icons of modern democracy, its legacy is as complex, or even as contradictory, as the meaning of "democracy" itself in the modern (and postmodern) world. Unlike its American predecessor, the French Revolution has always been claimed by many different political perspectives. This is hardly surprising, given that the Revolution produced a number of political forms beginning in 1789: constituent assemblies, a constitutional monarchy, republican governments, popular movements, emergency dictatorship, a "security state," and so on. One link between these often vastly different political experiences in the Revolution, something that again clearly distinguishes France from the United States, is the persistent, brutal violence that accompanied political action throughout the revolutionary decade. This experience of violent conflict, alongside the great number of transformations that affected government and law in this era, has always complicated the Revolution's political legacy. For moderate liberals who value constitutional government, for example, the violence and ideological foundations of the Terror can be understood only as some kind of irrational aberration. For socialists (whether moderate, radical, or utopian) the Revolution was a model of popular action, the overthrow from below of a repressive and illegitimate regime. The violence of "popular" government is justified, in other words, as an instrument of social change. Even the Terror that accompanied the Jacobins' radical social and economic policy is explained as an expedient response to specific crises and opposition. Neither liberals nor socialists, who look back to the French Revolution from different perspectives, understand violence as *intrinsic* to the ideals of this originary event.

Still, there has always been a fascination with the intense proximity between the ideals of the Revolution (however they may be defined) and the spectacle of violence in this era. Conservative thinkers, beginning with Edmund Burke and his infamous 1790 tirade *Reflections on the Revolution in France,* have always been willing to link the violent chaos that took place in France with the very goals of revolution and democracy. Indeed, the very birth of conservatism as a political ideology was a reaction to the severe disruptions occasioned by revolutionary democracy in France and abroad. And yet the identification of the Revolution as a kind of historical pathology was not limited to conservative or reactionary traditions. Liberalism was formed in reaction to more radical popular movements and ideologies that shared the revolutionary spirit. Early liberals, such as Benjamin Constant, who wrote in France in the wake of the Terror, therefore tried to distinguish the evils of radical Jacobin politics from the healthy goals of a proper constitutional liberalism. For someone like Constant, the violence of the Revolution should be linked not to democratic government or the idea of popular sovereignty, but rather to a particular, flawed form of democracy. In a famous essay on ancient and modern liberty, Constant denounced as dangerous anachronistic republican values such as "virtue," values resurrected by thinkers like Rousseau and enforced disastrously by the Jacobins in the Revolution. Like so many nineteenth-century European liberals, Constant believed that in a modern commercial society the only proper form of democracy was a liberal one that saw government as a means to protect the freedom of private activity for each citizen under the law.[1]

Throughout the nineteenth century, the liberal bourgeoisie fought traditional authorities for political power, repeating the struggles of 1789— and with varying degrees of success, as both Marx's *Eighteenth Brumaire of Louis Napoleon* and Tocqueville's *Souvenirs* brilliantly demonstrated in their own way. At the same time, socialists resisted the oppressions of both conservative and liberal regimes, often evoking the heady days of the sans-culottes' influence in the Jacobin republic of the Year II. Into the twentieth century, liberals and more radical socialists fought over this legacy of the French Revolution. There was essentially a battle between a vision of constitutional government, with its respect for individual rights and property, and a vision of radical revolutionary change, in which the state would act as a means of remaking society so that it would be more egalitarian and just.

This opposition would only intensify in the Cold War conditions that emerged in the wake of the Second World War. The French Revolution was adopted by Marxist states and scholars as a precursor of the communist revolutions of the twentieth century. Understood as a social conflict, the French Revolution was studied as a bourgeois revolution against feudal forms of property, with prophetic signs of the coming socialist utopia discernible in the sans-culottes movements, Jacobin economic policy, and ill-fated ventures such as Gracchus Babeuf's "Conspiracy of Equals" during the Directory. Meanwhile, liberal scholars considered the French Revolution one of the founding moments of constitutional democracy. The Declaration of the Rights of Man and Citizen, along with many of the ideas formed during the early constitutional phase of the Revolution, were textbook examples of the emergence of political modernity. The Terror, in contrast, with its dictatorial government, political repression, and elimination of opposition by means of the

---

1. See the various texts collected in Benjamin Constant, *Ecrits et discours politiques,* ed. Pozzo di Borgio (Paris, 1964).

guillotine, was understood as an early example of the "totalitarian" democracy characteristic of twentieth-century Marxist and Stalinist states. So for liberals, the Terror was a political aberration from the norms of democratic practice. For socialists and other radical political theorists, however, the liberal revolution of 1789 was itself an ideological distortion, masking the fundamentally violent nature of early bourgeois capitalism.

By the 1960s, this polarized opposition concerning the legacy of the French Revolution was fading, even though "revolution" dominated political consciousness in this era of student movements and decolonization. For one thing, academic historiography of the Revolution, like much professional history of the era, was turning increasingly to social history and social scientific methodologies. And although in France the Marxist historians who dominated the field of the Revolution had long championed a social interpretation, more and more research in this area by scholars with varied theoretical commitments revealed that the Marxist categories simply did not explain eighteenth-century France and the conflicts and transformations that emerged in 1789. As this particular paradigm of explanation broke down, the Revolution was increasingly fragmented by scholars who focused on the heterogeneity of society in this era, and by the numerous regional studies that decentered the Parisian political contexts. The decline in traditional political and intellectual history only exacerbated this tendency, since much of the polemic over the legacy of the Revolution centered precisely on the nature of the modern state and the structure of democracy, topics dealt with by political theorists and philosophers without a strong professional interest in the complexities of the French experience. In this context, the Terror ceased to fascinate many historians of the Revolution, as it became just another historically complex period that had to be understood in its (often local) specificity.

François Furet's *Penser la Révolution française* (published in 1978) radically transformed the study of the Revolution.[2] What Furet did was provide a new interpretation of the Revolution that focused again on its political culture and ideology. His argument was elegantly simple. Agreeing with the social historians who had shown just how complex eighteenth-century social and economic life was in France, he suggested that we would never find a coherent explanation for the revolutionary rupture in that context. Instead, Furet argued, we must rediscover the political nature of the Revolution, which for him meant not the political

2. François Furet, *Interpreting the French Revolution*, trans. Elborg Forster (Cambridge, 1981).

history of the period (told in such great detail by so many earlier historians) but the political culture that made revolution possible conceptually. In fact, Furet infamously argued that because of the complexity of French society, the Revolution could be explained only as an *imaginary* construction in the sphere of political ideology. The state, Furet said, collapsed almost by accident in the late 1780s, and yet the political leaders who took over the government of France interpreted this collapse as some kind of collective action. The "unity" of the Revolution, for Furet, lay not in some tangible historical reality but rather in its ideological self-projection as "event." Given that there was no such thing as a nation "one and indivisible," the revolutionaries in France constructed a peculiar form of politics that was grounded, according to Furet, on the nothingness of the People. Politics became a competition to represent a fiction. But because the revolutionaries took these ideas so seriously, Furet said, they could not help but see any breakdown of consensus in this new "nation" as enmity, an outbreak of a counter-revolutionary menace that became increasingly internalized as the Revolution wore on. The Terror, for Furet, was not a pathological aberration from some healthy democratic revolution, or an instrument of social transformation, as liberals and socialists believed. Rather, the Terror was an inevitable consequence of a revolutionary ideology that created a political form defined as a transparent representation of something nonexistent, the "nation." So the Revolution was from the start doomed to fail because of the inherent unreality of its founding principle.

The decade of the French Revolution has, in the wake of Furet's work, been described then as a helpless *errance* in the complex workings of democracy. The unsuccessful "wandering" originates, it is said, in the initial decision to found a new state on the idea of a "collective sovereign."[3] The revolutionaries supposedly failed because they attempted to identify the singular decisions of the state with the will of an elusive collective—"society" itself. They failed to recognize the radical difficulties (even contradictions) inherent in the relationship between society and state.[4] The Revolution, in other words, tried to make fully visible a collective voice that was essentially "ungraspable," making the whole revo-

3. Marcel Gauchet, *La révolution des pouvoirs: La souveraineté, le peuple et la représentation, 1789–1799* (Paris, 1995), 7, 9.
4. Brian C. J. Singer, "Cultural versus Contractual Nations: Rethinking Their Opposition," *History and Theory* 35 (1996): 309–37. Cf. J. A. W. Gunn, *Queen of the World: Opinion in the Public Life of France from the Renaissance to the Revolution*, in *Studies on Voltaire and the Eighteenth Century* 328 (1995); and Keith Michael Baker, "Sovereignty," in *A Critical Dictionary of the French Revolution*, ed. François Furet and Mona Ozouf, trans. Arthur Goldhammer (Cambridge, Mass., 1989).

lutionary process an "experience of the impossible."[5] The impossibility explains the proximity of democracy and terror: the Enlightenment introduced a new concept of sovereignty, one that grafted the singularity of monarchical sovereignty onto the complex heterogeneity of social reality. The revolutionaries erred, these critics declare, because they pursued an illusory end, the transformation of social multiplicity into political singularity.

Against this position, I want to argue here that the revolutionaries were very much aware of the complex problem of "error" that structured this particular transformation, and in the following chapter I will suggest that even during the Terror aberration was not always understood as enmity. Still, my analysis of revolutionary discourse does, like the revisionist interpretation, emphasize the importance during the Revolution of the critical concept of national identity. However, what I will demonstrate is that this idea of unity was hardly a fantastic delusion for the revolutionaries. Like "truth" in the Enlightenment, the very presence of "unity" in the Revolution was intricately linked with the problem of error and aberration, never taken for granted in the way Furet and other critics of revolutionary democracy would have us believe. In any case, it is worth taking a detour here to explain the historical conditions that are so important for the development of a revolutionary discourse of identity—namely, the nature of the French monarchical state and the political function of the Enlightenment in the eighteenth century—since I will ultimately suggest that this political identity was structured in much the same way as truth was within the epistemological discourse of Enlightenment.

The concept of unity that revisionists see as so problematic yet so essential to an understanding of politics and violence in the Revolution was not merely an invention of particular theorists or political actors. Furet's argument concerning the pathological faith in popular sovereignty as some metaphysical reality looked back to a long (if sometimes forgotten) tradition that explained this fascination with the singularity of a unified nation as a product of a very specific historical experience.

This "pathogenetic" tradition of thought—to borrow the language of Reinhart Koselleck's brilliant Cold War book, *Critique and Crisis: Enlightenment and the Pathogenesis of the Modern World*—shows how the emergence of the collective sovereign was part of a complex historical development in which France played a critical role. The French absolutist state had been created in the seventeenth century in response to profound so-

5. Gauchet, *La révolution des pouvoirs*, 18.

cial, religious, and political ruptures. This revolutionary move, what Marx in the nineteenth century called the "emancipation" of the state from society,[6] made politics a matter of pure *raison d'état*. Like the absolute sovereign Hobbes described in *Leviathan*, Louis XIV used his singular authority to secure a nation that was not an intrinsically stable social or political entity. The very success of the absolutist state in France is a crucial turn in the pathogenetic interpretation of the French Revolution. The monarchical regime consolidated its position by centralizing its administration and by neutralizing the regional powers of the nobility. Political power was reduced and concentrated in one location—the court—and participation in state decisions was denied to anyone outside the inner circle of the king. Moreover, the success of the absolutist state in securing the nation meant that French society became much more integrated, and therefore more stable. While society was still divided by feudal categories, the social barriers, as Tocqueville noted in his book on the French Revolution, were becoming in the eighteenth century more fluid and more artificial. Society was being transformed into a *commercial* society, and what prompted the very origin of the absolutist state—social and religious conflict—was disappearing.

Intellectually, the result of this transformation was that by the eighteenth century "society" was being described in its own terms, as an independent social and economic historical reality independent of particular political forms. Over the course of the century, the idea that government is merely conditional on society gained prominence in mainstream Enlightenment thought. The absolutist state itself was redefined as the servant of society, even by so-called enlightened monarchs themselves. In France, Jean Bodin had already redefined the authority of the singular monarch in terms of the nation. If, he said, sovereignty resided in the nation, then its very diversity demanded a powerful executive to manifest the unity of that nation.[7] The historical origin of absolutism is largely forgotten in the eighteenth-century debate, as society "discovers" its own internal unity and its own history. Society, however vaguely understood in fact, emerged as the ground of political structures for the philosophers of the time. Whether individuals were seen as naturally sociable or unsociable, theorists in the Enlightenment argued that

6. Karl Marx, "On the Jewish Question," in *Selected Writings*, ed. Lawrence H. Simon (Indianapolis, 1994). For the French experience, see Jeffrey W. Merrick, *The Desacralization of the French Monarchy in the Eighteenth Century* (Baton Rouge, 1990).

7. Jean Bodin, *Les six livres de la République* (Paris, 1576). See also Brian C. J. Singer, *Society, Theory, and the French Revolution: Studies in the Revolutionary Imaginary* (London, 1986), 73; and Keith Michael Baker, "Representation Redefined," in his *Inventing the French Revolution: Essays on French Political Culture in the Eighteenth Century* (Cambridge, 1990).

stability and order would emerge in some fashion from the very operations of society itself, and not from some force intervening from outside
the human sphere.[8] Government, as the French Physiocrats, for example,
argued, was an active force promoting and articulating these natural relations. Like the Deist universe, the social world ran according to certain
basic laws with minimal intervention.[9] In France, however, there was
still a fundamental gulf between the actions of the state and the life of its
citizens. This alienation from politics was a product of the development
of the state in the first place, that emancipation so necessary to security
in the previous century. By the eighteenth century, something like the
idea (and reality) of a nation was forming (due to a large extent to the
very successes of a centralized, absolutist state) yet because of the nature
of the state this nation could not express itself politically in any form.
The Enlightenment, in an important sense, was one effort to represent
society to the state and to itself (at least theoretically).

As many historians have now shown, this point in French history
marks an important turn. Those who were now trying to define and express the will of the nation in political terms (this was the era of a new
contest over "public opinion")[10] themselves had no practical political experience. The nature of the Ancien Régime precluded any political practice outside of state administration controlled directly by the crown.
Competing sources of authority had been largely neutralized. The
philosophes had to redefine the parameters of politics in order to open a
space for participation. They did this by denying that politics was confined to the plane of *raison d'état;* they aspired to the plane of truth,
Koselleck pointed out, since this was the only place they could do battle
with the existing power. The political critic engaged the absolutist state
in the sphere of philosophy, since he was excluded from the actual politics of the state.[11] Even members of quasi-political institutions like the
parlements had to redefine their roles in terms of Enlightenment theories,
if they wanted to adopt a new role as representatives of the "nation" before the king, given their historical position as representatives of the king
to the nation.[12] The Enlightenment removed politics from its radically

8. Peter N. Miller, "Citizenship and Culture in Early Modern Europe," *Journal of the History of Ideas* 57 (1996): 725–42.

9. See Carl Schmitt, *Political Theology: Four Chapters on the Concept of Sovereignty* (1922), rev. ed., trans. George Schwab (Cambridge, Mass., 1985), 36–37.

10. Gunn, *Queen of the World,* 388.

11. Reinhart Koselleck, *Critique and Crisis: The Pathogenesis of Modern Society* (Oxford, 1988).

12. Baker, "Representation Redefined," 229. See also Jean Egret, *Louis XV et l'opposition parlementaire, 1715–1774* (Paris, 1970).

limited sphere of operation and made it subject to something higher: the moral and ethical truths proclaimed by the philosophes. And one of the key truths of the Enlightenment was that society came before politics. From this point on, political action would be subjected to this test of legitimacy: whether or not it accorded with the "will" or interest of the nation, however this was defined.

Before the French Revolution, this kind of critique did not actually threaten political order. In France, the state continued to modernize and centralize throughout the eighteenth century, and effectively controlled political dissent in critical moments.[13] This only intensified the abstract quality of political criticism in the Enlightenment. Lacking any real political experience, the philosophes were forced to observe from the outside all the defects of the monarchical state. Their response was to construct a utopian counter-image, what Tocqueville described as an "imaginary society, in which everything appeared simple and coordinated, uniform, equitable and conforming to reason." Oblivious of the complex realities of French life, the writers located all the obstacles to this ideal community within the absolutist state itself. And, as Tocqueville wrote, even the population at large began to believe what these writers were telling them. "They disassociated themselves from what was, to dream about what could be, and in the end they lived intellectually in this ideal community [*cité*] that the writers had constructed."[14] The eighteenth century was a time when various bodies and institutions were created, not as practical exercises in political community but as antistates, modeled on the "truths" of natural social order and harmony. Masonic lodges and other secret societies, salons, the republic of letters itself, all refused to engage with the practical problems of actual states, a stance that some historians have seen as a retreat into hypocritical fantasies of apolitical sociability.[15] The main point here, however, is that in this historical tradi-

13. For example, during the Maupeou coup to suppress the *parlements*.

14. Alexis de Tocqueville, *L'ancien régime et la Révolution,* in *Oeuvres complètes,* ed. J.P. Mayer (Paris, 1950–), 2: 199.

15. Augustin Cochin, *Les sociétés de pensée et la démocratie moderne* (Paris, 1921); Koselleck, *Critique and Crisis,* esp. chap. 7; Ran Halévi, *Les loges maçonniques dans la France d'Ancien Régime: Aux origines de la sociabilité démocratique* (Paris, 1984). Those who follow Habermas and interpret these developments in the Enlightenment as indications of a growing public sphere, and not as pathological symptoms, include Daniel Gordon, *Citizens without Sovereignty: Equality and Sociability in French Thought, 1670–1789* (Princeton, 1994), and Dena Goodman, *The Republic of Letters: A Cultural History of the French Enlightenment* (Ithaca, 1994). Goodman addresses this question in her evaluation of Koselleck, Habermas, and others in her "Public Sphere and Private Life: Toward a Synthesis of Current Historiographical Approaches to the Old Regime," *History and Theory* 31 (1992): 1–20. However, these efforts to rehabilitate eighteenth-century sociability fail to address

tion the ideal of unity is taken to be essential to these political and intellectual developments.

This latent conception of national unity and identity emerged concretely when the extreme financial crisis of the 1780s resulted in the collapse of the monarchy. The state was paralyzed, and needed to find some kind of outside support to regenerate itself. The effort to secure that support, with the Assemblies of Notables and then the convoking of the Estates General, opened up a flood of the abstract political theory that had been constituted in opposition to the state in the eighteenth century. During the prerevolutionary events the idea of the "nation" could still be articulated negatively: against the defenders of privilege, against the crown's lack of reform. But with the emergence of the Third Estate as the National Assembly and the effective capitulation of the monarchy, what had been a purely *critical* position, grounded on fairly abstract notions of truth and identity, was now occupying a concrete political position of authority and decision. A position of singular sovereignty was taken over in the name of the people, society itself, and yet this "society" could be defined only negatively, at this particular point at least, as the obverse of the absolutist state.

As Furet effectively showed, the revolutionaries acted in an entirely new political context, because they were contesting to represent what was, according to Furet, a purely semiotic entity—a language, that is—whose origins, as Keith Baker has revealed so convincingly, lay in the complex development of eighteenth-century political and philosophical discourse.[16] Politics was taking place in a self-referential sphere of power where words (and not some social reality) legitimized action. For Furet and Baker, along with other historians such as Lynn Hunt and Mona Ozouf, the pathology of revolutionary politics was a function of the delusional idea that sovereignty was actually located in the people—who, as Furet repeatedly pointed out, were not actually "located" in any one place in particular. For Furet, then, power was therefore no longer political in the traditional sense, but ideological: "Language was substituted for power, for it was the sole guarantee that power would belong to the people, that is, to nobody." More important, for Furet at least, in order for this "empty" sign of authority to have any content, it had to create a new counter-image, one with some tangible reality, to replace

---

the revolutionary crisis and the origins of the Terror. We should note that even Habermas located the "failure" of revolutionary politics in France precisely in the lack of separation between state and society. See Jürgen Habermas, *Theory and Practice*, trans. John Viertel (Boston, 1973), 105.

16. Baker, *Inventing the French Revolution*.

the monarchy. From the beginning, the Revolution invented a whole new series of "negations" (aristocrats, counter-revolutionaries, enemies), and this is what made possible, according to Furet, the fictive reality of their opposite, the unitary nation.[17]

Linking so many critical perspectives on the revolutionary conception of national unity is the belief that there simply was no effective way of determining a "true" single national will. The revolutionaries, caught in the logic of unity, could not, many claim, envision a more pragmatic approach to political decisions, in part because this kind of politics lacked institutional support. There were no "reliable conventions" to locate public opinion,[18] nor were there traditional political forms that could represent and contain a diversity of positions (party politics); most important, there was, it seems, no *conceptual* space for any modern political negotiation that is grounded in the inevitability of social conflict. This was obviously not the case in Britain and the United States, where people had some experience of concrete political participation and recognized the need for compromise and negotiation.

The explanatory power of a pathological interpretation of the discourse of unity in France is clear. It explains the aspiration of the early revolutionaries to construct a new state based on popular sovereignty, while demonstrating the dangers that were inherent in this radically new invention. Without abandoning this radical concept of popular sovereignty, it is argued, the revolutionaries had no effective way of dealing with dissent and conflict in this context. They had taken over a model of singular sovereignty but applied it to the totality of society. There was no space for internal disunity, but this revolutionary consensus was, in Furet's words, only a "retrospective illusion."[19] The Terror, then, naturally developed as a method of guaranteeing the transparency of the unitary national will and the institutions of government.[20] Any conflict within the newly established representational bodies signaled *illegitimacy* in the Revolution, since the state was designed to represent, or manifest, the general will, which could be only one thing. Enlightenment, as Koselleck once said, effectively "prepared the way for the Terror and for dictatorship" because it constructed the fantastic ideal used to criticize the absolutist state, an ideal that did gain power, but because it had no real positive content, it ended up criticizing the very society it was supposed to govern. "The rational totality of the collective and of its

17. Furet, *Interpreting the French Revolution*, 27, 52–53.
18. Gunn, *Queen of the World*, 392.
19. Furet, *Interpreting the French Revolution*, 27.
20. Keith M. Baker, "Sovereignty," and Gunn, *Queen of the World*, 392.

volonté générale thus compels a constant correction of reality."[21] State and society were proclaimed one and the same by the early revolutionaries. The Terror simply tried to produce this unity in the face of critical resistances. Absolute, the sovereignty of the people "excluded pluralism of representation because it assumed the unity of the nation. Since that unity did not exist . . . the function of the Terror . . . was invariably to establish it."[22] A genuinely modern political culture was formed only in the aftermath of the Terror, with the recognition that the individual, and not the general will of the society, is the ground of the political sphere, as Furet in particular has emphasized.

But it is critical to point out here that something is missing from these pathogenetic narratives. There is no convincing resolution of a historical difficulty the revolutionaries actually faced. A merely pragmatic redefinition of the state would not have given any indication of what *constitutes* the very society to be ordered by this state, a very real problem once the state collapsed, as it did in France. And at this point, merely redefining the state in terms of "conflict" and opposing "interests" would have meant evading an essential question: What is the source of that fundamental and unanimous agreement that keeps the nation together in times of conflict? The Americans had a war of independence to identify the new nation opposed to the "loyalists." The French had a largely conceptual "war" against despotism and privilege, and the participants of this large and complex identity were not so easily demarcated in advance.

It is here, in the midst of an extremely difficult situation, that the Enlightenment concept of error emerged, I believe, to shape a critically important political form. As we have seen, it was believed, in certain strands of eighteenth-century thought, that the truth of identity—personal and cosmological—was concretely manifested only in aberrant forms. Attempts to reconnect with this truth were always in error, but these errors pointed the way to truth. If the collective sovereign was considered to be the transcendent source of legitimacy for revolutionary political practice, the revolutionaries, as representatives of the Enlightenment, were hardly unaware of the complex difficulties involved in making this legitimizing force appear in concrete situations.

The line of thought we have traced in the Enlightenment did, I will show, persist in the mainstream of revolutionary thought, suggesting another answer to the problem of identifying the unity of the nation in the face of disorder, violence, and aberration. The Enlightenment discourse

21. Koselleck, *Critique and Crisis*, 165.
22. François Furet, "Terror," Furet and Ozouf, *Critical Dictionary*, 149.

of error in its political form linked the absent unity of the communal voice with the irreducible differences of concrete individuals. The revolutionary theory of political error held out the possibility of a perfect integration of state decisions and the will of the nation, even as it recognized the very real dangers of inevitable aberration (in society and in political institutions). The revisionist historians are right to focus on the discourse of unity in the Revolution, since it was that discourse that *defined* the Revolution as a political reality. However, the conceptualization of unity in the midst of difference and aberration was much more complex than Furet and other critics of revolutionary democratic discourse have suggested. A focus on the language of error in the revolutionary texts will reveal a complicated and I think sophisticated understanding of how this absent, yet omnipresent, structure of unity in the nation operated.

NEGATION AND NATIONAL UNITY

When "national sovereignty" was declared in 1789, the concept was both familiar and highly elusive. From at least the late seventeenth century, visions of the "nation" had been constructed in opposition to ruling authorities. In other words, critiques of "despotism" had been grounded on various negations of that power. There was no common discourse of nation in France. The concept served as a vehicle for various principles that the crown (or ruling elites) were supposedly violating. Le Paige, Boulainvilliers, Mably, all sketched French nations that represented different negations of the absolutist state.[23] By the late eighteenth century, even the crown itself would represent its plan for political and financial reform as the interests of the "nation." The king's minister Calonne, for example, framed his own attack on privilege in the late 1780s from this perspective. This move radically reoriented prerevolutionary political discourse, for instead of the usual opposition between the state and the nation, for the first time socioeconomic *privilege* and the nation faced each other in a highly charged political crisis. Initially a financial concern (the nation could not, Calonne and Necker said, survive without the renunciation of certain privileges), this opposition was not

23. See François Furet and Mona Ozouf, "Deux légitimations historiques de la société française au XVIIIᵉ siècle: Mably et Boulainvilliers," *Annales* 34 (1979): 438–50; Keith Michael Baker, "A Script for a French Revolution: The Political Consciousness of the Abbé Mably," in *Inventing the French Revolution;* J. Kent Wright, "National Sovereignty and the General Will: The Political Program of the Declaration of Rights," in *The French Idea of Freedom: The Old Regime and the Declaration of Rights of 1789,* ed. Dale Van Kley (Stanford, 1994).

easily controlled; it would soon broaden to include all political privileges. The two assemblies of notables were denounced by critics for defending privilege, for the first time against the crown's desire for change, then against the nation once the crown had acknowledged the need for greater consensus.[24]

Consequently, in the discussions and pamphlet debates just before the revolutionary events, the nation was being defined less as an enemy of absolutist despotism than as a negation of privilege. For example, in his *Essai sur les privilèges*, Emmanuel Sieyes defined privilege negatively, as something necessarily "outside" of the common rights enjoyed by true citizens of the nation. If law was the product of national will, then privilege (literally "private law") was pathologically wrong—in Sieyes's term a *maladie anti-sociale*.[25] The nation, in this prerevolutionary context, could now be defined as something that was *not* divided by privileges, protections, preferences.[26] For Sieyes (and many others at the time) "this process of national assertion was intrinsically an act of separation and repulsion. The nation could become itself only by distinguishing itself from what was alien to it and by sloughing off this foreign element."[27] The pamphlet war that took place once the Estates General had once again been called to meet destroyed any lingering ideal of a "historical" political precedent for the institution.[28] The estates were going to embody the nation envisioned by eighteenth-century philosophy, something Sieyes argued in an early text, the *Vues sur les moyens d'exécution dont les représentans de la France pourront disposer en 1789*.[29] The real struggle would take place within the Estates General, over the definition of the nation. And it would be clear from the start that certain groups resisted this idea of the nation. Sieyes, for example, would soon abandon

24. See Michael Fitzsimmons's detailed account in *The Remaking of France: The National Assembly and the Constitution of 1791* (Cambridge, 1994), 7–17.

25. Emmanuel Sieyes, *Essai sur les privilèges*, in Sieyes, *Qu'est-ce que le Tiers état?* ed. Edme Champion (Paris, 1888), 1, 5–6, 9. I am adopting the eighteenth-century spelling of Sieyes's name, rather than the usual accented form that became standard in the nineteenth century, given that this was the way Sieyes himself normally signed his own works. See Murray Forsyth, *Reason and Revolution: The Political Thought of the Abbé Sieyes* (New York, 1987), 1, and William H. Sewell Jr., *A Rhetoric of Bourgeois Revolution: The Abbé Sieyes and "What Is the Third Estate?"* (Durham, N.C., 1994), 2n.

26. Sieyes, *Délibérations à prendre pour les assemblées de baillages* (1789), in *La déclaration des droits de l'homme et du citoyen*, ed. Stéphane Rials (Paris, 1988), 533.

27. Murray Forsyth, *Reason and Revolution*, 70.

28. See Lynn Hunt, "National Assembly," in *The French Revolution and the Creation of Modern Political Culture*, vol. 1: *The Political Culture of the Old Regime*, ed. Keith Michael Baker (Oxford, 1987), 413.

29. Published anonymously in 1789. See Forsyth, *Reason and Revolution*, 81.

his faith in the Estates General as a whole, reducing the "nation" in his most famous pamphlet—*Qu'est-ce que le Tiers état?*—to the Third Estate alone, given that the other orders seemed intent on preserving their almost ludicrously anachronistic roles.

From the very beginning, then, the Estates General was a confrontation over national identity. It is hardly surprising that the body never had the chance to act. The very call for common verification of the representatives' credentials challenged the ideological and institutional structure of the body, for many of the deputies had been specifically barred by their constituents from deliberating with the other orders on *any* issue. These representatives were bound by the *mandat impératif*, the condition of their election. The early debates on reviewing credentials and on the form of eventual deliberation, then, identified the real issue: were the representatives at Versailles there to protect the interests of their orders and particular regions, or were the estates going to act in concert as the voice of the nation in the quest for reform?[30] Some representatives, most notably the Dauphinois, symbolized an emerging ideal of national cooperation; all orders worked together, defying historical precedents. Others, like the delegates from Brittany, resisted this turn completely, remaining separated by order, planning to defend not only the structure of orders but the privilege of the province itself with respect to the state when the Estates General met in May. However, the Dauphinois soon became a focal point of public opinion, with their argument that the Estates General must be the means for furthering the interests of the nation as a whole.[31] Eventually this ideal of unity and national interest would come to be located within the Third Estate, a development that symbolized, for many public observers at least, this desire for reform in the name of the nation. The Third debated in public, for example, and did not retreat from the Common meeting room as the other orders did to deliberate. The modesty of many of the Third's representatives also strengthened their claim to represent the reasonable interests of the whole nation, and not just the elites.[32]

As the friction between the orders and with the crown only increased, the Third Estate eventually asserted itself as the voice of the nation without official approval, in the crucial Tennis Court oath, a powerful moment (psychologically and politically) in the creation of a positive source of unity for the nation. The newly formed National Assembly was the

30. On the importance of the verification question, see Ran Halévi and François Furet, *La monarchie républicaine: La constitution de 1791* (Paris, 1996), 117–18.

31. Fitzsimmons, *Remaking of France*, 24–26; see as well Jean Egret, *Le Parlement de Dauphiné et les affaires publiques dans la deuxième moitié du XVIIIe siècle*, 2 vols. (Paris, 1942).

32. Fitzsimmons, *Remaking of France*, 29, 35.

origin of the Revolution not so much because it broke with established protocols as because it effected a key transition: the nation was no longer merely a *negation* of certain political or social forces. Rather, the nation now claimed positive status and, more important, had a tangible location. The revocation of the binding mandates completed this transition, for it was now decided that the representatives spoke for the nation. Their task was the formation of a constitution, and this required that individuals be cut off from their merely local origins to work for the nation as a unified whole.[33] Having redefined national identity as a negation of social and political privilege, the National Assembly found itself enacting a negation predominant in Enlightenment political discourse: sovereignty was, for the first time, *not* in fact the property of the monarch. Supported by a public whose visions of change were threatened by ministers and armed troops, the National Assembly captured actual political power in a complex series of negative assertions.

The first major act of the newly established sovereign entity was also a radical negation. Whatever the circumstances leading up to and surrounding the evening of August 4, 1789, when the National Assembly voted to dismantle the entire feudal structure of France, there is no question that this event was understood by those participating as something "sublime," an emotional and powerful experience of this newly freed force, the "nation."[34] The nation was able to destroy many of the key negations it had in fact been defining itself against. There was consequently a profound absence in the wake of August 4, for the goals of the representatives had for some time been structured as oppositions, with no plan for the dismantling of the entire state and social structure.

The radical absence was filled by the constitution, itself preceded by the Declaration of the Rights of Man: these were *positive* acts of self-definition. The Declaration was, it is true, hardly a coherent document. Assembled in haste, it accommodated within its articles many strands of Enlightenment discourse, and perhaps inevitably reflected the basic principles of the largely bourgeois Assembly.[35] Its *conceptual* function, however, was clear: to define the principles of national identity, without using the critical technique of negation, the main rhetorical strategy of

33. "To become representatives of the people, that is to say enveloped in its sovereignty, they paradoxically had to break the link that chained them to their constituents and reinvent themselves as carriers of the national will": Halévi and Furet, *La monarchie républicaine*, 255.

34. See Fitzsimmons's excellent account, based on correspondence of representatives, *Remaking of France*, 53–60, esp. n. 84. See as well Jean-Pierre Hirsch, *La nuit du 4 août* (Paris, 1978).

35. See the various essays in Van Kley, *French Idea of Freedom*.

prerevolutionary action. The Assembly meant to show the French people, through the declaration of "universal" principles, that the new constitution was not going to be simply a reworking of the old relationships of power. It was to be, as Sieyes would say, a *chose nouvelle.*[36] Given that the very creation of the Assembly was an illegal act (in the context of the elections and the institutional procedures defining the Estates General), the Declaration served to base political action on higher principles. Legitimacy was to be derived from the basic rights of all citizens in the nation.[37] The ideal of national unity and these "higher" principles were only *strengthened* by the inevitable resistances that emerged during the early phases of revolutionary government—resistances from the crown to the new power of the Assembly, local resistances to acts such as the abolition of the old provincial identities in the name of the nation, resistance on the part of those affected by the renunciation of feudal privileges.[38] The constitution was necessary because the nation had to decide how to act in its own name against these resistances. The National Assembly had, up to this point, identified itself with the nation. State and society had been drawn together (at least conceptually), and this meant that the legitimacy of the representative body came directly from the nation. This was, of course, the very basis of "national sovereignty." Yet here some profound difficulties emerged for the revolutionaries, difficulties that have often been cited as the source of the extreme revolutionary violence that would soon develop.

It has been said that the revolutionaries failed to stabilize the French polity when they failed to establish the representative body as the one privileged location of sovereign will. National sovereignty escaped the borders of the Assembly and inevitably became an undisciplined and uncontrollable force, limited by no institutional forms. Perhaps this was unavoidable, given that the Assembly itself owed its very existence to the idea that the people could legitimately reorganize its institutions at will. But in deciding for this language of will (over the language of representation and limitation) was France already on the path to the Terror?[39]

By isolating the problem of error and its role in the concept of representation as it emerges in the early constitutional debates, I want to show how the politicians in the Assembly, with their work on the constitution

36. See Baker, "Fixing the French Constitution," in his *Inventing the French Revolution,* 263–67; and Sieyes, *Délibérations,* 540.

37. See Gauchet, *La révolution des pouvoirs,* 55, and his *La révolution des droits des hommes* (Paris, 1989).

38. See Fitzsimmons, *Remaking of France,* 75–80.

39. Baker, "Representation Redefined," and Furet, *Interpreting the French Revolution.*

of 1791, maintained the ideal of the unitary nation, but at the same time were also extremely sensitive to various kinds of "aberration" and the possibility of error in all political representation. This awareness of error in fact opened up an important gap between the mute will of the "people" and the concrete voice of the legislature. The nation, articulated first through a series of negations, had to confront at some point the possibility of its own errors: the will of the nation may have been opposed by certain obvious resistances, but how exactly would this will voice itself without any aberration? Rather than assuming an automatic transparency between the state and the people, as so many commentators have recently argued, the revolutionaries did I think directly confront from the start the essential *difference* between the voice of the nation and the voice of the government—not to mention the differences between the wills of individuals and the collective will as expressed in the institutions of government.

ARTICULATING THE VOICE OF THE NATION

In June 1789 Sieyes urged the Estates General to begin common verification and move from inaction to action. He linked this need for common verification with the goal of the Estates General itself. Sieyes said it was time for the representatives "to begin finally to concern themselves with the national interest, which alone, and to the exclusion of particular interests, appears as the great goal toward which all deputies must strive through common effort."[40] Sieyes continued in another speech to argue that the absence of particular representatives at any one debate or resolution vote did not at all invalidate any motions decreed by the Assembly. Since the body as a whole was trying to represent not the individual regions where the deputies were originally elected but the nation as a whole, there was no real doubt that the delegates present had legitimately discovered this larger interest. The verified representatives assembled to form the "national voice," and this assembly alone had the task of "interpreting and presenting the general will of the nation."[41] Despite all the difficulties and strong resistances, these "stormy circumstances" of the early revolution, the assembled representatives always have a "light to guide them," Sieyes claimed. The "mission" that they were fulfilling was not the subservient one of *mandataires* or royal offi-

---

40. Sieyes, "Motion sur la vérification des pouvoirs" (June 10, 1789), in *Orateurs de la Révolution française*, vol. 1: *Les constituants*, ed. Ran Halévi and François Furet (Paris, 1989), 1001.

41. Sieyes, "Motion sur la constitution des communes en assemblées des représentants connus et vérifiés de la nation française" (June 15, 1789), ibid., 1002.

cers, mere couriers of some other view or interest. Envoys of the people as a whole, the representatives had to adhere courageously to that task against all opposition. The people of France, he said, were pushing them not to stop but to form a constitution. "Is there a power on earth that can strip you of the right to represent your constituents?"[42] The real question facing the Assembly, then, was figuring out what this task of creation entailed.

For Sieyes, the task was clear. A constitution, he said, formed and organized public powers. He emphasized that a *nation* could not itself be "constituted," only its government. Assuming that it existed, the nation was not at all limited by any previous constitutional forms; the Assembly, therefore, was "free of all constraint, and of all form."[43] Sieyes was, in this speech, referring to points he had made previously in his immensely significant pamphlet, *Qu'est-ce que le Tiers état?* There, after locating the nation, via a series of negations, in the Third Estate, Sieyes finally addressed the positive "principles" of political action in the fifth chapter. The identity of the nation, Sieyes argues there, is not the product of some kind of *construction*. It is like the source of light, the origin of truth. Nothing predates it, conceptually or historically. "The nation exists before everything, it is the origin of everything." The nation would never exist if it had to wait for some positive act that would bring it into existence from component parts. The national identity, then, comes before all forms and procedures; it cannot be identified with any one particular mode of being. Large nations must exercise their common will through representative structures, but this does not mean that the common will disappears. For Sieyes, law does not define the limits of the nation but only serves its will, voicing its identity at any one particular time. The nation is "the source and the supreme master of all positive law" and "can never have too many possible methods of expressing its will."[44]

As a result, the nation can never be restricted in its movement, it cannot be limited to specific constitutional forms: the very particularity of any one form would eventually hinder the nation's ability to meet with varying conditions. There is always, Sieyes observes, the possibility of "unforeseen difficulties," and the institutions of a country would simply collapse if there did not exist a higher authority to deal with this emergency. "A body subjected to constituted forms cannot decide anything

---

42. Sieyes, "Après la séance royale," ibid., 1003.
43. Sieyes, "Préliminaire de la constitution: Reconnaissance et exposition raisonnée des droits de l'homme et du citoyen," ibid., 1013.
44. Sieyes, *Qu'est-ce que le Tiers état?* ed. Roberto Zapperi (Geneva, 1970), 180–84.

except what follows from its constitution." Once these forms are revealed to be inadequate to the problems at hand, the conflict between the
parts of the nation would descend into anarchy because the constitution
could no longer sustain order. As Sieyes argues, however, since the nation exists *independently* of these forms, it establishes a new order by
making a decision unfettered by the now inadequate procedures. An
order fixed for all time in specific forms would be fragile and transitory
"if it could encounter one single case in which it was impossible to indicate rules of conduct suitable to meet all needs." The nation must intervene and take any action necessary for the preservation of the community. Sieyes writes: "Whatever its will might be, [the nation] cannot lose
the right to change it as soon as its interest demands it."[45] Constituted
public powers were legitimate only if true to this will. A constitution
must organize these powers and make sure they remain accurate inter-
preters of will.

What is not so clear in Sieyes analysis is how the nation can make itself
present in times of crisis or emergency, those situations in which constituted authorities may well be in error. The central difficulty in this conceptual structure (a difficulty that would become a major concern of revolutionary politics at least until Thermidor) is that the sovereign force
has, according to Sieyes, no limitations on its power; it is the ultimate authority in all questions of law and order, and yet it cannot *by its very nature* be made fully present in any one specific space of representation. In
order to intervene, in order to amend any law, it must assume a visible
form to complete its task. As Sieyes significantly noted in an early pamphlet on the constitution, in the summer of 1789: "Although the national
will is, in this sense, independent of all form, still it must take one in
order to make itself understood [*se faire entendre*]."[46] The nation is essentially silent; it never speaks in its own direct voice. The necessary
organ—some concrete form—will as a result never be exactly the same
as the "national will" it serves to represent. Therefore, as the revolutionaries understood from the start, it is crucial to know just how *accurate* the
institutional manifestation of the ephemeral will would be. Because
there is an essential gap between constitutional form and national will,
at least potentially, all political decisions were potentially aberrant. But
in the absence of any one privileged path for the common will, how is
this gap measured? "With whom does the decision lie? With the nation,

45. Ibid., 184–87.
46. Sieyes, *Quelques idées du constitution applicables à la ville de Paris en juillet 1789* (Versailles, 1789), 32.

independent as it necessarily is of all positive form."[47] The real task of
the Assembly was to make sure that the will of the representatives of the
new legislative body would not vitiate the constitutional order by violating the will of the people; the Assembly had to create, that is, a method
for *identifying* these aberrations of political will, so as to avoid the collapse of the state in times of crisis.

"THE GENERAL WILL CANNOT ERR": REPRESENTATION AND
THE ROYAL VETO

After setting up a radically new relationship between state organization and society, one adopted by the early revolutionaries, Sieyes
confronted the problem of making sure that the representative body
would not be subject to conflicts and diverse interests, given that the nation's will must be unitary. Sieyes solves the difficulty with a simple, perhaps even simplistic, move. A political association, he says, is always a
unanimous will. The establishment of public institutions, however, can
be the result of only a majority decision. In effect, everyone agrees to
submit to the majority, which is the only practical way of arriving at decisions that are necessary in the first place only because society cannot
(as Sieyes had noted in both his *Vues sur les moyens* and *Qu'est-ce que le
Tiers état?*) exercise its common will effectively on its own once it has
grown to a certain size.[48] He concludes his speech by asserting: "The
general will is thus formed by the will of the majority."[49] The common
will must, he said, be assumed to be in the opinion of the majority. This
meant that the majority will of the Third Estate constituted its common
will, and that the will of the Third Estate (being the majority of the nation) itself constituted the general will. Sieyes claimed that a representative assembly "can speak then *without error* in the name of the entire nation."[50] While this assumption was certainly pragmatic, it seems
problematic in the context of the idea of national sovereignty. The veracity of the majority will would, in the constitution, have to be explained.

47. Sieyes, *Qu'est-ce que le Tiers état?* ed. Zapperi, 184.
48. Ibid., 178. Sieyes wrote: "It is thus absolutely necessary to resolve to recognize all
the characteristics of the common will in the agreed-upon majority. . . . Every citizen, by
his act of union, contracts the constant pledge to see himself linked by the opinion of the
majority, even when his particular will would be part of the minority": *Vues sur les
moyens d'exécution dont les représentans de la France pourront disposer en 1789* ([Paris], 1789),
18.
49. Sieyes, "Préliminaire de la constitution," 1014, 1015.
50. Sieyes, *Qu'est-ce que le Tiers état?* ed. Zapperi, 201.

If, as Sieyes and others claimed, each representative articulated the will of the nation, and not just the will of particular localities or interests, why was the majority *necessarily* right? If a minority could misinterpret the will of the nation, the majority was also potentially errant, as Rousseau had already admitted. This is something Condorcet reflected on well before the Revolution, as we saw.

The problem of error reemerged, in exactly this framework, during the September 1789 debate over the role of the king in the new constitution. Soon after proclaiming themselves the National Assembly and vowing to write a constitution for France, the representatives of France were immediately faced with the difficulty of creating a revolutionary polity that was founded on national sovereignty yet preserved a position for the monarch. For many conservative deputies, the debate on the place and function of the king was an opportunity to control the revolutionary turn without abandoning popular support for the Assembly. These representatives, while accepting the concept of national sovereignty, advocated strong monarchical authority, with an absolute veto over the decisions of the Assembly. Most resisted this subordinate position for the Assembly; at any rate, there was strong pressure from outside the sphere of government not to give the king such an absolute power.[51] Whatever the disagreements, the language of this debate on the veto is of some importance. The discussion was framed, inevitably, by the concept of "the people," the only concept that legitimized the authority of the Assembly in the first place; yet the elusive nature of what Rousseau, and now the revolutionaries, called the "general will" meant that the constitution could take on any number of forms. There was no reason why the monarch could not just as easily as an assembly "represent" the people, or why multiple chambers would not be more accurate than one legislature, given that the ultimate goal was to articulate the single voice of the nation. Since representatives were understood to be representing not their regional constituents but this abstracted *national* interest, the form of the constitution was, ideally, to be structured so as to limit the gap between the national voice and the eventual concrete will of the government (in the form of laws and executive decisions). In other words, the crucial task was to limit and control the possibility of error. Right, center, left, all agreed on this fundamental question; the political differences reflected divergent views on the relative likelihood of error in any one institutional structure. Would an assembly or a king be more mistaken (or corrupt)?

Most deputies were in favor of what was called the "suspensive" veto,

51. Baker, "Fixing the French Constitution," 271.

precisely because of the inherent ambiguities of the general will and the concept of "national" sovereignty. If both the Assembly and the king could be wrong in their interpretation, then the constitution should, many believed, allow for differences between them. And the best way to arbitrate any conflict would be a "call to the people," since it was the people's will that was the original measure of accuracy here. This seemed like a practical solution to many deputies, and the suspensive veto easily gained approval. Yet this framework opened up some serious theoretical difficulties. Once the possibility of error was allowed, even expected, the legitimacy of *any* representative or executive authority was seriously undermined. It has been argued that the Revolution could never have survived this constitutional position, one that made representatives and the king suspect, gave ultimate authority to an ephemeral entity, "the people," but did not create a prompt and efficient method for voicing the people's will in these crisis situations. This difficulty helped prepare the stage for the events of August 1792 and the overthrow of the monarchy and the Legislative Assembly. But was the instability of the 1791 constitution really a function of this conceptual framework? Again, I think that the problem of error can help resolve this question.

The problem of the veto, as Keith Baker has clearly demonstrated, was formulated in terms of error, the distance between the general will and any given political act.[52] One deputy who spoke in favor of the suspensive veto, Jean-Baptiste Salle, questioned the value of the absolute veto, noting that there was always a danger that the king's will might be an aberration from the will of the nation. The suspensive veto would call on the people to decide who was right: the Assembly or the king. If the truth of the general will lay with the people, then they ought to decide, Salle argued. Salle does bring up a potentially dangerous possibility. One could point out, he says, that "history is full of errors of the multitude"; in other words, perhaps even the people themselves do not always know the "general good." Salle, for his part, refuses to believe this. Error, he says, emerges only when the people actually govern themselves. As sovereign, the people can never make mistakes about their own interest. The nation could hardly desire its own harm. He goes on to cite Rousseau: "The general will cannot err, says the greatest political writer [*publiciste*] of the century. Why? Because when the nation makes the laws, everyone lays down for everyone: the general interest is necessarily only what rises above." The real threat of error arises with government; the problem, he observes, "is that *if the general will cannot err* when a nation makes a law, the Assemblies that it delegates can be mistaken, because if the will cannot be represented, they can, as in England, let themselves be corrupted, and prevaricate."[53] Salle's own attempt to control error is rather unsophisticated. He proposes a rapid turnover of representatives and a suspensive veto for the king. Error would not have a chance to take root in the Assembly, while the special status of the king would supposedly help protect the unerring general will.

Another delegate, Rabaud Saint-Etienne, made a similar point. Just as the people cannot err if they do not govern, the king cannot err if he does not legislate. "The king must never be mistaken, and he will never be mistaken if he will never make the law. But kings are men, and if you make them legislators, you give them over to the errors of humanity and consequently to the censure of peoples." The goal, as Rabaud Saint-Etienne put it, was to substitute "their [the legislators'] will, which can err, with the general will, which cannot at all be mistaken."[54] This was, of course, a rather circular argument, since the general will was exactly what required interpretation by representatives. Salle seemed to think that if every citizen expressed his opinion on a certain legislative decision, then differences would cancel out and only the general will would remain. This helps explain the appeal of the call to the people. But even Rousseau, invoked repeatedly here, was of course not so sure about this. At any rate, a constant call to the people (especially in this unstable revolutionary situation) was hardly practical.

The Comte d'Antraigues, who would soon become a counter-revolutionary and foreign spy, addressed this exact difficulty in his speech on the royal veto. He agreed that whatever power the king would ultimately have, it was accorded to him by the nation, the ultimate source of sovereignty. The question of the king's power was one of utility. What *function* could he best fulfill? Again, Antraigues frames this question in terms of error. If the people distribute powers as they see fit, as Sieyes already claimed, then these instituted powers can, by virtue of their separation, stray from the people: "The law being only the expression of the will of all, one cannot be assured that one man or an assembly of men will always want what all would have wanted." Antraigues, though, realized that because France was such a large nation, the will of the people could be *exercised* only through representational bodies. The will of the nation manifested itself through public organs. But how, then, could the gap between nation and aberrant organ ever be bridged? Antraigues's solution was to multiply the organs of national will, so that no one body

53. *Archives parlementaires de 1787 à 1860, première série (1787 à 1799)* (Paris, 1862–), 8: 529–31, 533. Cf. Baker, "Fixing the French Constitution," 291–292.
54. *Archives parlementaires*, 570–71.

or person could ever tyrannize the nation. He also suggested that if the representatives were charged with finding the general will, they would have to be carefully watched by the king, who will say when they had breached the limits set by the original constitution.[55] Of course, multiplying organs does not necessarily decrease the possibility of error, unless, as Condorcet once tried to establish with mathematical precision, one could ascertain the probability of error in these specific organs. Multiplying organs might, in certain conditions, even multiply the possibility of error disastrously.

Mirabeau, the great early leader of the revolutionary assembly, persuasively argued that the guardian of legislative error should be the king alone, precisely because the chance of error in this particular organ was so minimal. Acknowledging that a "secret terror" makes everyone want to limit the powers of the monarch, because someone who is above the law may very well rival it, Mirabeau claimed that if the question were considered calmly, and in the context of popular sovereignty, it was clear that the monarch was the *protector* of the people, and could not possibly be the enemy of the general good. The monarch, he said, intervenes not for personal interests but for the interests of the people. But why should the monarch intervene at all? It is true, Mirabeau notes, that if the Assembly, "made up of true elements," offers decisions resulting from careful, rational, free discussion and deliberation, "the product of all the knowledge they could gather," it seems that their will is not simply the general will but the general *reason*. However, Mirabeau introduces again the possibility of error. Imagine badly chosen representatives; imagine, he says, the "terror" of a secretive Assembly eliminating free debate and dissent. What would stop this development? "The prince is the perpetual representative of the people, as the deputies are its representatives elected at certain times." This perpetual representative must be given higher powers than the Assembly. If the power of the king were limited to the suspensive veto, he might be forced to sanction a bad law, for the suspensive option falsely assumes that a second legislative assembly cannot be wrong. Mirabeau does not bring up the possibility of error in the king's will; for Mirabeau, corruption is the main source of error, and the king, he implies, could never want to go against the voice of the nation, because it would not be to his advantage to do so.[56]

The *monarchiens*, a loosely connected group of representatives inspired

55. Antraigues, "Discours sur la sanction royale," in Halévi and Furet, *Orateurs de la Révolution française*, 1:7, 8, 10–11.

56. Mirabeau, "Discours sur le droit de veto," in Halévi and Furet, *Orateurs de la Révolution française*, 1: 674, 676, 677, 682.

by Montesquieu and an admiration for the British constitution, argued for a constitutional monarchy, but they distanced themselves from more extreme monarchical positions such as Mirabeau's.[57] Malouet, for example, also stressed the possibility of corruption in the legislative body, but he wanted to reserve ultimate authority not for the person of the monarch but for the constitutional document itself. He noted that sovereignty, in simple societies, is manifested without any obstacles every time the citizens meet collectively. Though sovereignty resides in the nation, when the nation becomes complex and large, it communicates some of its power to others. Now the true monarch, Malouet says, is the "organ" of the general will. But what makes the monarch an organ, and not just a despotic authority, is the constitutional demarcation of his sphere of power. The despotic will, Malouet observes, knows no limit, it is "always erring like a storm on the horizon, has no character, no inviolable asylum." Separated by the people by terror, the despot does not make law; he simply acts. The true monarch, then, is *limited by law,* a power maintained by the people and communicated to the representatives in the Legislative Assembly. This ideal situation is, according to Malouet, threatened again by the possibility of error, the straying of these organs from their origin—the people's will, that is. Malouet notes that the representatives are always going to be tormented by ambition. Their will, their interest can be in conflict with the general interest. The nation must guarantee that its interest is being represented by making sure the Assembly is watched by someone who can protect the constitution. Malouet argues that this is the role of the monarch, a figure who could not possibly act against the very document that defines and maintains his own position. Malouet goes even further. The representatives themselves should desire a strong monarchical presence, since they might become subject to the abuse of the people. The people might act "arbitrarily," so the representatives of sovereignty might need to be defended from the "anxieties and suspicions of the people."[58] For Malouet, the constitution is the only authentic voice of the national will, a position that is clearly opposed to that of Sieyes, who claimed that the people can be limited by no one single form, however legitimate its creation. Yet Malouet introduces an important if problematic point: If the general will is always right, is it always expressed through the people, at all times? Who exactly are the people? Can they never be mistaken when they

57. On the *monarchiens,* see Halévi's article on them in Furet and Ozouf, *Critical Dictionary.* On Malouet in particular, see Robert Griffiths, *Le centre perdu: Malouet et les "monarchiens" dans la Révolution française* (Grenoble, 1988).
58. Malouet, "Discours sur la sanction royale," in Halévi and Furet, *Orateurs de la Révolution française,* 1: 457–58, 460.

come together to act? What is the source of the eternal validity of the constitution?

Malouet's colleague Mounier addressed this very difficulty. He agreed, as all revolutionary politicians had to agree, that sovereignty was in the nation. However, it was a fact that the nation could not govern itself. And it was also true that having sovereignty and *exercising* it were two different things. The popular exercise of sovereignty would be dangerous, Mounier argued, because the nation wanted only what was best for itself, but since the nation was in effect a *collective* body, it could not always act in unity. It was prey to all the ambitions and interests that made it up. It was split by factions, and was an "empire of violence." Government, Mounier pointed out in a Hobbesian move, was created precisely to protect the people from this internal violence. And they could not organize a government without *delegating* their sovereignty to an outside force. The real problem was to make sure that this public organ of sovereignty really did act for the general will. But the concrete actions of actual people are not automatically the "general will." Mounier notes: "No government takes as its only guide the will of the multitude. In the ancient republics, one never subjected the people to a law they did not want; but one would not consider law everything they wanted." The key task was to identify "rules to distinguish an arbitrary will, an impassioned movement, from a reflective will, guided by the enlightenment of reason [*les lumières de la raison*]."[59] The measure of error was truth, not public opinion or mass desire.

Surprisingly, it is these conservative writers that take us back to the difficult problem first raised by Rousseau and taken up by Condorcet. How do we protect ourselves from error in the political sphere when the truth of the general will is threatened not only by the organs of representation but by the very actions of the citizens themselves? The fact that the general will was not immediately present as a guide to politics made politics necessary (as Rousseau noted), yet it also made politics potentially illegitimate. Most revolutionaries were not willing to agree, as the *monarchiens* were, that the "truth" could be enshrined in a single constitution and interpreted without error by a watchful, disinterested king. Sieyes, early in the Revolution, offered one of the most important and influential analyses of the concept of political truth.

REPRESENTATION AND THE ABERRATION OF WILL

In Sieyes's thinking, truth was what made politics legitimate, and political truth was a function of national interest. Sieyes explained

59. Mounier, "Discours sur la sanction royale," ibid., 895, 903–4.

the complex relation between truth and interest in one of the admittedly less incisive sections of his rhetorical masterpiece, *Qu'est-ce que le Tiers état?* There he wrote that "with a people accustomed to servitude, one can let truths sleep; but if you stimulate their attention, if you inform them of the choice between [truths] and errors, the mind clings to truth, as healthy eyes naturally turn toward the light." Clearly, the history of despotism had been the history of darkness and error, and the elections for the Estates General were the first manifestation of light. For Sieyes, in this prerevolutionary context, the role of the "patriotic writer" was to proclaim the truth. "If everyone's thought was *true* [*vrai*], the greatest changes, as soon as they offered a goal of public good, would be no difficulty. What better can I do than to help with all my powers to spread this truth that prepares the way?"[60] The people may err, he implied, but they will not intentionally stray from the truth. Truth, however, may at first appear as strange to prejudice as prejudice to truth. As Sieyes later noted, "reason itself must mature, and . . . to prepare the season of enlightenment, [reason] must precede it."[61]

The measure of truth in politics was for Sieyes the identification of a common national interest, the only proper object of political will. Only with the truth can the administration of the nation be properly conducted. The administrator, Sieyes writes, aims never to leave the right path. However, "this path [*chemin*] must have been cut through to the end by the philosopher. He must have arrived at the end, otherwise he could not guarantee that this is really the path that leads there." The philosopher, for Sieyes, is the pilot of political administration, the advance scout of the nation's own desire for its common interest. And like the pilot philosophers of the Enlightenment we encountered in epistemological texts, Sieyes's philosopher must reach political truth through error. "When the philosopher cuts out a road, he only has to deal with *errors;* if he wants to advance, he must destroy them ruthlessly."[62] The administrator, following after, knows the way but must confront all the interests that block the path blazed by the philosopher.

Sieyes poses an obvious question at this point of the text. How can we trust the guide in the wilderness when we have not seen the truth ourselves? In fact, Sieyes believes that there is no place for blind trust. The philosopher must be as open as possible, explaining everything as the path is formed.

60. Sieyes, *Qu'est-ce que le Tiers état?* ed. Zapperi, 194, 212.
61. Unpublished manuscript, quoted and translated in Forsyth, *Reason and Revolution,* 29.
62. Sieyes, *Qu'est-ce que le Tiers état?* ed. Zapperi, 216.

Everywhere I go I meet those who, in moderation, would like to *particularize* [*détailler*] the truth, or introduce it all at once only in weakened fragments [*légères parcelles*]. . . . We falsely suppose that truth can be divided, cut off from itself [*s'isoler*], and thereby enter, in small *portions*, the mind more easily.

Sieyes demands that truth be revealed in its full strength: "The truth cannot have too much of all its light, in order to produce these strong impressions that engrave it forever in the soul, impressions that evoke a passionate *interest* for everything recognized as beautiful, useful, and true." The "healthy eye" will recognize the light for what it is. The philosopher must work through error to reach truth.[63]

Yet what is truth for Sieyes? Not, he explains, something immediately tangible, "discovered" by the philosopher and then applied by the administrator and publicized in its totality. Truth is something more elusive, because, Sieyes suggests, it cannot make its appearance in the world without some degree of deviation, refracted and reflected in many directions. Sieyes claims that we never perceive the essential *source* of light, the "direct ray," only its manifestations as it travels and illuminates particular objects, reflecting some of its energy toward us. Truth is the relationship of all the particular truths expressed in different places, revealed by various reflections. "Without this ensemble [of truths] one can never feel sufficiently illuminated, and one often believes he holds a truth that will have to be abandoned as one contemplates further." Like the sovereignty of the nation, which comes before all else politically and legitimizes every political expression even as it never actually appears in any concrete location, truth is the source of authentic knowledge even as it conceals itself in its multiple refractions and indirect reflective appearances.[64]

Sieyes leaves the impression that the path to truth is not as clear as it sometimes seems. Significantly, he draws together the images of truth and nation. Knowledge, the gathering of all the reflections of truth, is the product of a collective enterprise, and thus a collective possession. Similarly, the nation is on its own path to truth: to find the common interest that itself is refracted through all the particular interests and conflicts in society. The nation, for Sieyes, is really a point of origin, and not some given entity. As the subject of the political quest for identity, the nation is defined by its unitary structure, yet this unity is purely conceptual, or rather existential. The first political act is the negative one of asserting the necessity of a national interest common to all, even if that interest is

63. Ibid., 213.
64. Ibid., 214.

still at the moment in question. Both the history of despotism and the gradual awakening of the dormant truths of human rights show that this goal has long been obscured. The desire of the nation to put itself on this path to self-identity is what interests Sieyes. This desire is manifested by the Revolution, a rejection of privilege and political secrecy. This is why Sieyes structured his account of national identity as a series of negations. Without a clearly defined final goal—the concrete manifestation of a positive general will or the identification of one concrete general interest—one could not accurately administer the nation. Yet while one searched for this common identity, it was possible to identify those groups or individuals who were not even moving toward the goal, or who were actively setting up obstacles along the path. "Privilege" is Sieyes's term for nonparticipation, a sign of self-isolation, or better, self-alienation from the community. The will of the privileged must always be bad for the citizens of the nation, and hence that privileged will was not even part of the national will. It had to be ignored.[65]

> Do not ask what place the privileged classes should ultimately occupy in the social order: that is like asking what is the appropriate place in the body of someone who is ill for a malignant tumor that weakens and torments him. It is necessary to *neutralize* it, to reestablish the health and activity of all the organs, so that these morbid combinations [*combinaisons morbifiques*] that poison the most essential principles of life will not form again.[66]

The neutralization of the tumor was not, politically speaking, the elimination of the error in the name of the truth. Rather, this cancer of privilege threatened the start of the journey of self-discovery. The truth was not already present to be protected; it must be formed, from all the reflections and refractions of the collective body. The acts of negation were aimed at protecting this space of formation. Once the nation had been purged (politically) of the tumor of privilege in the early days of the National Assembly, the formulation of a constitution could ensure the establishment of a space for positive decisions in France.

In the early constitutional debates of September 1789, Sieyes, like so many other deputies discussing the royal veto, looked at the general problem of the distribution of powers in terms of error. Sieyes could not believe that a veto would ever be necessary in the constitutional machinery of a politically cohesive society. Even if the royal veto was supposedly required because of the possibility of error within the legislature, the holder of the veto was of course also subject to the same possibility.

65. Ibid., 212.
66. Ibid., 218.

For Sieyes, it was therefore important to look closely at the degrees of potential error, since error could not be easily eliminated from the political space. And looking at the monarch, Sieyes noted:

> If we want to compare the chances of error to which he is subject with the errors menacing the legislature itself, it seems to me they cannot be balanced. The legislative body is elected, numerous, it is interested in the good, it is under the influence of the people. . . . On the contrary, the depository of executive power is hereditary, permanent; its ministers know how to make it a separate interest. . . . How, with such an inequality of chances [for error], do we always have the air of being afraid of the possible errors of the legislature, and fear so little the probable errors of the ministers?

Error was always possible in the assemblies, Sieyes admitted, but this danger was "infinitely more rare" than with even the most "impassive" minister.[67] Sieyes did not see the veto as a means of diminishing the possibility of error in the Assembly. However, although it is not clearly visible here, Sieyes did not frame the political error in quite the same way as the other deputies who argued this point, and his perspective on political organization points us in a rather new direction altogether.

During this period, when Sieyes participated in both constitutional debates and constitutional committee meetings in the Assembly, he did not believe that the general will was something preexisting, something to be represented, accurately or not, by individuals, assemblies, or monarchs. In his speech on the royal veto, Sieyes rejected the idea of any veto, suspensive or not, because he thought that a veto was simply arbitrary: "I can see it only as a *lettre de cachet* launched against the national will, against the entire nation." Sieyes understood why some deputies argued for the veto: they assumed that the national will was something to be discovered, by the Assembly or the king or whomever, and therefore error was possible. This was a mistake, for Sieyes. He pointed out that because of all the confusion, "we have succeeded in considering the national voice as if it could be something other than the voice of the representatives of the nation, as if the nation could speak other than through its representatives." "Here," Sieyes noted presciently, "false principles become extremely dangerous."[68] For Sieyes, the crucial constitutional question concerned the very *formation* of this general will: "With a numerous People, this common will can form itself through a Representative Body; the individual should not fear that its will might be

67. Sieyes, "Sur l'organisation du pouvoir législatif et la sanction royale," in Halévi and Furet, *Orateurs de la Révolution française,* 1: 1031.
68. Ibid., 1022.

turned against his interest."[69] He wanted to discover the best "channels" through which individual wills come to a common rendezvous, so they can then integrate to form a common united voice.[70]

Sieyes's point was an important one. If the people's will was already formed, at any level, what was the point of the national representative bodies? What bothered Sieyes in the end was less the veto of the monarch than the very idea of an "appeal" to the people to decide the question. What exactly was being appealed to? The representative was named by a locality to act for the totality of the nation, to make the acts of government conform to the national will. "This voice, where can it be, where can one recognize it, if it isn't in the National Assembly itself?"[71] Sieyes did not think that a comprehensive referendum (even if it would ever be practical) could evaluate the will of the Assembly.

Sieyes believed that even the most direct democracy was already a kind of representational system. He thought (with Rousseau and especially his friend Condorcet) that the formation of a national, general will was not simply a result of voting, a tabulation of individual wills.

> When we get together, it is to deliberate, for everyone to understand each other's opinions, to profit from reciprocal enlightenment, to confront particular wills, to modify them, in order to reconcile them, and finally to obtain a result common to the majority. . . . It is therefore incontestable that the deputies are in the Assembly not to report the already formed will of their direct constituents, but to deliberate there and freely vote according to their *present* opinion, illuminated by all the enlightenment that the Assembly can give to each.

The nation must therefore assemble in order to achieve this decision, and in a large nation, the assembly has to be a representative one. "The people or the nation can have only one voice, that of the national legislature."[72] Sieyes described the process of political decision making as a collaborative one, and the essential goal of this process was the best decision for the group as a whole. It was not simply compromise. The general will, as Rousseau had said, lurks within the individual, it is incarnated within the particular interests of the citizen.

And so the very juxtaposition of conflicting views, Sieyed had explained in 1789, prepared the possibility of a distillation of this general interest.

---

69. Sieyes, *Délibérations*, 537. On this point, see Singer, *Society, Theory, and the French Revolution*, 158.
70. Sieyes, "Sur l'organisation du pouvoir," 1023.
71. Ibid., 1027.
72. Ibid.

What appears to you a mixture, a confusion fit to obscure everything, is an indispensable prelude to enlightenment. It is necessary to let all particular interests crowd and collide with one another, to vie with one another, to seize the question and to push it, each according to his own power, to the particular goal he proposes. Through this trial useful opinions separate from those that would be harmful; the latter fall away, while the others continue to be active, and balance one another until, modified and purified by their reciprocal efforts, they finally come together by blending into a single opinion, just as in the physical universe a single and more powerful motion can be seen to result from a mass of opposed forces.[73]

When Sieyes wanted to protect the decision from error, he did not believe that the truth of the general will could serve as the mark of aberration. That was absurd, since the only reason government was necessary was to *form* this elusive will. Sieyes sought to protect the *space of decision*, first by eliminating the enemies of the nation, then by making sure that the process of formation was free of defects.

So Sieyes, like Condorcet, stressed the importance of the process of decision making. "The unity and indivisibility of an Assembly is in the *unity of decision*, it is not in the unity of *discussion*." If discussion was divided, the assembly would limit one of the main causes of error: the seductive oration. The conditions for a genuine decision could be created. There was no guarantee, however, that the decision was free of error.

Despite all our precautions, is it absolutely impossible that error slides into a decree of the legislature? I would respond, in the last result, that I prefer, in this infinitely rare case, to let the error reverse itself in the very legislative body, in the following sessions, than to admit into the legislative machine a foreign mechanism, with which one could arbitrarily suspend the action of its spring.[74]

In fact, Sieyes would protect decision from error on two fronts: first through the active elimination of these foreign elements, then through the purification of the internal space of politics.[75]

Since representatives did not represent given opinions or interests,

73. Sieyes, *Vues sur les moyens*, 91.
74. Sieyes, "Sur l'organisation du pouvoir," 1033–34.
75. Sieyes would reemerge after the Terror with a complex plan to preserve the authenticity of the decision-making process, to protect the formation of a single national will against the possibility of radical corruption from within. As he said during the debates on the Constitution of the Year III, "unity on its own is despotism, division on its own is anarchy; division with unity gives a social guarantee, without which all liberty remains precarious." Sieyes's plan was to separate within one "head" the various "faculties" of decision, to avoid both competition between independent powers and the dangers of "unlimited powers," which he called a "monster in politics, a great error on the

they had to represent the *labor* of formation, which was always going to be a collective task.[76] The true representative for Sieyes was not the person true to an existing view or interest, but someone who had both the interest and the capacity for the public good.[77] Defining these elements more precisely would occupy Sieyes (and other revolutionaries) for some time. The problem here was that the capacity of the individual could be measured only against the ultimate definition of the nation, which in some way relied upon the representative itself for its articulation. Sieyes, whose views on national identity were strongly influenced by the Physiocrats,[78] believed that the individuals who could best formulate the general interest would be those not limited by particular interests; in other words, those with enough leisure to have been well educated in social and political subjects, and who had enough money to be relatively independent.[79] This attempt to define a "capacity" for the general interest was the foundation of Sieyes's infamous distinction between what he called "active" and "passive" citizens.[80] Sieyes did not believe that everyone had the capacity or interest to seek out the general interest of the nation. Most would have the ability to choose someone in whom they could place their confidence, but those at the margins of society—the vagabonds, beggars, servile workers—should be completely excluded from citizenship, according to Sieyes. Only free men could be citizens.[81] "The qualities of man are to be *sociable* and not servile; to be capable of becoming an integral part of a society, that is, to be a citizen; to preserve in his heart the feeling of equality; not to have lost the inner

part of the French people." See Sieyes's speeches on the constitution in *Réimpression de l'ancien Moniteur,* (Paris, 1850–54) 25: 291–98, 442–52.

76. Sieyes believed that representation was the key factor in all social interaction, not just political relations. For Sieyes, the division of labor was a system of representations of labor. I represented you in one sphere of work, and vice versa. Politics was just another kind of work done by others for one's benefit. Sieyes's social thought has been well explicated in, for example, Forsyth, *Reason and Revolution;* Singer, *Society, Theory, and the French Revolution,* chap. 8; William H. Sewell Jr., *A Rhetoric of Bourgeois Revolution.*

77. Sieyes, "Préliminaire de la constitution," 1018.

78. See Forsyth, *Reason and Revolution,* chap. 2, and Sewell, *Rhetoric of Bourgeois Revolution,* chap. 3.

79. The constitution would include such a *marc d'argent* against the protests from the left, including Robespierre. See debates reprinted in Halévi and Furet, *La monarchie républicaine,* Annexes XVIII–XIX.

80. See Sewell, *Rhetoric of Bourgeois Revolution,* 176–80, and his earlier article "Le Citoyen/La Citoyenne: Activity, Passivity, and the Revolutionary Concept of Citizenship," in *The French Revolution and Creation of Modern Political Culture,* vol. 2: *The Political Culture of the French Revolution,* ed. Colin Lucas (Oxford, 1988), 105–24.

81. Sieyes, "Sur la nouvelle organisation de la France," in *Ecrits politiques,* ed. Roberto Zapperi (Paris, 1985), 254–56.

force of his soul and mind; to be indignant against the insolent, the tyrant, and the coward."[82] This was less an elitist conceit than an admission that only those individuals who freely participated in reciprocal exchange had an interest in the national good and an ability to locate a capacity for political action in others. Those who did not actively contribute to the *chose publique* could hardly become directors of its institutional structure.[83]

Sieyes, in his speech concerning the constitution and the rights of man, argued that "law, being a common instrument, the work of a common will, can have as its object only the common interest. *One* society can have only *one* general interest. It would be impossible to establish order, if one supposed it to run with many opposed interests."[84] Sieyes, early in the revolutionary process, knew that this general interest was outside any one individual's direct experience. His program was to eliminate those who self-consciously opposed the nation, *then* choose individuals who could actively determine that national interest. Moreover, it was necessary to prepare the space of decision making to protect against corruption and aberration, and to evaluate the legitimacy of the decisions. This last concern was the most problematic. Sieyes adamantly opposed the royal veto; he also opposed a "call to the people." What exactly was the standard of truth? Without a concept of a preexisting general will, was there any way to evaluate political aberrations?

EXTRAORDINARY INTERVENTIONS

The constitution of 1791 did include the suspensive veto, but the crucial call to the people was structured in such a way that instability was inevitable. The time gap between any royal veto and a new election was so long that it was bound to paralyze government. The king could sustain a veto for two sessions, and constitutional amendments could go into effect only after three successive sessions of the assembly.[85] Since the primacy (and unity) of the people's will was already enshrined in the same document, it is not surprising that once the king revealed himself yet again (this was after the infamous flight to Varennes in June 1791) to be largely hostile to the democratic process, the people would seek alternative channels of expression. The constitution proclaimed the representative assembly to be an accurate incarnation of the "will of the people,"

82. Sieyes, "Grèce—Citoyen—Homme," in *Ecrits politiques*, 81.
83. Sieyes, "Préliminaire de la constitution," 1014.
84. Ibid.
85. See the text of the constitution of 1791 in Halévi and Furet, *La monarchie républicaine*, Annexe I, 279.

even as it admitted the chance of error, and it created no institutions to mediate the inevitable gaps (between monarch, assembly, crowd, nation) that would soon emerge. The problem was there from the start.[86] Where was national sovereignty located?

The danger of the concept of the people as ultimate authority was real for many politicians in this period. It seemed obvious that the "multitude" could "stray," under the blind influence of a corrupt leader perhaps, so it was not clear why authority should be unproblematically located in the crowd, as Malouet noted in 1791.[87] This could mean the death of sovereignty. The vice of the constitution was that it made law subject to a sovereignty based on an abstraction, thus opening up dangerous possibilities.

> After having defined sovereignty without delegating it, and in a manner that favors the errors and passions of the multitude, we encounter the same danger in the definition of the law, which we say, after Rousseau, is the expression of the general will. But Rousseau also said that the general will is inalienable, that it cannot be represented or supplemented, it is formed by the immediate opinion of each citizen.

Given that the French government was representative, the idea of the general will as the origin of law could only lead people astray. "The recording of the general will is often uncertain and always difficult; the manifestation of public reason announces itself, like the sun, by streams of light."[88]

In a way, this was Sieyes's position: the general will intended the general interest, and this was something that had to be determined by rational, dedicated political intellects. Sieyes himself noted that a kind of political "ostracism" is always going to be necessary in a large society, to protect against ambition as well as the "errors of the multitude."[89] People generally consider anything outside their particular interest as purely "metaphysical" and somewhat suspicious. The fate of truth is to be unrecognized, even insulted, by those who have not risen to its level.[90] It has been argued that Sieyes's emphasis on the necessity and legitimacy of representational government, however elitist it may appear,

86. On the failure of the constitution from this conceptual perspective, see Halevi and Furet, *La monarchie républicaine*, 257–58.
87. Malouet, "Opinion sur la révolte de la minorité contre la majorité," in Halevi and Furet, *Orateurs de la Révolution française*, 1: 488, 498.
88. Ibid., 503–4.
89. Sieyes, "Sur la nouvelle organisation," 260.
90. See Forsyth, *Reason and Revolution*, 29.

was a solution that might have prevented the worst violence of the Revolution. His "brilliant invention" was to define this national sovereignty as *essentially* representative.[91] Thus he preserved the appeal of abstract sovereignty while confining it to one delimited place.

But this representational solution to the problem of the general will is not quite the end of the story for Sieyes. As he repeatedly noted in his pamphlets and speeches, the nation's will could never be completely "legalized" in this way. Sieyes's obsession with the pursuit of the truth in politics, his desire to create a purified space for the formation of a genuine political will, prevented him from ever being content with a merely pragmatic solution to this essential mystery of the identity of the nation.

In *Qu'est-ce que le Tiers état?* he explained that the nation comes before everything, it determines practically the modes of organization. And if it was true that the will of this nation was formed only representationally, it was also the case that there was no one sacred location for this process. "A nation must not and cannot bind itself to constitutional forms," because any disunity or aberration within constituted powers would violate the nation's will to promote the general interest. So who can evaluate any conflict, either within the government or between a nation and its government? "Power belongs only to the whole."[92] The nation must decide, and to express its will it must circumvent established procedures. If that will was essentially representative, it was nonetheless rather mobile.

> *Ordinary* representatives of a people are charged with exercising, within constitutional forms, that portion of the common will necessary for maintaining a good social administration. . . . *Extraordinary* representatives will have whatever new power the nation pleases to give them. Since a large nation cannot physically assemble itself every time circumstances outside of the common order might demand it, it must trust extraordinary representatives on these occasions. If it could meet before you and express its will, would you dare dispute it, because it exercised it in one form rather than another? Here reality is everything, form nothing.[93]

The problem of politics, then, in these revolutionary moments, becomes one of *recognition*, for if the nation must speak through its ministers, the representatives, and can choose these organs free from any visible constraints or precedent, how is the legitimacy of these representatives manifested? Sieyes seems to think this is not a real problem: election will al-

---

91. Baker, "Representation Redefined," 251.
92. Sieyes, *Qu'est-ce que le Tiers état?* ed. Zapperi, 183–84.
93. Ibid., 184–85.

ways be the natural voice of a national will. But there is no reason why this should be the case, especially in times of crisis. The sovereign force could potentially intervene at any moment and in any place, and its organs carry no visible identification marks. "Who is going to warn the nation of the need to send extraordinary representatives? . . . Is time going to be lost inquiring about who has the *right* to convene? Rather, we must ask: Who does not have the right? It is the sacred *duty* of all those who can do something about it."[94] Justifying the early revolutionary turn, Sieyes opens up the very possibility of terror in these passages. Given that the representative's mission is the formation of the will of the nation, and given that not every individual in the nation can know this will, the extraordinary representative might emerge from anywhere, his actions accountable only to the interests of the nation as a whole. The nation is not identical with its organs, but as we saw earlier, it must, according to Sieyes, take on a particular form to make itself understood.

What could possibly define and limit, in advance, a method for making this choice? Even Sieyes, during the period of the Directory, would support the idea that an election was not a sacred event. A preemptive coup could very well represent the nation's desire for its own general interest. Sieyes always relied, in the end, on an elusive negative construction: the nation, as he had said in 1789, could never act in a contradictory way; it could not desire its own harm. If the singularity of will was not directly available as an unproblematic standard of conduct, any move away from the unity of a common interest revealed itself as a mistake. "The common will cannot destroy itself. It cannot change the nature of things and make the opinion of the minority the opinion of the majority. We see that a parallel statute would be an act of madness [*démence*] instead of a legal or moral act."[95] This was the case with the nobility in the Estates General, the leaders of the Convention in the Terror, and eventually the people under the Directory, who voted for monarchists and Jacobins. Sieyes may not have known the ultimate truth, but he could identify the threats of disintegration. From the beginning, Sieyes was careful to protect the path of the true nation (one united in a common interest) from attack, even as he recognized that this path would not always be straight or even easy to determine.

In the earliest phases of the Revolution, given the radical uncertainties and instabilities inherent in the project of national unity, it was necessary to develop some idea of discipline. Stability was the main goal of most political leaders. The creation of institutions, the preservation of the

94. Ibid., 138.
95. Ibid., 188.

monarchy, restrictions on citizenship, the constitution itself, all were attempts to found a *self-imposed* location for the appearance of sovereignty,
precisely in order to control something already defined as the unfettered
origin of all political acts. The nation could always act, in an emergency,
through new agents—that described the founding moment of the Revolution itself. The nation had manifested itself in that strange, archaic institution, the resurrected Estates General, and reasserted its powers in its
confrontation with the privileged and a weakened monarch. The revolutionaries could hardly ignore that fundamental reality. The task, then,
was to create the space for a stable (if potentially errant) incarnation of
sovereignty, and to neutralize the forces of destruction that threatened
this space. Sieyes offered his solutions, his modes of discipline, while
recognizing the radical ineffability of the positive will.

His ideas would not, in the end, influence the Revolution in its movement toward terror. However, understanding how Sieyes framed revolutionary politics in terms of error helps us to see a continuity with the
leaders of the Terror, without seeing that violent phase of the Revolution
as inevitably deduced from its supposedly pathological origins. Revolutionary leaders were trying to demarcate a space for evaluating the authenticity of expressions of will. Radically different conceptions of this
space should not obscure the common effort to contain errant manifestations of this will, even though there was no clear visible form that would
ever define these political aberrations.

CHAPTER 6

The Terror: Marking Aberration
in the Body Politic

It is said that a vigorous government is oppressive; that is a mistake: the question is badly posed. Justice is necessary in government. The government that exercises justice is not at all vigorous and oppressive because of that, since only evil is oppressed.

SAINT-JUST, *Institutions républicaines*

The very gap between the nation and its representation in government is what allows the diversity of a large society to express its singular voice—this we have seen discussed in early revolutionary thought. At the same time, this essential gap opens up the possibility (perhaps inevitability) of error. Politics creates and preserves a space for the manifestation of national unity, a space that also would protect the nation as much as possible from the error that marks the translation of this immanent identity into concrete decision and will in the state. The Terror has been interpreted as an aberration of this political logic, in that the revolutionary state in this period, for whatever reason, tried to eliminate the gap between nation and state. The Jacobin dictatorship, it has been said, claimed an absolute transparency between the state and the people of France, which in reality meant that the "people" were displaced from concrete reality to rhetorical figure, for the only way absolute transparency could be ensured was by collapsing the relationship between these two discordant entities (state, nation) and effectively eliminating one of them from actual political power.[1] The government, defined by

---

1. See Lucien Jaume, *Le discours jacobin et la démocratie* (Paris, 1989), 392–93. Cf. Brian Singer, *Society, Theory and the French Revolution: Studies in the Revolutionary Imaginary* (London, 1986), 183.

the Terror, was the people, and so any opposition to the state (external or internal) was already identified as enemy activity.[2] This obsession with unity (in society and in its transparent symbolic representation, the state) caused all discord to be characterized as a sign of failure, and therefore all discord was violently eliminated.

Of course, revolutionary violence was not confined to the Terror alone. What distinguishes the violence of the Terror from previous phases of the Revolution is, supposedly, its systematic nature and the fact that the state instituted it. This is another way of saying that the Terror tried to eliminate the gap between people and state by taking over revolutionary violence into the state and monopolizing it, whereas more moderate politicians were always trying to establish a state (through the constitution) precisely to eliminate the need for revolutionary violence. But this need to contain and control radical popular violence was something that dominated revolutionary consciousness from the start. The very radicalness of popular action made it difficult to judge objectively. What was "authentic" action and what was merely criminal? Even in its earliest phases, the ambiguity of the "sovereignty" of the people was apparent, and the various political perspectives were in many ways efforts to define the marks of authentic sovereignty. The Terror, then, can be interpreted as one more effort to contain and control revolutionary violence, rather than an exceptional irruption of violence.[3] From this angle, the violence of the Terror would be a mark of the Revolution's initial failure to define adequately the "true" signs of the general will of the nation. It is a failure, in other words, of the attempt to base politics on a transcendent category that defies direct expression and thus is always open to interpretation (and therefore error and doubt).[4] Of course it is difficult to conceive of any polity that did not have recourse to some kind of foundational unity, however defined.

How did the theorists of the Terror believe it possible to distinguish between authentic expressions of sovereignty and the actions of the enemy? How was it possible to identify and correct error in the political sphere? Even more complex is the problem of distinguishing what Robespierre called the "error" of the citizen from the "crime" of the

2. Keith M. Baker, "Introduction," in *The French Revolution and the Creation of Modern Political Culture*, vol. 4: *The Terror*, ed. Baker (Oxford, 1994), xviii.

3. This argument is lucidly developed in Colin Lucas, "Revolutionary Violence, the People, and the Terror," in Baker, *The Terror*, esp. 71–76.

4. On the "unreality" of national unity and its effects on the Terror, see Jaume, *Le discours jacobin*, 395; Singer, *Society, Theory and the French Revolution*; and earlier, François Furet, *Interpreting the French Revolution*, trans. Elborg Forster (Cambridge, 1981).

counter-revolutionary, for the admission of error in the virtuous citizen (or even politician) introduces another dimension to the problem
of revolutionary politics. There was, as we will see, a fundamental gap
between the abstract but real legitimacy that derived from the unity of
the nation and any concrete manifestation of sovereignty, whether that
manifestation was popular action, legislative act, executive decision,
or emergency measure. Error, in other words, was always a possibility—something understood by most revolutionaries since the emergence of the National Assembly. Politics was for many the attempt to
create a space where that error would be reduced. The Terror, as expressed through Robespierre and Saint-Just, reconceptualized the gap
at the heart of the political. The Revolution had to battle the overt enemies of the nation—those mistakes to be eliminated—but it also had
to protect against inevitable internal errancy. Robespierre, and to a
certain extent Saint-Just, envisioned just such a political space, but it
was, in contrast to its conceptualization by more moderate political
leaders, an internal and moral space, rather than a constitutional or institutional one. Virtue (not "reason") was the necessary preparation
for insight into the national voice. The continuity between 1789 and
the Terror lies in this desire to formulate a space where an essentially
elusive identity might be manifested. The discontinuity was the radical shift from concrete institutional measures to highly elusive moral
ones. The role error played in this decisive shift in revolutionary politics was critical.

ROBESPIERRE AND THE POLITICS OF ABERRATION

Locating the Voice of the Sovereign

Robespierre heard Sieyes discuss the royal veto in the Assembly,
on September 7, 1789. Sieyes, as we saw, cut through the debate on the
relative merits of the absolute and suspensive vetoes with a powerful argument against any veto for the monarch. Robespierre, along with three
other deputies, demanded (unsuccessfully in the end) that discussion be
extended on this question, because Sieyes's "profound" speech had
given a "whole new important face" to the problem of the veto. According to one report, Barnave and Robespierre were "the two most distinguished men who revealed themselves most often favorable" to "strong
opinions" concerning the position of the king on legislative matters, and
who "wanted to push to the last consequences the maxim that all sovereignty resides in the people, a maxim that is so easy to render dangerous." Robespierre, another report noted, defended this position with the

most rigorous principles (6: 75, 76).[5] Still, when the vote was taken, on September 11, only 143 deputies voted against a royal veto. We have followed the attempt to establish a space for this essentially errant and mobile sovereign force, a space that would both prepare its manifestation and protect it from internal corruption and attack from outside. Through Robespierre we can track an alternative conception of this political space. We can begin with a common starting point for both these conceptualizations of politics: the problem of error as it emerged in the critique of monarchical authority and the debate over the formal structure of the new French constitution.

Although discussion of the royal veto was closed, despite his protestations, Robespierre printed his prepared speech on the topic as a pamphlet in late September 1789. His critique of the veto closely followed Sieyes's position. A large nation, Robespierre wrote, cannot as a body exercise legislative powers, and so it confers them on representatives. It is important to recognize that "this will of these representatives must be regarded and respected as the will of the nation." The nation has no other way of expressing itself, so this representative will is the "sacred authority, superior to any individual will." Executive powers can also be conferred by the people as they see fit, but these powers must execute only the predetermined will of the nation, a will formed in the representative body. The royal veto, "the right to contradict and fetter the will of the nation," Robespierre described as an "inconceivable monster," a kind of Lockean error of incompatible moral and political concepts (6: 87). Kings, like representatives, are in a subordinate position, *mandataires* and delegates of the people, public functionaries only. The monarch's function is to preserve the liberty and rights of the nation; clearly a king who opposes the national will is not fulfilling that role. Though this argument is consistent with Sieyes's constitutional position, Robespierre, unlike Sieyes, who for the most part argued these points logically, reveals, in this early text, his skill of binding his audience to the radical nature of the Revolution, placing these sometimes conceptual and political questions in the larger and more immediately dangerous context of the current unstable situation. Reminding everyone of the considerable accomplishments of the revolutionary assembly, Robespierre suggests that each step of this revolution would have been reversed if only those who were threatened by these measures (namely, the crown and all those with "feudal" privileges) had had any power to stop them. Why

5. References in the text (volume, page) are to Maximilien Robespierre, *Oeuvres*, 10 vols. (Paris, 1910–67).

should the nation construct a constitution that would only hinder its free action?

Robespierre, like other deputies who spoke on this question, was certainly aware of the problem of political error that makes possible the idea of a "constitutional monarch" who could serve as an alternative organ of the general will, as Mirabeau argued. Robespierre's answer to this objection foreshadows his later political thought. Admitting that representatives can abuse their authority, he refuses to admit that the solution would be to give a king authority over law: that is, to believe that "the legislature can err, therefore we must destroy it." This, Robespierre says, is not a convincing argument, since it demands absolute confidence in the executive power. As Sieyes already pointed out, the chance of error is in fact much greater in the executive than in the Assembly. Robespierre comments:

> As to error: besides the fact that it is a strange expedient to make the legislative power infallible by making it null, I see no reason why monarchs, in general, or their counselors should be presumed more enlightened concerning the needs of the people, or the means to fulfill them, than the representatives of the people themselves. (6: 91)

On what constitutes a good law, he goes on to remark, kings have very different ideas than those held by the people. But Robespierre's response here is really just a rejection of any *absolute* veto. The suspensive veto was, of course, an attempt to reconcile the crucial idea of national sovereignty with the need to protect the people from the possibility that the legislators themselves might act against them. The suspensive veto gave the final decision to the people, for in elections they could decide whether the king or the Assembly was "representing" their views accurately. Robespierre, again following Sieyes closely, denounced this seemingly reasonable compromise as absurd and especially dangerous.

How, he asked, is it possible to "appeal to the people" when the people have no tangible reality to begin with? Politics was necessary because the people could not make decisions as a whole. Like Sieyes, Robespierre pointed out the special character of representation. The people's will did not exist to be represented. The *labor* of forming this will (not the will itself) was being represented, precisely because the nation could not assemble to decide its will. "If the people could make laws by themselves, if the generality of assembled citizens could discuss the advantages and disadvantages, would they need to name representatives?" Since the people did not have the ability to deliberate as a whole body, what some were calling an appeal to the people would, in fact, turn out to be simply an appeal to some other local representative bodies. This would only destroy the national perspective, that common and uniform viewpoint embodied in the National Assembly (6: 92–93). Robespierre noted other disadvantages to the suspensive veto: the very possibility of a veto, he predicted, would force legislators to negotiate with the king while making law, which would in practice mean effectively sharing sovereignty with the monarch. As Robespierre's brother noted during these debates, even the "most mediocre minds" realized that the absolute veto would paralyze the legislature, but they did not seem to realize that the suspensive veto would do just the same. This idea would just be an "error of the moment," soon overturned, since it is an absurd notion that the executive can be the *judge* of what he is to execute: this power would destroy the monarch's own existence, since if he annulled what he was to execute, he would no longer have anything to execute (3: 51–52, 54). The "error" of the suspensive veto was passed easily, however, and these predictions of paralysis would eventually prove accurate, given the increasing impatience of the people with the king's resistance to the Revolution.

Despite the affirmative vote, Robespierre continued in October to resist the idea that the king should have any special powers over the nation. He refused to allow the king the right to sanction constitutional declarations, for example, when this question emerged as a dispute between the crown and the Assembly. "M. Robespierre says that the king's response presents him as superior to the nation," noted one journal. "Is it up to the executive power, he cries, to criticize the constitution made by the legislative power? No power can elevate itself above that of the nation," a comment that evoked some murmuring. Robespierre's declaration that "no human power can stop a nation from giving itself a constitution," however, was "loudly applauded" (6: 99–100).

Opposing royal power throughout 1790 and early 1791, Robespierre continually argued that the Assembly alone should be the location of the sovereign decision. On May 15, 1790 (when the question of war with Britain in a conflict with Spain over Nootka Sound had just been brought to the attention of the Assembly), he argued that the right of declaring war and peace should not be left to the king and his ministers, to that arena of "false" politics that valued individual ambition and greed over the people as a whole (6: 357–58). During the constitutional debate on this point later that month, Robespierre articulated his position more carefully. The king, he said, cannot be given the right to declare war as a *representative* of the people. "It is inexact to say representative of the nation. The king is the *clerk* [*commis*] and the delegate of the nation for executing the national will." While he softened this insult somewhat by saying that the king had the "sublime" task of executing the general will, his main point was clear—only the nation had the right to declare war, and the nation spoke only through its representatives. The king had to be constrained by their sacred authority. This was the position ultimately adopted by the Assembly (6: 364). On another occasion Robespierre repeated his Sieyesian position on representation, arguing that the sovereign people "can exercise their supreme authority only through representatives." Here he was trying to persuade the Assembly that only the legislative power should be able to intervene in matters that concern the nation as a whole (such as the validity of elections) (7: 126, 127).

This was especially important in the judicial sphere, Robespierre warned. He spent a great deal of effort establishing the point that if any outside force could interpret the law, or decide when it was not being accurately implemented, it effectively (but erroneously) could *make* the law. If, for example, judges could err in their application of law, the force of correction must emerge from the very source of the law, the legislature. Robespierre's proposed appeal tribunal (*tribunal de cassation*) ought to be located, he said, in the "heart of the legislative body" (6: 376). It was reported that Robespierre "thinks that just as the legislative body must always stay alert in maintaining the constitution, it falls to it alone to repress the violation of the laws emanating from its heart, and to rectify the errors of the judges charged with their application" (6: 580). Error could be identified and corrected only by the truth emanating from the origin, that is, the sovereign as embodied in the Assembly (7: 218). Of course, this logic of error could be extended in other directions. Even Sieyes allowed for the "extraordinary representative" who emerges to "correct" the normal legislative body when the people decide it no longer has that sacred authority. While Robespierre always opposed the constitution of any power above the representatives of the people, he did not hesitate to argue at the same time that the people, even if they could not act politically for themselves in normal circumstances, could well voice their desire to "correct" their own representatives.

The Ambiguities of Intervention

As he already noted in his speech on the royal veto, Robespierre knew that the legislature might err. And if it was true that Robespierre opposed the idea that a superior power such as a monarch could be the source of correction, he seemed to be arguing, as we saw, with Sieyes in saying that the people themselves were not in a position to be arbiters of truth and error in the political sphere because of the size of the nation. At the same time, it was very clear that Robespierre, from the start of the Revolution, warned that this did not mean that representatives could effectively usurp the people's authority. Robespierre continually evoked all the ambiguities of representation, ambiguities he would manipulate throughout his political career. It was never entirely clear what exactly constituted usurpation and when exactly the people had the right to contest their own representatives.

Some of Robespierre's earliest interventions are comments on various disorders in the nation, and his main point was to highlight this latent ambiguity concerning resistance and order, an ambiguity created by the process of revolution itself. Robespierre tried to persuade his fellow politicians that defining "disorder" in a revolutionary context was not a simple task. Since the Revolution was itself a disordering event, the distinctions between legitimate and oppressive order, as well as legitimate disruption and criminal action, were extremely unstable. As early as July 20, 1789, Robespierre was saying that "it is necessary to love order but do not harm liberty." We cannot, he said to his fellow deputies, indiscriminately declare all those who cause disorder "rebels" when, as in the example he was referring to, the "trouble" was the "generous" efforts of citizens to destroy a conspiracy formed against the citizens themselves. These disturbances may well have caused death for the guilty, but no political harm emerged, and liberty was gained (6: 39). The point is that the people had a right to act outside of normal political channels.

A series of interventions by Robespierre in 1790 repeated this argument from different angles. At one point he said that even an uprising against army officials could be an authentic act of the people, when they genuinely feared for their liberty, especially when one considered the past abuses of the military (6: 187). The act itself is not intrinsically criminal; the context and history of the situation must, he argued, be ascertained. Complicating the matter was the fact that since the Revolution the relationships of authority were in flux. Until the revolutionary government could sort out administrative questions and fix the constitution, it was not at all obvious that "authority," which may well have been continuous with Old Regime oppression, should be respected by the people. "M. Robertspierre [*sic*] has revealed the dangers of placing the power of quelling riots back into the hands of those enemies of the people's liberty" (6: 229). On another occasion he warned that care must be taken to prevent administrative bodies from being made up of enemies of the public good, or using troops to disrupt elections on the pretext of maintaining order, as in England (6: 256). The external forms were no guarantee of legitimacy—only intentions could define that.

Robespierre did not, then, like some others, use the argument for representative government as a kind of political shield. In his earliest interventions, he repeatedly invoked the need for a close connection between the people and their government. Speaking once again on the problem of popular disturbances, Robespierre rather ominously suggested that the true representative, the one with the people's confidence, would be able to calm them and prevent an outbreak of violence, in one move both precluding repressive measures and questioning the authenticity of particular representatives or government officials (6: 269). Robespierre also, in this context, suggested another, perhaps even more important difficulty: the people may well go "astray" and commit "errors." According to Robespierre, this problem would be solved if the government acknowledged its responsibility to correct the situations that initiated these errors. It was not a question of punishment. It is not possible to conserve liberty, he noted, with the "means of despotism." There was no need, in other words, to declare martial law every time "errors of the people" created victims (6: 255–56). Robespierre would always defend the patriotism of the citizens, even when it might have been "reduced" by the "errors in which we have thrown them" (6: 287–88). True crime, he was saying, must be distinguished from the momentary lapse of the patriot in trying circumstances (6: 497). The question that was emerging for Robespierre, however, was how to make these distinctions. Robespierre defended representation against monarchy and the people against representatives while acknowledging the possibility of the people's own errors. He raised the elusive question of error and the even more problematic question of truth—the truth that could correct all these variations of political error was constantly shifting, with no clearly established point of reference.

So well before the Terror, even though Robespierre was at the margins of the revolutionary course, he exploited the latent ambiguities of sovereignty. If representatives were the authentic national will (in opposition to the monarch), and therefore the source of truth against the errors of judicial and political usurpation, these same representatives had to be careful to *identify* with the people for whom they spoke. Conversely, the people might stray into error, hence there was no unproblematic space for the expression of the popular will. This duality emerges in comments starting in 1790. On the one hand, the people are being deceived, he noted in March, led astray by the commissioners of the executive power. Law is of no use, he implied, if it is not properly executed. "It is not at all sufficient to make laws when establishing liberty; your first duty [*soin*] must be to ceaselessly keep watch to repel all the dangers that surround its cradle." The government protects the space of liberty from the enemy. On the other hand, Robespierre knows that the enemy is as much internal as external. In December he would claim that among the first principles guiding the legislature, "the first duty [*devoir*] is to form morals, to extend the sentiment and love for liberty, without which the constitution is only a ghost, laws only formulas" (6: 663). Echoing Rousseau, he endows the legislature with divine duties: it must bring the truth to the hearts of a potentially errant people and protect the space of law from evil opposition. The problem, as should be clear, is that Robespierre (along with many others) had already admitted that the legislators who create the constitution and make the laws might err. There was no one privileged source of truth in Robespierre's conceptualization of politics at this point.

Robespierre in fact recognized this as the fundamental question. He would forcefully argue, for example, that the Assembly must not bind itself to its own decrees, precisely because they may not be entirely right on every occasion. Against those who saw the acts of the Assembly as inviolable, Robespierre countered:

> How have we been able to surrender to this supposed maxim, this inviolable rule: that the safety of the people and the happiness of men is always the supreme law; and to impose on the founders of the French constitution that of destroying their own work and of halting the glorious destiny of the nation and of entire humanity, rather than correct an error of which we know all the dangers. Only an essentially infallible Being can be immovable; to change is not only a right but a duty of every human will that has failed. (7: 173)

However, some measure of truth must be available to identify the errors of the multitude, the errors infecting administration, and the potential errors of the legislative body. Each organ of the nation might, theoretically, be the one to hold the truth and correct the errors of the other, something explicitly argued in the debates over the royal veto. There was no "infallible" location for sovereignty to make its appearance.

Robespierre would effectively play both sides of this ambiguity, invoking alternatively the authentic action of the people against their government, the authentic will of the representatives against the administration (and sometimes the people), and the authentic voice of the revolutionary state against virtually anyone during the Terror. But was Robespierre opportunistically abusing the unstable concept of popular sovereignty in revolutionary France (even out of a sincere desire to help the people)? Clearly, the question for Robespierre was not so much the articulation of the truth in its essence (however that truth was conceived politically) given that humanity was not, he said more than once, infallible (7: 439). Robespierre opposed the death penalty, for example, precisely for this reason. He observed that the "voice of reason and justice" tells us that no human judgment is so certain that society could punish by death someone condemned by other humans "subject to error." Even in the most enlightened and upright judges there remains a place for "error or prejudice" (7: 439). Robespierre was attempting to mark out a politics on the edge of error, one that would protect the *space* of the truth from all attacks, internal and external. The main task of this politics was less the imposition of truth than drawing the line between error and crime, between a failed truth and an attack against the truth.

The Voices of Will

Attempting to delineate these distinctions, Robespierre began with the Rousseauist opposition between individual interests and the general will that had only the nation's interest in view. The sphere of the political was marked by this generality that united everyone in the nation, and this space had to be protected from the intrusions and resistances offered by individuality. The revolutionaries, while they recognized from the start the diversity and heterogeneity of social "reality," did not believe that the unity of the nation was merely a fiction, as it was in the Hobbesian state. The nation existed in a transcendental sphere of identity in which all citizens participated.[6] The essentially ephemeral nature of this identity is what makes revolutionary politics so difficult to understand, though in the context of Enlightenment thought on error, its elusiveness is hardly surprising. At any rate, Robespierre saw that the identity of the political individual was a product of this intangible yet higher dimension of social life, rather than the other way around. The desire for a new foundation in the Revolution was tied to this faith in a substantial *origin* of identity. The revolutionaries could not envision free individuals simply coming together to form a new state. Politics, in this revolutionary context, was inextricably tied to a traditional conception of national identity as a real, if elusive, foundation. Moreover, it was often the case in French culture that the excesses of individuality were, as in Rousseau, understood to be *opposed* to this collective reality (as they were not in Britain or America at this time).

This suspicion of individual interest runs through the early constitutional debates. Robespierre couched the problem in explicitly Rousseauist language. He first argued this point when he discussed the problems of government. All individuals, all corporate bodies have an individual will, he asserted, and it differs from the general will. This is

6. Eighteenth-century origins of this concept of national identity are explored in Sarah Maza, "Luxury, Morality, and Social Change: Why There Was No Middle-Class Consciousness in Prerevolutionary France," *Journal of Modern History* 69 (1997): 199–229. See esp. the concluding remarks, 228–29.

entirely natural (7: 264). Men were, he later said, naturally weak (10: 264). Of course, in government, where so much is at stake, this inevitable straying was particularly dangerous. Robespierre believed in construct- ing the political space in such a way that individual desires could not function. In April 1791 he referred to Rousseau, noting that "to inspire the most confidence and respect for the laws, the legislator must in a way isolate himself from his work, and emancipate himself from all per- sonal relations that can link him to the great interests that he is to de- cide." He went on to propose that no member of the Assembly should be a minister of the state (7: 201, 202).

One of Robespierre's most popular early motions was based on this same ideal. He argued that the framers of the constitution should not be eligible for election to the new legislative body. This restriction would help produce the most disinterest on the part of the deputies who cre- ated this foundational document. Robespierre would also note, in a later speech on this topic, that the representatives must see themselves as es- sentially without personal existence in the political sphere. Individuals had no rights in politics. Laws were not dictated by the sovereign to the people: rather, "the nation produces them through the organ of its repre- sentatives. As long as they are just and conform to the rights of all, they are always legitimate. Now who can doubt that the nation can make the rules that it will follow in its elections, in order to defend itself against error and surprise?" (7: 386). The perfect organ is one that allows the voice of the sovereign to manifest itself purely. Robespierre was not denying the possibility of error and interest, but he was outlining the ideal space where political actors could effectively strip away these (nat- ural) aberrations from what constituted the national good.

> What is the principle, what is the goal of making laws concerning elections? The interest of the people. Wherever the people exercise their authority and manifest their will not by themselves but through representatives, if the rep- resentative body is not pure and closely identified with the people, liberty is annihilated. The great principle of representative government, the essential object of laws, must be to ensure the purity of elections and the incorrupt- ibility of the representatives. (7: 404)

Here we find a critical juxtaposition in Robespierre's thought, one that informs Jacobin politics in the Terror: the possibility of error is linked to the possibility of corruption. If the individual, or legislator, may err, it is because the general will does not speak purely in his heart. Politics, for Robespierre, was moral because of this relationship.

Robespierre was constantly warning against weakness in government, since this moral virtue was a constant effort to resist individual desires. He saw, for example, the dangers in July 1791, when the counter-revolutionary "menace," as he called it, was wearing down France. He pointed out that just as an individual tires after prolonged activity, so an assembly feels the effects of weakness after concentrated efforts. This was a danger because a weak body is, he explained, prone to infection. However, the *true representatives* of the people, Robespierre claimed, will be able to rediscover the appropriate sentiment for the nation (7: 587). In opposition to someone like Sieyes or Condorcet, Robespierre did not advocate an *intellectual* asceticism as a means for gaining insight into the national interest. He saw that one would become more closely identified with the people (and therefore less subject to error) if one practiced a kind of *moral* asceticism: the purging of any individual interest that would block the pure expression of the general will. Robespierre was, however, acutely aware of the difficulty of this task.

If early in the Revolution he had celebrated representational government as the "sacred voice" of the nation, he would soon qualify that idea, pointing out that this was the case only if these representatives were truly identified with the nation, the people. In July 1792, when France and the Legislative Assembly were approaching the most intense crisis of order since 1789, Robespierre (at this point not a representative, because those who had participated in the National Assembly were excluded) spoke on the crisis in the government at the Jacobin Club. Here he invoked the idea of a "representative despotism," which had violated the constitution. The representatives, he declared, had usurped sovereignty, and had become absolutely independent, not consulting the "nation." The great crisis was nothing less than the "conspiracy of the majority of the delegates of the people against the people" (8: 416, 417). In itself, this was hardly a conceptually radical move on Robespierre's part. The radical point was that the "people" (and not some kind of objective "interest") would identify the errors of the legislators or executors. Which returns us to the problem originally envisioned by both Sieyes and Robespierre: how to make an appeal to the people outside of the representational system itself?

Robespierre and other "radicals" were willing to admit that the authentic sovereign voice might flash up in extraordinary moments of crisis in unpredictable ways, outside of the constituted powers that were no longer embodying the spirit of the nation. The revolutionary events of August 1792 were just such an occasion, perhaps the perfect expression of this principle. The people had risen to remedy the faults of their government (8: 449). The people, that amorphous entity, could, as Sieyes had (perhaps unconsciously) admitted, form their own organs of expression when the present forms are no longer adequate to the task. And Robespierre, conscious of the ambiguity involved in identifying the authentic national voice, interpreted these acts of popular violence as themselves essentially representative, in a way consistent with Sieyes. In moments of crisis, the nation itself cannot assemble to act, but a fragment of the people can act in its name. (Recall Sieyes's claim in defense of the Third Estate's revolutionary action: who does *not* have the right to defend the nation when the opportunity arises?) In a stable nation, Robespierre pointed out, the National Assembly would be the authentic voice of all France, no matter in what particular city it might reside in fact. Similarly, in a situation of crisis, the people of Paris, for Robespierre, *were* the people of France, acting for the whole, since the crisis happened to be in this particular concrete location (9: 36).[7] "To affirm liberty, this vast empire needs a foyer of enlightenment and energy, from which the public spirit can communicate itself to the infinite multitude of all the tiny sections that make up the universality of the French people" (9: 39). The nation cannot appear as itself; it requires a conduit, an organ, that can concretely manifest this "spirit." Paris is a real space ("foyer") for the appearance of an invisible spirit, and as such is essentially limited temporally and spatially in its function as representative. It is not the extravasation of the nation but the radical formation of an alternate representative organ.

Robespierre constantly reminded his fellow political actors that the Revolution was founded on just such a violent act, one that opened up a space outside of all the traditional political forms then in place. He would make the same point, in November, in the newly elected emergency body, the Convention:

> Citizens, do you want a revolution without revolution? What is this spirit of persecution that has just audited [*réviser*], to put it this way, those who have broken our chains? But how can we submit to a certain judgment the effects that can incite these great commotions? Who can mark, after the fact, the precise point where it is necessary to quell the tides of popular insurrection? At this price, what people could ever shake off the yoke of despotism? (9: 89)

Without pretending to evade the terrible spectacle of the September massacres (9: 90–91), Robespierre argues in effect that the authentic sovereign voice, the voice of 1789 and August 10, was still in operation, and however errant its expression, the government had no right to mark, after the flash of revolutionary truth itself, the boundaries of appropriate

---

7. See, on this point, Lucas, "Revolutionary Violence," 69.

action. The people were represented by these revolutionaries, and in a sense had an inviolability as long as they were acting in this authentic manner.

> Because if it is true that a large nation cannot raise itself in a simultaneous movement, and that tyranny can be struck only by the part of the citizens closest to it, how would they dare to attack it if, after their victory, delegates from remote parts can make them responsible for the duration and the violence of the political torment that saved the country? They must be considered as tacitly authorized to act by proxy for the entire society together. (9: 89)

This is a perfect example of Sieyes's "extraordinary representative" force in action.

Yet Robespierre was acutely aware that this manifestation must be seen as essentially temporary, the exceptional product of crisis and not a permanently disruptive force.[8] He realized, like any revolutionary politician, that long-term stability relied on a disciplined and protected space of sovereign decision. Rather than impose from above, however, the limits of sovereign expression, something he denounced as unrevolutionary, Robespierre offers the example of self-discipline. After August 10, he pointed out, the people did not continue to "agitate tumultuously" without any goal. The people naturally form more stable organs. After solemnly regaining their rights, he says, the people "named, in all the sections of Paris, delegates [who were] *charged with their full powers* to ensure public liberty and safety." This is a "great and sublime" idea, Robespierre adds, because this process of localizing the decision in a limited space is the only way the people can act in a normal situation. Without this self-limitation, "insurrection would flow away like a torrent, without leaving any traces, and the people would fall again into the hands of intriguers who had deceived them until then" (8: 449). This unfocused energy, however necessary in times of emergency, is ephemeral without the concrete signs of a representative authority.

So Robespierre was not contradicting himself, despite having earlier argued that insurrection is something to be avoided. In August 1791 he tried to point out in constitutional debates that insurrection was built into a document that made it necessary to correct any "errors" of representation with the very mechanism of this representational order. Some way had to be indicated, Robespierre believed, for reclaiming the rights

8. See Singer, *Society, Theory and the French Revolution*, 184.

of the nation against its representatives if radical change became necessary.

> Insurrection can never be a constitutional means, since on the contrary it is
> only the effect of violence and reversal even of the constitution. Since it is
> possible that there exists a case where the nation would like to review the
> foundations of the constitution, it is obvious that it leaves only insurrection
> as a means in this regard. . . . M. d'André does not indicate any kind of
> means by which the nation could reclaim its rights, in the case I mention; he
> is content to simply say, if the desire of the nation was universal, to change
> the totality of the constitution, agreement would have taken place. He is cer-
> tain that there would be no need of law, or any mode of deliberation for that.
> This is, then, to put insurrection in the place of all constitutional forms and
> means. (7: 691)

Robespierre is especially concerned that the people may be hindered by
their own representatives, that the legislators may err in their constitutional duties. If it takes three consecutive legislatures to change constitutional clauses, Robespierre points out, the people would have to please
the very authorities that abused their power, that violated these rights.
The nation is, and here Robespierre uses the language of Sieyes, "subor-
dinated to the constituted power" (7: 691). Robespierre is trying to persuade the deputies that in order to avoid complete violence, the people
must have another way of expressing themselves when they want to re-
order the constituted authorities. Insurrection, observes Robespierre, is a
"rare, uncertain, and extreme" remedy, a "terrible right" (8: 59). Although it is clear that he supported the convening of extraordinary
elected bodies, like the Convention, to address severe constitutional
crises, in reality the exceptional crisis can never be truly anticipated, and,
as Sieyes pointed out, this meant that the nation could never be limited
to any formally established procedure. But Robespierre's main concern
was not constitutional. His main fear was that insurrection would be
necessary because the people could always be misled by authorities, and
would need to rise again to recover their rights. Robespierre spent most
of his effort making sure that this terrible right would not need to be exercised. Insurrection would be avoided, he said simply, if the elected assembly did not abandon the people, and would fight their enemies itself
(8: 59).

It is clear that in this framework the Jacobin society could function as
an important mediating body, a space between the people (who might
resort to insurrection) and the representative bodies (who might err or

lead the people astray).[9] As Robespierre wrote in a letter, patriots throughout France were affiliated with the society, forming a "holy league against the enemies of liberty and of the country." It was a "holy confederation of all friends of humanity and virtue" (3: 69–70). Robespierre resolved Sieyes's difficulty of accurate representation not with a fixed constitutional mechanism, which was not, it could be argued, really possible anyway, but by advocating measures that would serve to increase the identity between the people and their representatives. This was, for him, a dialogical process, for the people could stray and the politicians could err: there was no solid, preexisting foundational space of legitimacy. This instability was, however, the key difficulty. Robespierre cautioned against any simplistic and dangerous assumption of what "the people" were. One of the duties of the representatives was to defend the people, to protect them against their own defaults. As Rousseau said (Robespierre points out): "'The people always want good, but they do not always see it.' To complete the theory of the principles of government," Robespierre continued, "it would be enough to add: the *mandataires* of the people often see the good, but they do not always want it" (8: 90). Here in essence is Robespierre's conception of the political sphere, a place that can arbitrate both the errors of the citizens and the crimes of corrupt delegates.

Clearly, this space was not just an institutional one, though institutions were of course crucial. For Robespierre, the space of politics opened up by the Revolution was an internal space, the moral sphere of the self and its intentions. Political legitimacy was inherently a question of epistemology, an "epistemology of virtue," in Carol Blum's apt phrase.[10] Robespierre situated himself and the Jacobins in this ephemeral political space. The societies were mediating bodies, locations that involved both the people and their representatives, without a predetermined order or hierarchy. But of course the revolutionary leaders were in fact the ones who established (or rather tried to establish) the borders of this intersection, none more successfully than Robespierre in the period of Jacobin control.

We can see Robespierre continually operating in the shadowy border zones of political legitimacy, claiming always to identify the authenticity of the sovereign voice in its sometimes errant movement between people and representative. Speaking against Brissot and his Girondin colleagues in March 1793, for example, Robespierre evoked the instability

9. On this point, see ibid., 190–91.
10. Carol Blum, *Rousseau and the Republic of Virtue* (Ithaca, 1986), 244.

of the true revolutionary spirit, raising the complex problem of untangling the distinctions between errancy and authenticity.

> In this way, the Brissots, the Rolands, and all the other rogues have led public opinion astray since the glorious event that saved liberty [Aug. 10, 1792]. The public spirit has remained behind the Revolution, because since this epoch all the rogues were leagued in order to lead astray public opinion. . . . The people must know their true enemies. . . . Our enemies have seized the postal system, they are masters at defaming us; they can spread error, we cannot spread the truth. They have all the channels of opinion and public wealth, we can overcome so many obstacles only by extraordinary measures. (9: 297)

Public opinion, Robespierre says, is not always the "opinion of the people." And the representative of the people is not always the "true representative." Just as the people are not corrupt but may be led astray, so the Convention may err, according to Robespierre, when it is being misled by a coalition within (i.e., the Girondins at this point) (9: 399). Who is to make this decision of legitimacy, though?

At this point Robespierre is careful not to claim that role for himself. On May 26, 1793, we find him making this strange invitation at the Jacobin Club: "I exhort each citizen to preserve the sentiment of his rights. I invite him to count on his force and on that of all the nation. I invite the people to rise in insurrection in the National Convention against all the corrupt deputies" (9: 527). Robespierre does not himself make any decision. The people must place themselves in this position (*se mettre . . . en insurrection*). Only two weeks after the enforced purge of the Convention, Robespierre made these remarks on representation:

> The word "representative" cannot be applied to any *mandataire* of the people, because will cannot be represented. The members of the legislature are *mandataires* to whom the people have given first power, but in the true sense we cannot say that they represent them. The legislature makes laws and decrees; laws have the character of laws only when the people have formally accepted them . . . their silence is taken for approbation. (9: 569)

This last point was perhaps the most important. Robespierre was not advocating formal public approval. He was, it is true, leaving open the possibility that the people might correct the errors of their representatives. Silence meant approval, though: this was critical because it was always possible to deny the authenticity of any one particular objection. Remember that even "public opinion" might be in error. Again, Robespierre left open all the ambiguities of representation, and could resolve them only in each concrete instance. And each time, he managed to act as a kind of arbiter of the truth, rather than its privileged representative. Accepting the demands of the sectional leaders—for example, in the case of the Girondin prosecutions in September 1793—Robespierre described the situation in terms of truth and not in specific predetermined relationships of power. "The National Convention must be worthy of such a people; it will be. It has appreciated for a long time the great truths of which you just reminded them; it has made them [truths] the measure of its duties" (10: 99). Truth, however, was never permanently located anywhere in particular.

A Political Epistemology of Error

The true representative of the people (not simply the sitting delegate) was always vigilant, identifying the threatening crimes of the enemy, while guiding the people, who might, in the wrong circumstances, stray from the truth of their own good. In the chaotic and transformative atmosphere of the Revolution, one of Robespierre's key concerns was maintaining the distinction between the errors of authentic citizens and the crimes of counter-revolutionary enemies. The complex ambiguities of this opposition are outlined in this intervention supporting the modes of arrest in late 1793:

> When public notoriety accuses a citizen of crimes where no written proofs exist, but where the proof is in the heart of all indignant citizens, are we not going to recover judicial order with the first decree? Are we annihilating completely the wisdom of revolutionary measures? Humanity wants the people to be saved and the country to triumph; but it wants crime and tyranny to be punished without pity. Humanity also wants patriots oppressed by revolutionary measures to be helped and delivered. But do not go and reduce the friends of the country to discouragement. It is not the time to paralyze the energy of the nation; it is not the time to enfeeble great principles. . . . Be kind and humane to innocence and patriotism, but be inflexible to the enemies of the country. (10: 157)

This language would recur in Robespierre's speeches right up to his last appearance at the Convention in Thermidor. The distinction here, between an error of patriotism and a criminal attack, certainly makes sense within the framework of a late Enlightenment epistemology of error. The errant citizen may stray but he is on the path to redemption (politically), whereas the criminal, the enemy, sees the path but rejects it, and attempts to seduce the people away from it.[11]

We can follow a number of these references in Robespierre's public interventions. This ongoing question of the incarcerated patriot in revolutionary politics was an obvious occasion for expressing this distinction clearly. In December 1793, during debates concerning potentially innocent prisoners, Robespierre observed: "There is a measure to be taken so that the patriot may no longer be confused with the counter-revolutionary." The difficulty is making sure that this delicate procedure is made by someone with the right insight: there are no clear objective rules for knowing the authentic voice of the patriot, which can always be mimicked. Robespierre, again, wants to resolve this difficulty by neutralizing as much as possible the effects of individuality. The decision must be made by those with no personal authority (again, a process of self-isolation) and who remain unknown to the public, so that they may avoid the "natural weaknesses" of man. These individuals must not listen to solicitation, they must turn their ears only toward those "places where the patriot groans" (10: 264). Later that same month he warned the Convention about the importance of keeping the distinction between error and crime present, in his speech on revolutionary government. "It is dangerous," he said, to leave to these two "monsters" (moderatism, aristocracy) "the means to lead astray the zeal of good citizens; it is more dangerous still to discourage and persecute good citizens who have been deceived." What was to be done? Robespierre declared that it was necessary to "protect patriotism, even in its errors, to enlighten patriots, and ceaselessly elevate the people to the height of their rights and of their destinies" (10: 276). This was something he had already noted when he defended the liberty of the cults in November. The Convention will proscribe fanaticism and punish rebellion, and "it will protect the patriots themselves from their errors" (10: 209). In one of his most famous speeches during the Terror, on "political morality," Robespierre repeated this important point:

> Misfortune to those who would dare direct toward the people the terror that must approach only its enemies! Misfortune to those who, confusing the *inevitable errors of patriotism* [*civisme*] with the *calculated errors of perfidy*, or with

11. The distinction here was not between good and bad individuals among the people. The virtuous one moved away from individuality itself toward the good of the whole. "The people are always better than individuals," Robespierre once wrote. Again, his main concern was those in power. "Now what are the depositories of public authority, if not individuals, more exposed to error than others?": *Lettres à ses commettans*, Jan. 10, 1793, in *Oeuvres*, 5: 209.

the attacks of conspirators, abandons the dangerous intriguer to pursue the peaceable citizen! (10: 359; my italics)

Robespierre has identified a familiar opposition: the difference between error on the way to truth and the crime that intentionally leaves the path altogether. Robespierre also identifies a familiar predicament: How to make this distinction in the absence of the destination, especially when it is admitted that *everyone* is fallible, everyone might be suspected of leading the people astray? "Who then will disentangle all these nuances?" he asked, and "who will trace the line of demarcation between all these contrary excesses?" Robespierre's answer: "Love of country and of truth" (10: 276–77).

It is important to notice Robespierre's wording in this response: it is not truth that will decide, since truth is exactly what is in question here. *Love* of truth, of the nation, will give us insight. What exactly does this mean? Robespierre has no faith in particular institutional or procedural forms: they can all (they all will) become corrupted. With almost Platonic resignation, Robespierre cautions:

> It is necessary to take in advance precautions to put the destiny of liberty in the hands of truth, which is eternal, rather than those of men, who are transient, in such a way that if the government forgets the interests of the people, or if it falls into the hands of corrupt men, according to the natural course of things, the light of recognized principles will illuminate their treasons, and so every new faction finds death in the thought of crime alone. (10: 351)

A space must therefore be cleared for the possibility of insight into these difficult problems. This space was essentially internal: if the individual could purify his love for the truth, for this higher identity of the nation, then he should see the truth when it appears to him. There will be no possibility of straying even in the event of a total collapse of authority. To recognize truth, one must be pure. Robespierre was not the "infallible" but the *incorruptible*. No man could have total access to the truth, yet the pure man would be its haven when it appeared. Robespierre wanted to make a similar claim for the Convention during the Terror. Again, he did not claim that this body was itself the truth: it was, he said, the "sanctuary of truth," a place of refuge for this elusive appearance (10: 366).

The creation of the revolutionary state was not, then, for Robespierre, a symbolic appropriation of political truth. It was the creation of a point of stability in "stormy circumstances," so that the enemies of the nation could be eliminated and the long (and errant) path to internal order initiated. The legitimacy of its authority was existential. It was self-protection, and not explicitly a "government" that aimed to protect citizens within the state (10: 274). Robespierre did not evade this foundational principle. The Republic was not defined by any abstract criteria and its identity had no predetermined boundaries. "The Republic is in those who defend it" (10: 299). In this situation, a clear *site* for decision was more crucial than hard and fast rules of judgment. There was, literally, no time for error in the emergency situation. So against his own thoughts of May 1793, Robespierre focused on the centrality of representational authority, justified not constitutionally but existentially. The goal of the factions, he said in January 1794, was to steer the people astray and detach them from the Mountain. The people, once they have lost their way, lose their confidence in the representatives, leaving open opportunities for the enemies of the Republic to gain control. "One can excite the people to revolt and lead them to some excesses, and the people deceived [*égaré*] by villains will lament their error, but too late" (10: 315,317). The government must eliminate the factions and avoid this disastrous error.

It was not immediately clear to many conventionels that the actions of someone like Danton were crimes against the nation rather than errors of patriotism. Robespierre's attempt to convince the Convention in this case—a short speech delivered on 11 Germinal—never in fact tried to prove Danton's guilt objectively. Instead, Robespierre questioned the Assembly as a whole: If this accusation is suspect, what legitimacy was there to all the many previous purges that the Assembly had authorized? The ability to detect error and crime had already been claimed by these representatives. Authority was not derived from their representational status, since this was, as we have seen, highly ambiguous and hardly permanent (as the Girondins knew). If the representatives saw themselves in Danton's place, Robespierre was quick to say both that "guilty men always fear seeing their fellows fall, because, no longer having before them a barrier of guilty ones, they are left more exposed to the light of truth," and that "the number of guilty is not so great." Robespierre then confidently asserted that "patriotism, the Convention, have been able to distinguish error from crime, weakness from conspiracies. . . . They do not strike without discernment" (10: 415).[12] Terror had become, in a sense, infallible, according to Robespierre, or at least in order to function legitimately as protector of the nation it had assumed infallibility. Robespierre returned to this issue in his infamous speech on religious principles, a month before Prairial and the introduction of the laws that

---

12. On this particular speech, see Claude Lefort, "The Revolutionary Terror," in *Democracy and Political Theory*, trans. David Macey (Cambridge, 1988), 59–69.

would intensify the application of Terror. Here Robespierre ridiculed "aristocrats" for accusing patriots of crime, "sincere patriots," he noted, "whose involvement in suspicious activities (*démarches indiscrètes*) was due solely to their hatred of fanaticism. You do not have the right to accuse," Robespierre continued, because "national justice, in these storms whipped up by factions, knows how to distinguish errors from conspiracies; it will seize, with a sure hand, all perverse intriguers, and will not strike a single good man" (10: 457).

Robespierre's goal in his speech on national religion was to create in the people, in all citizens, the means for making these distinctions accurately themselves, so they would not have to rely on the emergency government, or any government, for guidance in the uncertain future. The cult of the Supreme Being was a way of creating a space for insight in each individual. "Passion" and "reason" both were human characteristics that could lead the self away from recognizing the appearance of truth. Robespierre thought that the "masterpiece of society" would be the construction of internal barriers to such errancy. We should, he advised in this famous passage,

> create in him, for questions of morality, a swift instinct that, without the tardy aid of reasoning, would make him do good and avoid evil; for individual reason, led astray by the passions, is often only a sophist who pleads their cause, and human authority can always be attacked by the self-love of man. Now what produces or replaces this precious instinct, what supplements the insufficiency of human authority, is the religious sentiment that impresses on souls the idea of precepts of morality given by a power superior to man. (10: 452–53)

What was becoming clear by this point, though, was that Robespierre believed he and his fellow Jacobins had such an instinct, an unusual ability to disentangle all these nuances. The Mountain, he would claim in the days after the introduction of the laws of Prairial and the escalation of the Terror, was that portion of the representative body designated by the people to "struggle against error." The Montagnards, he added, will always be "the bulwark of liberty [*le boulevard de la liberté*]" (10: 493).

Robespierre would again claim this ability to see the truth, speaking at the Jacobins in favor of an accused representative on 1 Thermidor. He condemned those who threw away denunciations on those representatives who were "beyond reproach, or who had failed only by error." For Robespierre, "nothing is easier than giving justice to citizens with complaints to lodge, without finding guilty those representatives who were only deceived. Measures taken in a moment of error must be distinguished from those that have been planned with deep malice." We will, he observes, "avoid shipwreck" because the Convention is, for the most part, pure, above crime, above fear (10: 536).

Robespierre's last speech continued this theme: he alone was perhaps the only true sanctuary for truth. By this time, the Convention, that "temple" (a consecrated space for the appearance from "outside") was now in discord, he noted, and he would soon reveal the causes of this dangerous rupture. Here, he says, "I need to open my heart; you need as well to hear the truth. . . . I come, if it is possible, to dissipate cruel errors." Again, only the guilty need fear Robespierre's truth.

> Conspirators would never be conspirators at all if they did not have the art of dissimulating so cleverly, to gain after some time the confidence of some good men; but there are *certain signs* by which one can discern dupes from accomplices, and *error from crime*. Who will make this distinction then? Good sense and justice. (10: 552; my italics)

And what exactly were good sense and justice? Robespierre is caught in the epistemological complexity generated by a conception of truth whose essential reality remains a mystery and yet still functions as the only foundation of legitimacy. Robespierre, who was never really the agent of God but rather the self-appointed protector of the foyer of the Supreme Being, was painfully aware of the omnipresence of error and crime in this world, and sought to guide the people to the luminous truth when it appeared. But what was the basis of his insight, his Socratic, Christlike power in the political sphere? Robespierre, that "pure man [*l'homme vièrge*], the incorruptible man, who never strayed from the path of patriotism and virtue" (7: 514) was caught in a political sphere that could never reveal the veracity of his own claim to authority. Robespierre's ultimate failure can be located in this late turn, when he no longer emphasized the essential ambiguity of this moral space of politics, when instead he implicitly declared himself the privileged organ of the nation, of truth itself. Here Robespierre strayed at his own peril from the Enlightenment understanding of error.

SAINT-JUST'S NEGATIVE (POLITICAL) THEOLOGY

Unlike more experienced and mature figures like Sieyes and Robespierre, Saint-Just did not participate in the early constitutional phase of the Revolution. In 1791, however, he did publish a short book, *L'esprit de la Révolution et de la constitution*, which reflected the largely moderate position of the National Assembly. Saint-Just supported the idea of a "popular" monarch, one without nobility attached to it, who executed the law "religiously," and he maintained the ubiquitous position that the people were sovereign.[13] He also argued against the death penalty, as did Robespierre, of course (325). This text may not read like the preparatory work of the future radical politician. Still there are traces here of Saint-Just's own at times idiosyncratic perspective on political and social questions that will occupy us here.

One of the important claims he makes concerns law, the main objective of the revolutionary assemblies. Laws, he wrote, are not at all conventions, even publicly sanctioned ones. Society is the foundational "convention," and laws are simply the "possible relations" emerging from the nature of that origin (324). This rather simple distinction opens up many difficult problems for Saint-Just, problems in what might be called political epistemology that he would be able to work on in the very center of power in the Revolution. How, according to Saint-Just, does the legislator discover (literally unconceal) these relations in society, and more important, what exactly is the point of laws if they are merely the expression of a preexisting natural relation? Saint-Just needed to explain (as Rousseau did in his *Second Discourse*) "natural" society, the origin of corruption, and the possible path for recovering this original society. The political theory Saint-Just developed, first privately, then in the intense environment of the Convention, the Committee of Public Safety, and as representative *en mission* during the war, was a kind of negative politics, one that fitted perfectly into the program of the Terror and the revolutionary state. Saint-Just spent less time articulating the "nature" of society than claiming that through negation (the elimination of aberration) this reality would reemerge on its own. At the same time, Saint-Just was aware of the possibility of corruption in any postrevolutionary state, since corruption is what had led France to the degenerate condition of the Old Regime. And so he envisioned a program (fragmentary, idealistic, and fantastic in parts) that would not so much institute a politics authorized by truth as manifest nature in tangible, concrete forms, to elaborate an impersonal guard against the straying of citizens and their government.

Politics as Aberration

Saint-Just began thinking about these questions after he had come to Paris, only to find that he was excluded from participating in the newly called Legislative Assembly (although he had been elected) because he failed to meet the minimum age requirement. During this period, roughly

13. Saint-Just, *Oeuvres complètes*, ed. Michèle Duval (Paris, 1984), 296–98. Further references to this edition are in the text.

September 1791 to the following September, Saint-Just sketched a draft of a manuscript he titled "De la nature, de l'état civil, de la cité, ou Les règles de l'independance, du gouvernement."[14] This text, rediscovered only in the 1950s,[15] is the starting point of much of his political thinking during the Terror, and it often makes its appearance in (at times cryptic) references in his public speeches. A fundamental distinction is first laid out here: Saint-Just's critical opposition of social and political spaces. The historical aberration that marked the development of modern societies was, according to Saint-Just, a confusion between these two categories, a confusion that had persisted so long that they were now seen as fundamentally related in some way. This concept of history, something that separates Saint-Just from Robespierre, his closest political colleague, redefines political and social error in the context of the Revolution. Saint-Just believed that political power became criminal when it strayed into the social sphere, and that individual citizens in society erred if they strayed from the natural relations of society. He therefore proposed two protective spaces that would allow society to move toward a stable and harmonious order: a political space of defense and a social arena of guidance.

Saint-Just always emphasized the "natural" origin of social life. This origin cannot, as Sieyes said, be explained as the result of any positive, deliberate act. "People are united by the relations of man as a social being," wrote Saint-Just in *De la nature* (932). Relations in society are not particular, individual conventions. In a series of statements, revised and reformulated in a number of ways, Saint-Just pointed out that the starting point of identity was itself the unity that bound together disparate individuals considered to be related in some fashion.

<The nature of relations is the homogeneity of things that unite them.> . . . Nature ends where convention begins. Social life is therefore the relation of homogeneity that unites <genders [*sexes*]> men, sole eternal principle of their preservation. The social state does not at all derive from convention; the art of establishing a society through a pact, or by the modifications of force, is the very art of destroying society. (922)[16]

14. For the composition of this manuscript, see Jean-Pierre Gross, "L'oeuvre de Saint-Just: Essai de bibliographie critique," in *Actes du colloque Saint-Just* (Paris, 1967), 350–51.

15. Published by Albert Soboul as "Un manuscrit inédit de Saint-Just," *Annales historiques de la Révolution française*, 1951, 321–59.

16. Saint-Just's manuscript fragments are sometimes difficult to unravel because of their syntax, incomplete punctuation, and conceptual obscurity. I have often included material that Saint-Just had crossed out (indicated by angle brackets, as in the *Oeuvres complètes*) if it gives a fuller sense of the passage, at the price of some confusion. I have translated these fragments as literally as possible; thus their rough quality.

Identity of the whole establishes relations between individuals, and this identity is described as coming "existentially," from a common need for preservation. As in Rousseau's *Social Contract*, the people are formed by a common relationship produced by the threat to survival: all subsequent social distinctions take place within this clearly demarcated space.[17] For Saint-Just (as for Rousseau), it was clear that the modern states of Europe no longer operated according to these natural social relations. In this fragment, Saint-Just gives his version of Rousseau's story of the degeneration of natural society.

> The world is today populated only by savages. . . . <All the arts have produced marvels, the art of governing has produced only monsters; for we have looked for the skill of representing [*l'art image*] in nature, and for principles in our pride.> Whatever might be the source of the present order of things, it is impure, it is a work of shadows. (923)

This is the first indication of Saint-Just's negative political strategy: those shadowy errors of the modern world, once stripped away, will give way to nature, something outside of direct human construction. In fact, as he will explain, it is human intervention itself into society that is the source of these errors. Saint-Just's account of this political original sin is deceptively simple. Society, he claims, is naturally peaceful, internally. However, each individual society is in a relation of force with respect to other societies. Each society must resist conquest: this relation with the potential enemy is the only one that deserves the term "political." As Saint-Just puts it, then, "the social state is the relation of men among themselves, the political state is the relation of a people with another people" (923). The moment of aberration is perfectly clear, for Saint-Just. Political force at some time intervenes in the social sphere. "We see that men, treating one another as enemies, have turned against their social independence the force that is appropriate only to their exterior or collective independence" (923). This force cuts through the homogeneity binding independent citizens, and introduces a relationship of oppression. Saint-Just argues that this moment of aberration was not a spontaneous (that is, irreversible) movement. He points to the example of the Franks and the Germans, people with no "magistrates"; the people and the sovereign were a single entity. At some point, however, "when peoples lose the taste for assembling to negotiate, to cultivate the earth or to conquer, the prince is separated from the sovereign, here ends social life and begins political life or convention" (928). There are now two relationships:

17. Rousseau, *Contrat social*, bk. 1, chap. 6.

between citizens and between the citizens as a whole and the prince (whether in the form of senate or king). This last relationship is for Saint-Just unnatural, a monstrous aberration. The question he addresses, then, is how to eliminate this error and rediscover natural harmony. The goal is not to "improve" this relationship of government and society, the goal of most Enlightenment political theorists and, of course, the revolutionary politicians influenced by them.

The majority of what Saint-Just calls "errors in the political community [*cité*]" stem from the mistaken belief that human society in its present state can somehow be the object of political action. Legislation, he asserts, is not a "science of the actual." Once social and political categories have been confused, only perverse "aggregations," and not true societies, can be formed (924). "It is an error to believe that men were savage and that they united first in the civil state to preserve themselves." Against Hobbes, Saint-Just thinks that people united out of a feeling of mutual support. Society is not then linked originally with a politics of force: societies were unified long before the state of war. This society was not the "prey" of politics; "it was ruled by the law of nature and men became savage as they <swerved from> confused <political and social law> the laws that ought to rule peoples, those that must rule men" (925). The introduction of political force into social relations has "denatured" human beings. No possible progress can be made as long as we continue to ignore ourselves and take pride in our "false nature," for we will not be able to rediscover our "veritable" nature (927). There are, for Saint-Just, two kinds of "sovereignty" that must be disentangled: one is the "force by which [a people] resists <conquest> oppression," and another, rather confusedly defined as "the individual sovereignty of all men by which property, possession, <safety,> is maintained, this sovereignty is what we have called independence. . . . <The sovereignty of the people with respect to themselves would be illusory, they have no need of force against themselves>" (934–35).

This at times rather strange analysis is an essential part of Saint-Just's later approach to the actual practice of politics in the Revolution. Saint-Just rejected the elusive idea of a sovereign people acting through various (and, as we have seen, problematically defined) representatives. For him, politics was only about war, the war against the people's enemies. Politics was *essentially* terror, and would, Saint-Just believed, effectively disappear with the Terror, at least in one important sense. Does this mean that he thought society, once recovered and protected, was self-governing? Saint-Just did express this idea often. "The social body," he suggested, "resembles the human body, all its relations contribute to a harmony" (937). Saint-Just realized, however, that the social body at the time of the Revolution was anything but naturally harmonious; otherwise the Revolution would not have been necessary. So Saint-Just did, even in this early text, probe the problem of corruption, to isolate the opportunities for aberration so that they could be eliminated in the future state. Saint-Just notes that although many philosophers were aware of the "disorders" in the social body in the modern world, too few were willing to take an active part in rectifying these disorders. "Seneca, Montaigne, and so many others show with a great deal of spirit that everything is going badly, but the cure? I do not like doctors who speak, I like those who heal" (939). Saint-Just's own plans for social medicine emerged from his crucial distinction between the political and the social. Politics would not bring about social correction. Rather, intervention would be necessary only to cure those pathologies that resulted from the intrusion of the political into the social space. Saint-Just took a great deal of care to emphasize that the social would essentially take care of itself if left alone and protected from external enemies. He would then, later on, look again at the possibility of aberration in the social body itself.

In this text *De la nature*, however, Saint-Just reduced law to its absolute minimum: it was simply the manifestation of "nature." "Laws," he explained, "are the natural relations of things and not at all relative relations or the effect of the general will." For Saint-Just, will is often a source of aberration. The less positive will that intruded into society's self-government, the less opportunity there would be for error, the transgression of nature.

> Rousseau, speaking about laws, says that they can only express the general will, and finishes convinced of the necessity of the legislator. Now a legislator can express nature and cannot express the general will. Moreover, this will can err, and the social body must no more be oppressed by itself than by someone else. (941)[18]

This is a rather remarkable statement, and it contains an idea that will recur in Saint-Just's political thought into the Terror. The general will for Saint-Just *can* very well err. What does not stray is nature; if only its laws could be discovered, social health could be maintained. It is not, Saint-Just says, that will is necessarily opposed to nature; rather, the "true" goal of a collective will is independence and survival, "but that is in the nature of things before being a will, positively a will" (951). Moreover, human will itself is what allows humans to stray from this law in the

---

18. Cf. this remark: "Law is therefore not the expression of will but that of nature" (951).

first place. "The social life is corrupted by the abuse of an intelligence that was not at all animal. It was the relation that the divinity had placed between itself and man so that he would be grateful and noble; without this intelligence, man would have followed only mechanical relations like animals" (956).

The error of politics is possible only because of this independent will. But this means, for Saint-Just, that any social "medicine" would be largely surgical, the elimination of anything foreign to this initial ordered state. In other words, anything that was a product of human invention (the result of radical will) was suspect, since it was at best unnecessary and at worst a dangerous threat to "nature." Saint-Just described his program in this way: "I do not break the links of society, but society has broken all those of nature; I do not seek to establish novelties, but to destroy novelties themselves; I am not at all set against truth, just error"(944). For Saint-Just, the elimination of errors would in fact lead to the reemergence of truth. The operation to cure the social body of its ills was entirely negative. Saint-Just assumed that a society was a preexistent unity, bound by a relation of homogeneity shared by all citizens. This society, by definition, was indivisible: it was the foundational ground of all other relations. "The *cité* is the social body, from this perspective, it has no other laws than those of nature formed by the legislator, the king or the sovereign, consequently, it is indivisible, since a society that divides ceases to be a society" (950). Once this body had been corrupted, the key task was identifying this original community so that it might flourish again. This meant purging it of "political" forces; it also meant repelling the enemy on the outside. This was the source of Saint-Just's negative political theology. Destroy what is *not* society, and you will be left with that pure identity.

Refounding the Social Body

Saint-Just's first speech at the Convention, and his first major political act, was a short but radical discourse concerning the king's trial. The argument was straightforward and uncompromising. The king, alleged Saint-Just, was by definition above the law (since he created it), and therefore outside of the "social contract." He could not be tried as a criminal, someone who has violated the agreed-upon laws, since this would assume that he was already a citizen. The king, above the people but not of them, can be tried only as an *enemy* of the people. His guilt, then, was not a matter of specific transgressions: the mere fact of being the monarch in the Old Regime was enough to prove his status as an enemy to be destroyed. This was a matter not of civil law (laws among citizens) but of the law of nations (laws between potential enemies). For Saint-Just, the judgment of the king was an existential act, and one that had to be done decisively. If the nation engaged in a debate with the enemy, it would only get lost in a "vicious circle." The king "must reign or die," Saint-Just claimed; there was no middle ground. Any questions about the internal organization of the state must await this foundational decision: "By the price we put on our errors, we play at wrestling with them, instead of marching straight to the truth." He went on to say that monarchy "is one of those offenses that even the blindness of an entire people cannot justify." No man could reign innocently, Saint-Just noted in one of his most famous epigrammatic statements. This was not a matter of fact to be decided, but was built into the logic of sovereignty itself (378–79).

In his second speech on the trial, Saint-Just again highlighted the existential character of the decision: "Have the courage to pronounce the truth," he said. "Truth burns in silence in all hearts, like a blazing lamp in a tomb." For the nation to survive it must escape this tomb, destroy these oppressive constraints. Saint-Just challenges his audience with this call: "If there is anyone who is not touched by the spell of the republic, let him fall at the feet of the tyrant, and let him give back the knife that immolated his fellow citizens; let him forgive all his crimes" (401). The republic would not be formed out of a preexisting political framework. It could only be founded, and those who bound themselves together into a social body were those who recognized the common threat of the enemy.

Having read *De la nature*, we can see more clearly what Saint-Just was really arguing here. For him, any political intervention (that is, outward-looking protective force) into the social is a crime. The first step toward a legitimate order is not the correction of any internal "errors" but the eradication of the most radical error of all, the intrusion of force into society. Saint-Just, in a rather cryptic passage in his first speech, seems to indicate that the king's trial must not be a singular act, limited to this specific situation. He reminds the Convention of the ongoing importance of the independence of the people from their government.

> It is not enough to say that in the order of eternal justice sovereignty is independent of the present form of government, and then to draw this consequence, that the king must be judged; natural justice and the principle of sovereignty must yet be extended through to the very spirit in which it is appropriate to judge him. We will not have a republic without these distinctions that place all the parts of the social order in their natural movement, as nature creates life from the combination of elements. (380–81)

Saint-Just would continue, throughout his relatively short but intense career, to draw all the implications from this crucial distinction between political force and social harmony.

In one speech, on the nature of the minister of war, Saint-Just succinctly outlined his basic theory of power. Declaring a state of war, he says, is really a problem of *external* relations. For Saint-Just, "it lies only with the sovereign to discuss the acts of force that involve citizens' lives and public prosperity." He goes on to warn that "if these acts are a part of the governing power, the magistrate has the opportunity to misuse against the people a force established only against external enemies" (496). The one with power, for Saint-Just, is always subject to corruption. As he noted when he declared the minister of war a traitor in March 1793, "I have not found a single good man in government; I have found good only in the people" (414). Force, Saint-Just would always say, is to be used only against the enemy. The people did not need to be coerced. Eliminate the enemy and protect the people from their government, and everything would run harmoniously.

Saint-Just's constitutional proposal, presented to the Convention in April 1793, elaborated this theory of government in greater detail. He began with this declaration, an echo of his earlier reflections in *De la nature*: "In general, order does not result from movements of force." Force was an entirely negative operation for Saint-Just. "Nothing is ordered but that which moves on its own and obeys its own harmony; force keeps away only what is foreign to this harmony. . . . Laws repel only evil; innocence and virtue are independent on the earth" (416). It is precisely this structure that makes force and its object, the "alien," so important for Saint-Just. Since order and harmony cannot be imposed, they need not be the subject of action. In fact, as long as foreign elements are eliminated, this harmony will reemerge spontaneously. If, as he says here again, the art of governing has so far produced only "monsters," it is because governments have treated the people as something to be ordered. "I have thought that social order was in the very nature of things, and borrowed nothing from the human spirit but the care of putting diverse elements in their place" (416). Politics, the art of resisting conquest, has nothing to do with the social, which precedes it. "Men in the same society are naturally at peace; war is only between peoples, or rather between those that dominate them" (416). Therefore, Saint-Just argued, the main goal of the constitution would be to "separate in the government the energy needed to resist external force from the simple means necessary for governing" (416). Saint-Just evokes the literal sense of *gouverner* here: to govern is to steer, to gently pilot in the right direction, but not to impose an order by force. The government ought to efface itself as much as possible, even when it has to guide the nation to harmony. Act, he advised at one point, to encourage justice without seeking renown, "similar to the supreme being, who puts the

world in harmony without revealing itself" (778). Saint-Just himself always tried to maintain this distinction: between eliminating the errors
of force and gently steering the people, preventing any straying from
their own natural order.

There is no doubt that for the most part Saint-Just was concerned
with this first problem, the elimination of enemies and the need to
maintain the political/social division. Like Robespierre, however, Saint-
Just was faced with the difficulty of identifying these divisions. The difference between the crime of the enemy and the error of the citizen had
to be determined. Again, this was an epistemological task: intentions
were critical, because Saint-Just, like Robespierre, believed that the
people could very well stray; indeed, the fact of the Revolution indicated there had been a long-term historical aberration. Saint-Just outlined this ambiguous structure when he discussed the problem of the
Vendée and the emergence of civil war in the west. The initial anarchy
in the region, Saint-Just suggests, was the result of understandable confusion, given the early history of the Revolution, but once the people
there had seen the truth of the general will (here, in contrast to his earlier statement, Saint-Just says this will "can never err"), a general will
expressed in the recent plebiscite that resoundingly approved the Jacobin constitution, everything would have calmed down and the Revolution would have been stabilized. What happened, Saint-Just observes,
is that the proscribed Girondin leaders, in spite of the visible "truth" of
the people's will, acted to stir up trouble, in effect leading the people
astray. "It is a crime to take up arms when the people have assembled"
(458). These criminals must be punished, Saint-Just says, not the innocent who erred unintentionally. "The people can be mistaken; they are
mistaken less than men" (521). So Saint-Just tells the Convention not to
condemn everyone arrested in the aftermath of May 31. "Not all of the
detained are guilty; the greatest number only strayed. However, since
during a conspiracy the safety of the country is the supreme law, you
confused for a moment straying [*l'égarement*] and crime, and wisely sacrificed the liberty of some for the safety of all." This confusion was
hardly surprising: as Saint-Just declares, "nothing resembles virtue like
a great crime" (459). Individuals stray because these crimes have the
false prestige of truth; even the best citizens can be deceived. This is
why, Saint-Just argues, insurrections in a free state are dangerous for
liberty, because "the revolt of crime usurps the sublime pretexts and the
sacred name" of legitimate revolutionary action.[19] "The imitative spirit

---

19. Saint-Just, "Fragments diverses," in *Théorie politique*, ed. Alain Liénard (Paris,
1976), 303.

is the mark of crime" (725). Clearly, special insight is necessary to combat crime of this kind. This was the duty of the revolutionary government.

But as Saint-Just observes in his speech against Danton and his "accomplices," the difficulty of determining error and crime in the critical phases of a revolution is almost overwhelming.

> A new regime establishes itself with difficulty, especially a great empire, where the multiplicity of the wheels of government, of relations, and of dangers means that the majority of abuses escape justice and survive wisdom. How to disentangle intrigues that break all the threads and confuse attention? How to listen to the tranquil voice of good sense in the midst of traps set by the mind? (764)

To be sure, Saint-Just was not worried about the nuances of this particular problem. Without exactly claiming perfect "good sense," he told the Convention that it was their duty to uncover and punish enemies of the Republic. The role of government was to combat enemies, and also to protect the people from abuses of power. Like Robespierre, Saint-Just outlined a privileged space for authentic revolutionary action, one occupied by an elite circle of political actors. So the "government" (which was not an institutionally demarcated entity) must be vigilant. In fact, the government had to be most vigilant against itself, given that this was the very location of pathological aberration, the transformation of political into social force. The "debris" of any remaining faction would prove to be the breeding ground for more infection of the social body, he noted in this speech against Danton. External enemies were not so problematic: they revealed themselves in outright armed opposition. The internal enemy, the one who disguised crime as truth, was much more dangerous, and much more difficult to track. In the end, however, it was Saint-Just's conception of social harmony (and not some internal space of virtue) that would allow him to identify error and crime. "Today, when nature and wisdom have regained their rights and truth has rediscovered sensitive ears, it is up to the love of country to make its austere voice understood" (997).

The enemy, according to Saint-Just, is anyone outside of the sovereign. Since Saint-Just defines the sovereign in terms of mutual relations and a mutual desire for preservation and harmony, it is possible to identify enemies negatively: those not fully supportive of the Republic, those who act in a spirit of division. "You have to punish not only traitors but even those who are indifferent; you have to punish anyone who is passive in the Republic and does nothing for it, for as long as the French people have expressed their will, everything that is opposed to it is outside the sovereign, everything outside the sovereign is an enemy" (521). While this would seem to lead to a crucial problem—knowing the will of the people—certain truths were apparent to Saint-Just from the very logic of sovereignty. "The solidity of our Republic is in the very nature of things. The sovereignty of the people desires that the people be unified; it is therefore opposed to factions. Every faction is an attack against sovereignty" (734). Foundation was a matter not so much of positive creation as of critical negation. This was the heart of Saint-Just's negative political theology: "You wanted a republic. If you do not want at the same time what constitutes it, you will bury the people under its debris. What constitutes a republic is the total destruction of what is opposed to it" (700). The birth of the Republic is necessarily violent, because it introduces something new into the present. The liberty of the Republic "emerged from the bosom of the storms; this origin is common to the world, coming from chaos, and man, who cries on being born" (812). This identity would be rediscovered through the process of destroying all opposition. Saint-Just, in his speeches, usually defined the people through negation: in opposition to government, the rich, the counter-revolutionary.[20] Since "the people" were naturally harmonious, the revolutionary state was less concerned with managing this social sphere than creating it and protecting it from all threats. "Let the factions disappear, and there will remain only liberty" (819). By his own account, Saint-Just was absolved of the need to articulate the positive outlines of the people at this point.

The critical problem of representation and sovereignty was, therefore, simply not a major conceptual problem for Saint-Just. In the postrevolutionary state, order would be the norm, he assumed. So for Saint-Just, the end of revolution marked not the beginning of a moral, virtuous government but the near total dissolution of government. By 1794, he was trying to articulate what this post-Terror society would look like, as he started to draft fragments on "republican institutions" and suggest, in his later speeches, the nature of the state in a republican society. "Terror," he wrote in a fragment on "society," "can relieve us of monarchy and aristocracy, but what can deliver us from corruption? . . . Institutions. We do not doubt this: we believe everything to have been done when we have a machine in government" (976). "Render politics impotent by reducing everything to the cold rule of justice" (912). At one point he supported the need for a revolutionary (temporary) government by noting that the present one was only a "hierarchy of error and outrage" (521).

20. See Annie Geffroy, "Le 'peuple' selon Saint-Just," in *Actes du colloque Saint-Just*, 231–37.

Later he would observe: "We have a government, we have this common link of Europe, which consists of public powers and a public administration. Institutions, which are the heart of a republic, we lack." The very advantage of the republican state, Saint-Just was saying, is that it has this internal means of protection. Institutions restrain *moeurs* and "arrest the corruption of laws and men" (699).

And so in a late speech on public order (*police générale*) Saint-Just reminded the Convention that the true unity of the nation was not in the government but in the interests and relations of the citizens themselves (810). Authentic order, then, would arise from the people, and not through forceful repression. "We must commit ourselves to forming a public conscience—that is the best way to keep order [*police*]" (811). "Form civil institutions. . . . There is no durable liberty without them. They support the love of country and the revolutionary spirit itself when the revolution is over" (818–19).

Institutions and Social Aberration

The facts of corruption, the long history of a pathological "denaturation," proved to Saint-Just that however good the people were, aberration was always a possibility. Since government itself was the most likely source of both corruption and political aberration, Saint-Just believed that the construction of institutions should protect the nation from its own government. At the same time, the will of men threatened even this natural harmony, and so Saint-Just also envisioned institutions that would steer the errant citizen back into the order of nature. This was the dual role of institutions in a republic. "Institutions are the guarantee of the government of a free people against the corruption of *moeurs*, and the guarantee of the people and of the citizen against the corruption of the government" (967). Institutions would guard against two kinds of error.

"There are few men," Saint-Just noted, "who do not have a secret desire [*penchant*] for fortune. The calculations of ambition are impenetrable; destroy, destroy all the paths that lead to crime" (424). This was in fact the main goal of those institutions that would severely limit government authority. As he wrote, the state had to be structured so that it substituted a permanently "true" foundation for the potentially errant human individual.

It is essential in revolutions, where perversity and virtue play such large roles, to state very clearly all principles, all definitions. A moment comes when those who have the most intellect and cunning [*esprit et politique*] prevail over those who have the most patriotism and probity. Misfortune to those who live in a time when virtue lowers its eyes, flushes the brow, and passes for vice compared with shrewd crime. (969)

Saint-Just, like Robespierre, seeks a way to distinguish crime and patriotism, to reveal truth and error in the political realm. In a world of corrupt, factional politics, everything becomes reversed. The simple, artless man is found to be criminal simply because he does not understand crime. Here, in this world, all useful deliberation ends. No longer is it a question of a body of citizens trying to determine among themselves possible errors and the true path of virtue. "There are no longer clear ideas of things and the safeguard against so many errors is just that everything apparently goes as it should go. What is virtue in one century and for one people is a crime for another people and in another century" (963). Power is the only factor: "One no longer finds either the one who was right or the one who was in error, but the one who was the most insolent and the one who was the most timid" (969).

Saint-Just has very few doubts about *knowing* the truth of virtue. As he says, "I do not like new words at all; I know only just and unjust, these words are understood by all consciences." As for Robespierre, this internal moral space was essential for authentic and legitimate action. Therefore, it was essential that all definitions be reduced to conscience; "the mind [*esprit*] is a sophist that leads virtues to the scaffold" (969). Institutions, Saint-Just believed, would relieve individuals from the possibility of aberration. The "inflexible justice of laws" would take the place of the power and force of individual influence (969). Institutions, he extravagantly claimed, "have as their goal to establish in fact all the social and individual guarantees in order to avoid dissension and violence. < . . . Institutions have as their goal to substitute principles of morality in all actions for [. . .]> to substitute the ascendancy of *moeurs* for the ascendancy of men" (970).

Saint-Just in effect evaded the complex epistemological/moral problem Robespierre addressed, how to distinguish, that is, outside of the very institutions and identities that were potentially errant, the error from the crime, false virtue from authentic. Robespierre looked to the self, and particularly his own self, for an answer to this question. The space of morality must be cleared of all corrupting influences so that the truth of justice will be recognized and obeyed when it appears to us naturally. Saint-Just was somewhat less reflective. For him, institutions were the weapons of truth. Institutions, he wrote, "establish the delicate distinction between truth and hypocrisy, innocence and crime, they ground the reign of justice" (966). Without these tangible (yet essentially transcendent, in terms of authority) guides, "the strength of a republic would rest either on the merit of fragile mortals or on precarious means" (966). This is not to say that a state structure of institutions would simply impose order on these "fragile mortals." Saint-Just envisioned a naturally peaceful and ordered people who needed only these "guarantees" in the event of error. "Do not let the government be a power for the citizen, let it be a source of harmony for him, let it be only a force to <preserve> protect this state of simplicity, against force itself" (968). But what exactly is the force of the institution? Saint-Just gives institutions transcendent authority, yet does not discuss the method of discovering them. What is clear, though, is that institutions are not mere laws. For laws, he rightly points out, are problematic. "To obey laws, that is not so obvious, for law is often nothing but the will of the one imposing it. One has the right to resist oppressive laws." For Saint-Just, only an institution can be the touchstone of legitimacy. "A law contrary to institutions is tyrannical" (976).

Saint-Just avoided Robespierre's tendency to mystical structures, seeking instead to derive these foundational institutions, the standard for all political and social aberration, from a logic of national identity. In one condensed passage, Saint-Just tries to make this point.

All beings are born for independence <and society.> This independence has laws <that are the principle of society> without which <each> beings would languish isolated, these laws in bringing them together form society, these same laws derive from the natural relations, these relations are the needs and affections. (971)

The very independence of an individual, then, has a certain character: one can be an individual only with a certain independence and freedom within a preexisting structure of some sort. Pure independence is isolation, and does not make sense of natural organic identities. As he writes, independence "is founded on the relations and the laws that unite them [individuals]. United by these laws, they find themselves in a state of force" against another identity: with animals, this is the enemy relation between species, and in humanity, the enemy distinctions between individual societies (970).[21] And so, for Saint-Just, the construction of institutions has as its end the manifestation of all these "relations and affec-

---

21. Saint-Just did not think that the Revolution could be universal, that it could spread through other nations and form a great harmonious whole. "The good souls who indulge these illusions know little the extent of the path that we have made away from truth. This dream that it is possible is in a future that is not at all made for us. We must, then, without fruitlessly seeking to put social relations between peoples, limit ourselves to reestablishing them between men"(972).

tions" that bind individuals together in the first place, into one society. "The country is not the soil, it is the community of affections, which ensure that, each fighting for the safety or liberty of those dear to him, the country finds itself defended" (977). The institution would operate in this space of affection. It would not impose these relations; rather, it would express them in a legal form so that straying from them would not be possible. Institutions produce "guarantees" and form "limits" to human aberration (907).

Friendship and Aberration

Saint-Just identifies the essential relationship of society as friendship [*amitié*]. Individuals without this link to others in the community are, quite simply, not members of the community. This, for Saint-Just, is quite obvious. The "institutions" that follow simply articulate what is a natural and usually tacit aspect of human social life. Saint-Just does not want to impose an artificial link on all citizens. He wants to make explicit what is usually unclear. So he envisions a republic where "every man aged twenty-one is bound to declare in the temple who his friends are, and this declaration must be renewed, every year, during the month of Ventôse" (983). Friendship was a kind of "cement" for the republic,[22] and these institutions would make this cement visible and hence subject to correction. This could take strange forms, but Saint-Just's intent is clear. "Friends are placed next to one another in battle" (983). "Those who remained friends all their life are buried in the same tomb" (984). "The people will elect the tutors of children from the friends of their father" (984). Friendship substituted for external relations administered by a central authority. One's membership in the *nous* of the nation was predicated on common links of affection. The only guarantee of social unity lay in the preservation of these links. "If a man leaves a friend, he is bound to account for the reasons that made him leave, to the people in the temple" (984). Rejection of *amitié* meant rejection of the nation. Saint-Just declares: "If a man has no friends at all, he is banished" (984). This was necessary, because for Saint-Just, the order of society was to be maintained only through these natural preexisting relationships, and not through abstract laws or artificially imposed relationships.

Since the only way the possibility of error could be reduced in government was to severely limit its authority in social matters, Saint-Just had to make sure that error would not infect the social body. He thought he could do so by strengthening the individual *rapports* in society that al-

22. See Françoise Fortunet, "L'amitié et le droit selon Saint-Just," *Annales historiques de la Révolution française*, 1982, 187.

ready defined it as a society. "No one can contract without the presence of his friends, otherwise the contract is nul." "Friends receive contracts," and not any state administrative authority (990). Because *amitié* was so pervasive in society, the link that consolidated national identity, Saint-Just thought that any straying from the public good could be isolated and corrected in this private but very tangible space. "If a man commits a crime," Saint-Just proposed, "his friends are banished" (984). These institutional forms enforced a mutual responsibility that was already the very foundation of social solidarity. The political for Saint-Just was really founded on the social, expressed concretely as friendship.[23] "You must construct a community [*cité*], that is to say citizens, who would be friends, who would be charitable and brotherly," he recommended to the Convention in his speech on public order. Although guilt by association was a common enough mode of the Terror, Saint-Just gave this theme a certain theoretical ground.

So for Saint-Just, it was one thing to make an error of judgment; it was another to knowingly support someone who was guilty of counter-revolutionary activity. Traces of Saint-Just's concept of friendship as a natural rapport appear in his public pronouncements during the height of the Terror. Addressing Danton directly (though he was not, as it happens, in the Convention at the time), Saint-Just remarks: "You are the friend of Fabre; you defended him; you are not man enough to implicate him; you were not then able to defend yourself in your complicity" (772). "Whoever is the friend of a man who negotiates with the court is guilty of laxity. The mind has its errors; the errors of conscience are crimes" (769). The factions are, for Saint-Just, antisocieties, groups of accomplices, friends in crime. Citizens may err, but other citizens will guide them to the truth and virtue. The factions err intentionally, against the public good. They will reject the opportunity for redemption. Note how Robespierre, for example, is able to denounce his friends when it is a matter of public good.[24] Note also how Saint-Just claims that the tyrant (Louis XVI) had no personal friends—supporters were interested only in preserving the crown (466). Of course, it would turn out that Saint-Just and Robespierre would not have enough friends on the ninth of Thermidor. Although Saint-Just never did get to complete his speech in defense of Robespierre, it is clear he was caught in the same predicament: he needed the support of those who could not in fact see through error to truth. "What language am I going to speak to you?" he planned to ask

23. See Patrice Rolland, "La signification politique de l'amitié chez Saint-Just," *Annales historiques de la Révolution française*, 1984, 327.
24. Robespierre, *Oeuvres*, 10: 414.

his colleagues at the Convention. "How to describe to you errors of which you have no idea?"(907). Saint-Just's insight into the nature of aberration and the essence of "nature" could be confirmed only in the fantastic future society he alone could envision. Lost in fantasies of Spartan social life, he was unable to locate that elusive identity he so vehemently protected with the negative machinery—discursive and otherwise—of terror. Yet however fragmentary or immature his response, the problems Saint-Just addressed were embedded in the political reality of the revolutionary beginning, of the very beginning of democracy.

CHAPTER 7

A Counter-Revolutionary Politics of Sin

The problem of a conservative politics opened up in the wake of revolutionary disruption is a particularly difficult one. The destruction of traditions and institutions denies any practical idea of conservation; the idea of tradition has to be reinvented to accommodate the creation of new forms, which nonetheless constitute a restoration of an underlying identity. The counter-revolutionary theory of politics (at least in its more sophisticated forms), when seen from this vantage point, was in many ways concerned with exactly the same issues that confronted the revolutionaries. The question of practice and the relationship between order and an origin that was no longer clearly present was a shared concern. Each movement introduced its own recuperative force of order. The theological dimension of counter-revolutionary political thought was not, then, simply a retreat from reality.[1] Both counter-revolutionary and revolutionary thought had to reconcile the reality of disorder with a faith in the possibility of order, an order legitimized by the genuine original foundations of the community.

The Enlightenment structure of error intervenes at precisely this point. The errant fragment of the revolutionary citizen was to be overcome through spiritual or political discipline. For theocratic writers of the right, social and political errors would be transcended through a political theology, and yet these writers did not avoid the difficult problem of discovering and maintaining order in the very heart of disorder and un-

1. As George Boas, for example, implies, writing dismissively that both Maistre and Bonald "[shrink] from the temporal into the eternal, from the mutable into the unchanging": *French Philosophies of the Romantic Period* (Baltimore, 1925), 85.

certainty. Theology (mediated through politics) was not, in other words, a ready-made answer to the problem of social and political fragmentation. The question of authority and the possibility of error continued to be basic difficulties for any social order.

It has been argued that the theocratic counter-revolutionary thinkers in effect rejected any idea of political legitimacy, and sought out instead ways to establish order on a model of obedience. They elaborated a dictatorial system of political authority, emphasizing not the rational grounds of legitimacy but instead the urgent need for intervention.[2] This theocratic idea was, however, rather more complex than it appears. The very need for decisive intervention was bound up with an interpretation of human society that recognized the inevitable and fundamentally irreconcilable individual differences that animated any situated human community. For writers like Joseph de Maistre and Louis de Bonald, this radical differentiation would be framed not by some idealized national identity, as it was in the Revolution, but instead by the foundational unity of the divine. Difference, transgression, error—these were all manifestations of humanity's essential separation from the perfection of divine order; the manifestation, that is, of human sin, at the individual and social level. Political authority was, in this context, less the imposition of an arbitrary religious order on society than a way of preserving an inevitably imperfect social order so that the historical movement *toward* a new and better condition might take place. The political theology of the counter-revolution was a politics structured by human errancy, the endlessly repeated wanderings from the straight path of God's will.

TRUTH'S ABERRANT TRANSLATIONS

As we have seen, the problem of error in the late eighteenth century was often directly related to the dialectic of unity and difference in the world. Error revealed a disruption of unitary identity, and was understood to be a condition of the concrete appearance of that transcendent reality. This link between an epistemology of error and an ontology of aberration persists in the counter-revolutionary tradition. As Louis de Bonald, for example, once explained, error is like a curve that deviates from the perfect linearity of an infinitely straight line. For Bonald, error is the disruption of a perfect form, a local aberration from something defined in its generality as inherently unified and self-identical. "Every

2. See Massimo Boffa, "Maistre," in *A Critical Dictionary of the French Revolution*, ed. François Furet and Mona Ozouf, trans. Arthur Goldhammer (Cambridge, Mass., 1989), 970.

time we deal with the general, truth is absolute, since absolute and general are synonyms. [Truth] is relative only when we are dealing with the *particular*."[3] It is not clear exactly what a "relative" truth is for Bonald. What he does say is that the application of general and absolute truths to the material world *demands* a certain deviation from the strict formality of the abstract rule. The relative truth is really a kind of error. Although in the abstract, Bonald explains, we can assume that lines, for example, are straight, surfaces flat, bodies absolutely hard, and so on, once something *concrete* and hence unique comes into play, this idealistic mathematical model must be adapted, it must be transformed if it is going to describe something real. The exact scientist may well manipulate abstractions in their purity, says Bonald, but the artist, who works with the particular, "is forced to take account of the deviations of lines, the roughness of surfaces," in short, the manifold irregularities of the material world. The important point is that these imperfections inherent in the concrete do not necessarily invalidate the abstract truths; they are the inevitable results of a fundamental disjuncture between absolute and particular that can never be effaced. The error, in other words, does not so much contradict the truth as mark a translation of truth into the world. Errors are the "local and particular" deviations from "universal" truths, which could never, of course, be located anywhere in particular.[4]

This basic structure, the aberrant relation between the universal and the particular, also lies at the heart of Bonald's conception of human identity. Principles, Bonald writes, are of an absolute good [*bonté*]. "Application and practice are imperfect, or are good only as a goodness relative to men, to specific moments and circumstances." As Bonald explains, this relational structure follows from the human relationship with the divine. "All principles, even those of the physical sciences, are first truths, essential [and] fundamental: they are from God or in God, the essential order, *supreme reason of all things*, as Leibniz says, and they are necessarily perfect, like their author and the source from which they emanate. Application is from man, and is imperfect like him." Bonald gives us this example: Even the best human attempts to construct an accurate measuring device—a ruler, for instance—made out of a material such as copper or wood, always reveal an essential flaw, manifested in *défectuosités* and countless curved deviations, most of them beyond our observational limits.[5] Human sinfulness, we might say, is explained here

3. Louis de Bonald, *Législation primitive considérée dans les derniers temps par les lumières de la raison*, in *Oeuvres complètes de de Bonald*, 3 vols. (Paris, n.d.), 1: 1052.

4. Bonald, *Recherches philosophiques*, in *Oeuvres complètes*, 3: 58, 394.

5. Bonald, *Considérations philosophiques sur les principes et leur application* (1819), in *Oeuvres complètes*, 3: 453–55.

analogically as the wandering of error, a concrete aberration. We are not even capable of defining our own aberrations, since any measure we construct will be subject to radical error.

Crucial here is the idea that neither the errors of the material world nor the irregularities of our human existence on earth ever invalidate the truths that define them as aberrations—just the opposite. And so Bonald, in this text, was seeking not so much to correct the aberration as to maintain its connection with legitimacy. What is clear is that error is intimately related to truth, error marks an imperfect *application* of truth, something that exists in perfect, absolute clarity only in God. Reflecting on the errancy of human knowledge, Bonald wrote:

> We say *the errors* of Aristotle, of Luther, of J.-J. Rousseau, the errors of a century. Why can we not say *the truths* of Plato, of Leibniz, of St. Augustine, the truths of a century, as we say the truths of the Gospel? Error is from man, and truth is from God: the one is invented, the other discovered.[6]

What most people call "error" is in fact "incomplete truth." Our thoughts are "true [*vraies*]," but they are often misdirected and misapplied. Reworking a theme popular in eighteenth-century psychology, Bonald argues that error is mistaken judgment, not a true negation. But Bonald's understanding of a mistake is very particular: it transforms a truth that the merely human organs of thought and sensation cannot fully comprehend.[7] The error of judgment is a deviant version of something already existing. The key concept for Bonald is application. The concrete act of knowledge is not merely crooked, it *makes* the straight crooked, the human action wanders by *leaving* the straight path. Error, for Bonald, is not so much the difference between truth and the concrete world as an imperfect image of truth in the limited sphere of human existence. More clearly, he declares that "errors are only disfigured truths [*vérités défigurées*]."[8]

Within the theological framework of writers such as Bonald, there was no absolute division between the divine realm and human reason. The link between error and truth was an intimate one. Humanity was not "erring" in a space cut off from divine truth; the human mind can, as Joseph de Maistre wrote, only "ignore the truth or abuse it."[9] What is

6. Bonald, *Pensées sur divers sujets*, in *Oeuvres complètes*, 3: 1358.

7. Bonald, *Législation primitive*, 1112, 1159.

8. Bonald, *Démonstration philosophique du principe constitutif de la société*, in *Oeuvres complètes*, 1: 95.

9. Joseph de Maistre, *Eclaircissement sur les sacrifices*, in *Les soirées de Saint-Petersbourg, ou Entretiens sur le gouvernement temporel de la Providence, suivies d'un traité sur les sacrifices*, 2 vols. (Paris, [1888]), 2: 279.

clearly worked out in Maistre's political and religious writing and Bonald's social theory is the precise nature of this relation between truth and error, the dual presence of rule and aberration in the human world. If humanity itself is radically imperfect, an abuse of truth, or at least a disfigured image of divine perfection, how can we ever recognize the truth, how can we participate in its powers when by definition it is impossible to know it in its entirety?

Maistre, in one of his last works, published only after his death, said: "Original sin, which explains everything, and without which we do not explain anything, unfortunately recurs every moment of time." Man is always capable of prevarication, capable of committing a crime, always susceptible to error. Here Maistre introduces two critical theocratic concepts that will frame our discussion of counter-revolutionary thought: error and repetition. Humanity is involved in a constant process of transformation, a process that continually produces errancy. At the same time, human minds, unlike the minds of beasts, have some awareness of their degraded condition. This "sentiment is at the same time the proof of his greatness and his misery."[10] The political theology of the counter-revolution centers on this dualism, humanity's existence not so much in error as on the boundary between error and truth.

Seen from this perspective, the political action advocated by theocratic writers like Maistre can be understood as the task of reintroducing order into crisis, but with the awareness that human knowledge was always threatened by the limitations of the human spirit. Although figures such as Bonald and Maistre are quite often dismissed as reactionary thinkers willing only to maintain outdated traditions and institutions, it is more accurate to say that their idea of "restoration" involved integrating new *forms* of order that would preserve a certain hidden continuity obscured by revolutionary fantasy. They realized that "traditions would not persuade and thus they must discover new truths which would make possible the reestablishment of order, hierarchy, and authority."[11] Their aim was not a return to some idealized past order of things.[12] They sought a return to the proper course of history, the *restoration* of a course that was perhaps always errant, a series of steps that were painful and violent, but that might ultimately lead to a better future. They were not simply denying the revolutionary ideals of popular sovereignty, of a democratic social and political order. Nor were they simply clothing a starkly decisionist concept of authority in the mysteri-

10. Maistre, *Soirées de Saint-Petersbourg*, 1: 58, 63.
11. Albert Salomon, *The Tyranny of Progress: Reflections on the Origins of Sociology* (New York, 1955), 38.
12. See Guido de Ruggiero, *The History of European Liberalism*, trans. R.G. Collingwood (Oxford, 1927), 89.

ous shrouds of religious faith. These counter-revolutionary thinkers began with the assumption of human weakness, the constant tendency to error, and constructed a political system that would accommodate both the reality of aberration and the promise of redemption implied in the very recognition of weakness.

According to counter-revolutionary theory, the crisis facing French society in the aftermath of revolutionary disruption, a crisis affecting societies throughout Europe, could not be resolved by simply restoring the institutions destroyed by the Revolution. The decay of social and political order had led to this disaster, according to this tradition of thought, so the Revolution had in effect produced a sort of purification. The ideal of restoration, then, would be the reintroduction of order in a radically new form, a form that would *refound* the original spirit of the nation, before its infection. But this origin was problematic. There was in fact no one golden age of society that would serve as a model, however much these writers looked to the past for their inspiration and specific examples. Yet in the absence of any legitimating origin, order never became a question of mere human utility. The restoration of order was, in this counter-revolutionary discourse, framed in relation to an origin, but it was an origin defined by its inaccessibility.

ORIGIN AND DIFFERENCE IN MAISTRE

In some reflections on the nature of the "origin" in human life, Maistre carefully avoided two extreme answers to the question of existence. The diversity and incompatibility of world cultures, languages, political systems, religions, and so on could lead to the conclusion that all these aspects of human life were simply constructions, arbitrary conventions whose forms depended on contingent circumstances and historical developments. In other words, society was an agreement maintained through traditional practices. If this contractual approach was taken, it seems as if one must either accept that each system was equally legitimate in its own particular context or, alternatively, believe that some universal and rational system applicable to all humanity ought to be found to replace what were in fact outdated prejudices. Maistre rejected both pluralism and Enlightenment universalism, as he saw it, in favor of an analysis of origin itself that would focus on the conceptual difficulty of tracing back any form of organization to some perfect starting point. Maistre showed, in other words, how the very notion of origin was contaminated by the reality of change and development.

Maistre highlighted a paradox: How could we ever penetrate the origin of something that could never come into being unless we assumed its very existence in the first place? Discussing language, for example, Maistre points out that it must appear in the world as an "explosion" since it is impossible that humanity could pass, in some gradual way, from a state of total aphony to speech. There was an absolute discontinuity that defied analysis. "Languages could not be invented either by a single man, who would not have been able to enforce obedience, or by many men, who would not have been able to agree among themselves."[13] Maistre therefore rejects the fashionable idea that we could somehow trace the origin of language through so-called primitive languages. A particular tongue arrives in the world, he writes, only when a society "is in full possession of language." The primitive language is not closer to some mythical origin; it is in fact more likely to be a disgraced language that has fallen from a state of perfect wholeness.[14] "Speech is as essential to man as flight is to the bird," Maistre wrote, but the variations of particular languages precluded any single origin.[15] Language (as a faculty) is the origin of languages: it comes before the various forms but in itself cannot be rediscovered in its general purity. This lost origin, language, can be sought only within its particular (and hence *disfigured*) forms of existence. The origin is an absolute appearance, but the very fact of appearance in a concrete form obscures the nature of the origin.

According to Maistre, an obsession with development constitutes one of the main errors of modern philosophy, which always avoided the true problem of origin by focusing attention on a series of secondary causes instead of confronting the fundamental causes that defied any logical or empirical analysis. Basic principles, Maistre once suggested, can themselves never be explained with recourse to the concrete application of those principles, those worldly *forms* that are the products of more fundamental realities. "In effect, the essence of principles is that they are anterior, evident, nonderived, undemonstrable, and *causes* in relation to the conclusion, otherwise they would need to be demonstrated themselves, that is to say, they would cease to be principles."[16] The genuine origin—whether logical or historical—must stand outside of the system it produces, and therefore this origin is always occluded.

This structure is crucial to an understanding of Maistre's political ideas. The origin of society, he maintains, is as obscure as the origin of

---

13. Maistre, *Examen d'un écrit de J.-J. Rousseau,* in *Oeuvres complètes,* 14 vols. (Lyon, 1884–86), 7: 554. Cf. Bonald, *Législation primitive,* 1068.

14. Maistre, *Soirées de Saint-Petersbourg,* 95, 101–2.

15. Maistre, *Examen d'un écrit,* 555.

16. Maistre, *Soirées de Saint-Petersbourg,* 323.

humanity itself. The idea of a compact emerging from a collection of isolated beings is intrinsically paradoxical. Any deliberation concerning the origin of a society assumes from the start a preexisting sociability among the people involved, and if it were to be argued that one single person created a society, it is impossible, Maistre holds, to imagine anyone with enough power and authority to forge cooperation among individuals who had no common language, no common interests that would have already united them into a group. The origin of society is not a passage that humanity could have gone through gradually at some distant part of its past. The presocial, for Maistre, is like a prebirth in that there is no link of continuity between the anterior conditions and the subsequent development. Society is an organization humanity receives from outside the boundaries of its own being, from the divine source of all existence. Society is, Maistre believed, "the immediate result of the will of the Creator," "the direct work of nature, or, to say it better, of its author."[17] The point here is that the analysis of various particular societies will not lead us to this origin: different communities and nations are forms of something that arises within the universality of humanity itself. Therefore, Maistre says, primitive cultures, like primitive languages, are not at all closer to this origin, and in fact, they may actually be further from it, as a result of some prevarication in their history.

At any rate, Maistre wants to say that the foundational principles of social order cannot be found in the early stages of its development. Maistre seems to have reached an impasse, for if there is no true origin that could legitimize contemporary order, what exactly does provide the necessary foundation for it? Of course, one eighteenth-century approach, which culminated in the Declaration of the Rights of Man in the Revolution, tried to look beyond local differences to locate the true identity of humanity, its universal character, so that particular forms of social organization could be reformed and corrected according to this measure of aberration. For Maistre, this "enlightened" approach was seriously mistaken. Humanity simply does not exist as a tangible unity, he claimed: "There is no such thing as *man* in the world. I have seen," he wrote, "Frenchmen, Italians, Russians in my life; I even know, thanks to Montesquieu, *that one can be Persian*. But as to *man*, I declare that I have not met one in my life; if he exists, he is unknown to me."[18] This might seem to lead to the idea that political and social organization is simply a function of local circumstance, and legitimacy only a matter of success,

17. Maistre, *Etude sur la souveraineté*, in *Oeuvres complètes*, 1: 317, 324.
18. Maistre, *Oeuvres*, vol. 1: *Considérations sur la France* (1797), ed. Jean-Louis Darcel (Geneva, 1980), 123–24.

measured by the duration of order.[19] For Maistre, however, the radical fragmentation of the human world was not evidence that all social forms were essentially arbitrary and unconnected with one another.

Maistre had noted that all human beings have languages, and that these different languages can be learned and translated. However, there is no one pure human language that would be the perfect and uniquely sufficient expression of the abstract potential for speech. Language has to appear in some particular form, as a *langue*. Each of these tongues has its specific rules, rules inapplicable to others, and yet they are all fundamentally related to this inaccessible originary power. There was, Maistre would imply, an analogous relationship in the social and political forms of life. There was no universal constitution applicable to all peoples, Maistre always argued, but this did not mean that there was no continuity between constitutions. There was a humanity, but it could not appear in any one place. Maistre defined even the basic idea of national identity not in positive terms but as a result of a fracture: to constitute a nation, he says, is to define it in opposition to all the others.[20] The task of politics was of course bound to these contingent differences, but it was not limited by them: the political act also had to relate to the divine origin of all things. All human life was interdependent, whatever the fractured nature of actual existence. The various structures of human order were incompatible taken in their concrete form,[21] but they all looked to a higher authority that gave them value. The goal was to reestablish the order constantly threatened by the contingent and transient nature of human existence in history. Successive forms of social order could not be stripped of their contingency, Maistre implied, but there was a danger of losing sight of the universal value inherent in any order. As Bonald wrote, "truth is, like man and like society, a seed [*germe*] that unfolds in the succession of time and of men, always old [*ancienne*] at its beginning, always new in its successive developments."[22] This complex interaction of the ancient and the new, of truth and error, the absolute and the relative, structured human society, and this process demanded a certain form of political authority.

19. Maistre does seem to suggest a kind of political pragmatism in this passage of the *Considérations sur la France:* "What is a constitution? Is it not the solution to the following problem? Given *the population, customs, religion, geographical location, political relations, wealth, good and bad qualities of a certain nation, find the laws that suit them*" (124).

20. Maistre, *Essai sur le principe générateur des constitutions politiques et des autres institutions humaines* (1809), ed. Robert Triomphe (Paris, 1959), XLVII, 83.

21. See ibid., XLVIII, on the impossibility of transplanting the Olympic games into a French context, and LIX, on the "degeneracy" of borrowing foreign words.

22. Bonald, *Législation primitive*, 1199–1200.

As Maistre explained in a key text on constitutions and other human institutions, politics should not be formulated on the basis of human activity alone, but neither should it be understood as the unmediated transcendent imposition of some sacred power. Political activity, Maistre suggested, operated in the space between God and man. The relation between God and humanity was a relation between the universal and the particular. "God calls himself: *I am;* and every creature calls itself: *I am this.*"[23] God is unnamable, in that he encompasses everything: "I AM WHAT I AM."[24] The individual human can be only one thing; his name is relative to his limited action. He is always concrete and particular, and thus is always imperfect, impure in the sense that he never reaches the perfect unity associated with the divine principle of creation. This is in fact what lies behind the fundamental fragmentation of the human world: everything historical is the local and therefore slightly defective appearance of the universal, which exists outside of all space and time while incorporating it entirely. What is unique in human beings, Maistre repeatedly pointed out, is an awareness of imperfection, an awareness that points to some kind of prior knowledge of perfection.

Human existence is, therefore, not simply transient but *errant.* Human history represents a fall into a successive, earthly life, from one characterized by special intimacy with the divine. Stripped of its specific narrative content, this image represents an important structural dimension of theological political theory such as Maistre's. The conservative approach does not resurrect some past perfection, because this state has been lost. Politics must seek out the path to the truth of our existence, and the fact that this path has been lost means that humanity always faces the danger of lapsing completely into a transient, corporal life. Here, deaf to the spiritual voice, humanity can pretend to control life, yet it is this tendency that, according to Maistre, can lead to inevitable disaster. "Distracted by his vain sciences from the only one that truly interests him, he believed that he had the power to *create,* although he has not even that of *naming.*"[25] The distinction here between creating and naming is crucial. Maistre denies that man has any real creative power. He also denies the power to name, which is a more puzzling accusation. However, this idea of the name informs the political theory Maistre develops. The explanation of the name and its relation to human language and divine creation is located in Genesis.

23. Maistre, *Essai,* L, 86.
24. Exod. 3:14. Citations from the Bible in this chapter are from *The New Oxford Annotated Bible, with the Apocrypha,* ed. Bruce M. Metzger and Roland E. Murphy (New York, 1991).
25. Maistre, *Essai,* XLVII, 82.

For God, the linguistic form and pure creative energy are perfectly congruent, expressed together in the verb. As God names, he creates. In Genesis this process is represented by the narrative structure "Let there be . . ." God "has *named* everything because he has created everything."[26] At the moment when God creates the human being in his own image, there arises a special relationship between humanity and the rest of creation. Man participates in Creation by naming the beasts, which God brings to Adam in order to see what he calls them.[27] "He did not wish to subject him to language, but in man God set language, which had served *Him* as medium of creation, free."[28] The purity of this "creative" knowledge of the world is altered after the Fall; once God is disobeyed, no longer can humanity freely participate in the Creation. The Fall, it might be said, introduces the *human* word. The knowledge of good and evil is not *new* knowledge, for nothing is evil in the Creation: "God saw everything he had made, and indeed, it was very good."[29] The knowledge gained by eating from the tree is in a sense the awareness of self, the introduction of vanity into consciousness. Adam and Eve now see themselves as naked, and are ashamed.

The "evil" is, as Walter Benjamin has suggested, nameless; it does not designate a space of reality but separates humanity from its real relation with divine creation. Evil is not an actual force, physical or spiritual; it is the term for disruption, a way of describing the disharmony introduced by the freedom to deviate and wander from the created order that is God's universe. Evil appears when things are out of true, when error has been committed.[30] Language is no longer an intimate collaboration with the divine but rather a means of communication among human individuals which operates outside itself, with material forms. With the introduction of the human word, the plurality of languages becomes possible, since in communicating something other than itself, the word is now somewhat arbitrary, it has become a sign of something, not the actual medium of expression as it is in the divine word. Humanity approaches the original ideal of naming only by assigning the proper name, which is not at all representative, but seeks the true nature of the individual by describing its relation with God.

This is the structural point where Maistre tries to reestablish an au-

---

26. Ibid., L, 87.

27. Gen. 2:19.

28. For this reading of Genesis, which accords well with the theocratic doctrine of the name, see Walter Benjamin, "On Language as Such and on the Language of Man," trans. Edmund Jephcott, in *One-Way Street and Other Writings* (London, 1979), 115.

29. Gen. 1:31.

30. Maistre, *Considérations sur la France*, 95.

thentic order in a corrupted and diverse world. We can overcome our limitations if we abandon the conceit of invention and seek the authentic, which is named in accordance with its true place in the order of things. The name is the path to a truth no longer fully present to a fallen humanity. The "first chapter" of metaphysics, writes Maistre, is "that of NAMES."[31] Error is invented, truth discovered: so a purely human invention will never establish a solid institution. The name expresses the true relation between human works and the divine: if the sign is by nature arbitrary, the name is "not at all arbitrary." The name is the medium of communication with God. "Man in harmony with his Creator is sublime, and his action creative." Left to itself, humanity can produce nothing of real value. This marks the limit of human action; it also marks a difficult and almost paradoxical predicament. For humanity, the origin is necessarily a mystery, and so order is not a matter of articulating or representing fundamental principles visible there. Separated from an origin it cannot retrace, the human mind must seek to regain a lost state. Alone, humanity cannot produce this truth. *"Man has not, or has no longer, the right to name things."* The name, Maistre suggests here, must germinate. Humanity must work through the humble means of the human word back to the divine; through disciplined activity, man can regain this relationship with the divine: "If he has worked legitimately, the vulgar name of the thing will be ennobled by it and will become great."[32] This legitimacy must be clarified—there is no evident foundation that would point us in the proper direction.

Maistre approaches the difficulty with the idea that we can sense the truth when it is awakened by a threat. We often find in Maistre's work the idea of resistance. The truth may never appear to us unproblematically, he maintains, yet attacks against it reveal an order that we feel must be defended.[33] This same structure arises in Rousseau's discussion of the general will, which can be felt only when it appears in opposition to individual wills. The universal, whether sacred or secular, must reveal itself in concrete local circumstances. The difficulty is trying to work through the variant incarnations of this universal source in order to regain the purity of the origin. Maistre believed that this continuing identity could be ascertained in some form, even if it could not be revealed in its original purity: "Every belief enduringly universal is true; and whenever certain articles particular to different nations are sepa-

---

31. Maistre, *Du Pape* (1819), ed. Jacques Lovie (Geneva, 1966), 318.

32. Maistre, *Essai*, L, 86, LIII, 91.

33. On resistance as a key concept in the structure of political authority, see Julien Freund, *L'essence du politique* (Paris, 1965), 709.

rated from any belief, and there remains something common to all, this remainder is true."[34] In practice, however, this process of abstraction was incredibly difficult. Maistre's political thought was therefore resolutely practical, intensely concerned with the immediacy of political action. In a situation of crisis, some way had to be found to extract the universal truth from all its local variations, all its particular aberrations.

For Maistre, it was crucial to recognize that the articulated dimensions of the social order, manifested in laws, institutions, customs, are not somehow *representative* of this higher order, but signs of its vulnerability in the world. If humanity were perfect, there would be no constitution, written or unwritten; in fact, no nation would even need a government. Government arrives in society to preserve order, and various laws come into existence to protect this order against dangerous attacks. This is the role of human action: it does not create or impose order in society, it strives to *protect* order. The difficulty, as Maistre will describe, is that human action is inherently imperfect, it always tends to stray from the proper path. In other words, Maistre was emphasizing how an imperfect human will is at once exactly what threatens order and the only possible means for restoring order. It was not always easy to transcend this imperfection, Maistre pointed out, even in defense of a divinely inspired truth.

ABERRATION AND ORDER

Maistre's famous text on the French Revolution, the *Considerations on France*, opens with a stark portrait of human imperfection:

> In the works of man, everything is feeble [*pauvre*] like its author; views are restricted, means rigid, motives [*ressorts*] inflexible, movements painful, and results monotonous. In divine works, the riches of infinity appear openly in the least part; its power is exercised without effort [*en se jouant*]; everything is supple in its hands, nothing resists it: even obstacles are a means for it, and the irregularities produced by the operation of its free agents come to arrange themselves in the general order.[35]

In this passage Maistre seems to be saying that human action is, historically speaking, completely blind, totally random, redeeming itself only in some mysterious integration within the great providential course designed by a higher intelligence. Yet Maistre links the irregularities of human action with the divine plan. This is not to say that human error

34. Maistre, *Essai*, xxx, 58n.
35. Maistre, *Considérations sur la France*, 63.

will be fitted into some grand design, like the pieces of a puzzle we will never see in its complexity. What Maistre alludes to here is the idea that human error is in fact a distorted version of this grand truth, linked to both the corporeal conditions of the individual and the purity of divine principles. Although it is true that as concrete historical beings we never will see the complete picture, we participate in that reality even through our wanderings.

But Maistre does not think that we are completely blind to the divine plan—again our awareness of error indicates the crossing of that border between individual human nature and divine truth. Inspiration, in other words, is a possibility. "It is pleasurable," writes Maistre, "to have a presentiment of the plans of the Divinity amid general upheaval. We will never see the totality during our voyage, and often we will be mistaken, but in all possible sciences, except the exact sciences, are we not reduced to conjecture?"[36] This conjecture is possible (if not always accurate) only because whatever the errant tendencies of the human species, all beings are "linked to the throne of the Supreme Being by a supple chain, which restrains us without enslaving us." The attempt to transcend the wandering course is an attempt to follow this chain to its source, and this is the basis of authentic action for Maistre. The distinction is not that between pure truth and pure error; to be human means always to be in error in some sense, but humanity can potentially lose sight of the truth and descend into total anarchy. A higher order might manifest itself in the "irregularities" of history, without ever eradicating this errant tendency, but if humanity lost its way completely, complete disorder, total violence, and not simply irregularity, would be the result.[37]

Maistre looked, then, beyond historical and social variations to find some kind of inner continuity. For the most part, Maistre was confident that this continuity would be recognized by anyone prepared to see it.

> Let us not at all confuse the essences of things with their modifications: the first are unalterable and always reemerge; the second change and vary the spectacle a bit, or at least for the crowd, since every experienced eye easily penetrates the changing cloak with which eternal nature is clothed according to time and place.[38]

The task, according to this conservative view, was to identify the lasting elements of social and political order, to penetrate the spirit or force of a

36. Ibid., 95.
37. See Bonald, *Législation primitive,* 1197.
38. Maistre, *Considérations sur la France,* 98.

nation's vitality instead of being overwhelmed by the merely contingent forms taken on at any particular time. Bonald would write that these variations are always only temporary. "Truth, though forgotten by men, is never new; it is from the beginning, *ab initio*. . . . Error is always a novelty in the world."[39]

This is why writers like Maistre and Bonald looked to tradition as a source for truth. "For Bonald," wrote Carl Schmitt, "tradition offered the sole possibility of gaining the content that man was capable of accepting metaphysically, because the intellect of the individual was considered too weak and wretched to be able to recognize truth by itself."[40] As Maistre put it: "Human passions may well tarnish, even falsify [*dénaturer*] original creations; if the principle is divine, that is enough to give them an amazing duration."[41] For Maistre, the key problem was not so much some kind of mystical attempt to gain the truth for all time. Although Maistre was throughout his life very interested in the illuminist traditions,[42] he never attempted to structure political action on the "revealed" truths of the mystic traditions. Maistre believed that the greatest dangers lay in the revolutionary idea that humanity could construct its own political institutions. "He believed, he who has not even the power to produce an insect or a tuft of moss, that he was the direct author of sovereignty, the most important, holy, and fundamental aspect of the moral and political world."[43]

For Maistre, then, politics was not about instituting, or even "restoring," a perfected human social order, but instead about acting as a force of order in an eternally imperfect and dissonant condition. Order would not flow automatically from some fundamental constitutional organization; it could result only from repeated interventional activity. This recognition of fundamental conflict, and not some simplistic rejection of democratic values, informs Maistre's claim that the fundamental national laws establishing the highest political authority could never be based on some kind of universal agreement. "The essence of a funda-

39. Bonald, *Pensées sur divers sujets*, 1349–50. Bonald makes reference to Ecclesiastes here, but the book reference (24:14) is inaccurate. However, cf. Eccl. 3:14–15. "I know that whatever God does endures forever; nothing can be added to it, nor anything taken away from it. . . . That which is, already has been; that which is to be, already is; and God seeks what has gone by."

40. Carl Schmitt, *Political Theology: Four Chapters on the Concept of Sovereignty* (1922), rev. ed., trans. George Schwab (Cambridge, Mass., 1985), 54.

41. Maistre, *Considérations sur la France*, 111.

42. See Emile Dermenghem, *Joseph de Maistre mystique* (Paris, 1923), and Maistre, *Ecrits maçonniques de Joseph de Maistre et de quelques-uns de ses amis franc-maçons*, ed. Jean Rebotton (Geneva, 1983).

43. Maistre, *Essai*, XLVII, 82.

mental law," wrote Maistre, "is that no one has the right to abolish it: for how could it be above *all* if *someone* had made it? Popular agreement is impossible, and were it otherwise, an accord is not at all a law, and does not obligate anyone, unless there is a higher authority that guarantees it."[44] The freedom of human agents means that some *consent* to the law is always necessary, since it is possible that even the most sacrosanct law might be rejected (as even Genesis recounts). Consent, however, can never *produce* anything but a temporary agreement no more stable than the transient interests of those who participate in it.[45] Genuine law does not arise from these ephemeral circumstances, Maistre would explain; authentic law stands above the individuals in any one epoch, though it must be transformed in the light of ever-changing circumstances.

So for Maistre, authority has to come *before* the law. Written law is the merely human articulation of an established force, and in fact the particularization of its power in codified expression can only weaken it. Consequently, Maistre does not confine the law to any fixed, eternal principles that could be enshrined in some tangible constitution—even a theocratic one. Sovereignty, he makes clear, is not the representative of some defined order: it is an active force that *establishes* order in any time of crisis. Government does not "represent" the people. As Maistre succinctly puts it: "Since man is sinful [*mauvais*], it is necessary that he be *governed*." It is the disorder of multiple wills that must be decided by a "superior power." Without this force, society would be a constant battle for supremacy.[46] "Man, with his quality of being at once moral and corrupt, just in his intelligence, and perverse in his will, must necessarily be governed; otherwise he would be at once sociable and unsociable, and society would be both necessary and impossible."[47] Unity is essential to this force. As Maistre explains, the more locations for this force to be expended, the more likely that it will be turned in contradictory directions. Expressed through merely human organs, the power of the sovereign is subject to their imperfections. As Bonald once commented, "the particular will of any man is necessarily depraved and destructive."[48]

Never fully expressed at any one time in a completely adequate fashion, this sovereign force must always be free to intervene in any new or uncertain situation. This is why the written laws and constitutions gen-

---

44. Ibid., II, 16.

45. Maistre, *Etude sur la souveraineté*, 312.

46. Maistre, *Examen d'un écrit*, VII, 563. See as well Maistre, *Du Pape*: "Man must be governed precisely as he must be judged, and for the same reason: that is, because wherever there is no *sentence*, there is *combat*" (129).

47. Maistre, *Du Pape*, 128.

48. Bonald, *Théorie du pouvoir*, in *Oeuvres complètes*, 1: 182.

erated by any individual community can never be the genuine foundation of the true supreme authority in politics. As Sieyes pointed out early
in the Revolution, the exceptional case opens up the need for a reaffir-
mation of sovereignty. Maistre described the problem this way:

> It is not within the power of man to create a law that has no need of any ex-
> ception. This impossibility stems equally both from the human inability to
> foresee everything and from the nature of things, where some things vary to
> the point of leaving the circle of law by their own motion, and others,
> arranged by insensible gradations, under common genres, cannot be
> grasped by a general name without being false in its nuances.
>   This results in the necessity, in all legislation, of an exempting authority
> [*puissance dispensante*].[49]

When it is said that "nothing is missing, all is foreseen, everything is
written," then it must be that the laws are worthless, Maistre writes.[50]
The effective government is one that can deal with exceptional and critical situations with the least interference. The tradition that is so important to writers like Bonald and Maistre is not the accumulated productions of human history but the eternal spirit, which has always
transcended them. As Maistre declares:

> Another very deadly error is to be too rigidly attached to old monuments. It
> is no doubt necessary to respect them, but it is above all necessary to con-
> sider what jurists call *the last state*. Every free constitution is by nature flexi-
> ble [*variable*], and flexible in proportion to its freedom.[51]

Clearly, the legitimacy of the deciding authority relates less to the specific codes of law than to the authorizing force itself, and the competence
of those who exercise this force. The appearance of the critical situation
demands action, and this action cannot be circumscribed ahead of time.
Indeed, even the determination of what constitutes a "critical" situation
cannot be defined in writing. The true decisive power is an "admirable,
unique, infallible public spirit, above all praise."[52]
    Genuine political action essentially manifests this unique spirit of the
nation. This is a notoriously evasive entity: limited by no one location, it
could appear, potentially, anywhere in the nation. This difficulty
emerged most clearly in the Revolution, but it is omnipresent in any po-

49. Maistre, *Du Pape*, 134–35.
50. Maistre, *Essai*, xxvi, 53.
51. Maistre, *Considérations sur la France*, 142.
52. Maistre, *Essai*, v–vii, 20–22.

litical system that denies a representative model of political action. The political actor, according to Maistre, must participate in this legitimizing force—he is not merely representing various interests or beliefs lurking among the citizenry. In other words, the politician is reaching for the source of all order in his efforts to establish a specific political order: he is searching for some kind of divine inspiration, Maistre suggests.

> Every time a man puts himself, following his own strengths, in harmony with the Creator, and produces any institution whatsoever in the name of the Divinity, then no matter what his individual weakness, his ignorance, his poverty, the obscurity of his birth, in a word, his absolute lack of human means, he participates in some manner in the Almighty, of which he has made himself an instrument.[53]

Authentic action is instrumental action. The structure here is very similar to revolutionary models, if one substitutes "nation" for Maistre's divine creator.

Maistre, however, much like the early revolutionaries, thought that the essentially elusive character of sovereign force could be contained by a formal institutional space. In this way, the appearance of sovereignty could be limited and controlled, even if its particular actions were not. Maistre unites, in a way, the early revolutionary concept of institutional stability with the idea of inspirational decision making. Maistre criticizes the republican political space on these grounds. The diffusion of power would lead to weakness and inevitable conflict. Again, it was not a blind faith in absolutist tradition that led Maistre to the idea of monarchical power. Rather, Maistre knew that in conditions of crisis the decisive force of the sovereign had to be expressed in one unique location. The boundaries of an institutional structure would provide the only measure of limitation.

In a monarchical system of government, Maistre saw, the uniqueness of the sovereign force is exercised through one leader. But it does not follow, he said, that distributing this force among many citizens, as in a republic, would allow everyone to participate equally in the divine energy that is the essence of sovereignty. In fact, just the opposite occurs in a republic, Maistre observes. In a monarchy, sovereignty "possesses enough brilliancy [*éclat*] to transmit [*communiquer*] a part of it, with necessary gradations, to a host of agents, which it distinguishes to a greater or lesser degree. In a republic, sovereignty is not tangible as it is in a monarchy: it has a purely mental existence, and its greatness is incommunica-

---

53. Maistre, *Considérations sur la France*, 112.

ble." In the republic, in other words, the force of sovereignty has no privileged location where it may appear with all its force, and thus its energy is never fully realized. And although everyone is theoretically entitled to express this sovereignty, Maistre points out that inevitably, only an elite few will ever really share that energy; "the imagination is staggered by the amazing number of sovereigns condemned to die without ever having reigned."[54] Furthermore, as Bonald noted, the fact that each citizen can, theoretically, exercise power means that there will always be competition for this privilege.[55]

This dissipation of sovereign energy could only weaken the power of any one of its individual agents. Each office in a republican government, then, has only a tenuous connection with national sovereignty. "Therefore it is the man who honors the office, it is not the office that honors the man: the latter does not shine as an *agent*, but as a *portion* of the sovereign." This is what constitutes, for Maistre, the difference between rank and power, the difference between increasing intimacy with the full light of monarchical sovereignty and the struggle for mere control of unstable republican institutions. In a republic, people understand the "deputy" to be just a small portion of the sovereign power, a "seven-hundred-and-fiftieth" part. The deputy who is respected "is not at all [respected] because he is *deputed* [i.e. delegated], but because he is respectable."[56] Of course, it is dangerous to rely on the respectability of individual representatives. If power, Bonald observed, is fractured, it eventually will cease to operate in any ordered way. Power must remain unified to be effective in conditions in which different interests have to be decided. This unity cannot be *represented*; the individual can act only as its agent or envoy for specific tasks.[57] Power cannot really be shared: it must remain one. It is not based on any principle that legitimizes its appearance, it simply *is*, and all definitions come after the fact.[58]

Clearly, the most important point Maistre wants to make concerns the basic structure of political institutions that allow for the best exercise of

---

54. Ibid., 102.

55. Bonald, *Théorie du pouvoir*, 986.

56. Maistre, *Considérations sur la France*, 166, 130–31. The true deputy, for Maistre, must be "deputed" by the legitimizing sovereign force: he is an envoy of this sovereignty, and shares in its brilliance. The English translation of this passage obscures this structure, by rendering *il est député* as "he is a deputy." The confusion is that the noun and the verb form (*député*) are the same in French, while the English verb form (deputed) is an archaic one. See *Considerations on France*, trans. Richard Lebrun (Montreal, 1974), 105.

57. Bonald, *Théorie du pouvoir*, 301, 150.

58. Bonald, "Du pouvoir: Réflexions politiques" (1839), in Bonald, *Réflexions sur la Révolution de juillet 1830, et autres inédits*, ed. Jean Bastier (Paris, 1988), 160.

sovereign power. As Maistre writes, it is impossible to construct a perfect order that will endure unchanged through history.

> If perfection were the natural accompaniment [*l'apanage*] of human nature, each legislator would speak only once; but, although all our works are imperfect, and since as political institutions become corrupted, the Sovereign must come to their aid with new laws, still, human legislation approaches the [divine] model by this intermittence of which I spoke earlier. . . . [T]he more it acts, the more its work is human, that is to say, fragile.[59]

An imperfect mediator must intervene only when necessary, so as not to risk introducing error. However, the human imperfection of even the celebrated foundational legislators means that the imperfect institutions of any nation will inevitably require modification and reform if they are to survive successive attacks, Maistre is saying. Nonetheless, an initial inspiration marks the true origin of any real institution or nation, and this originary brilliance will maintain national identity if it is cultivated and respected. God invests the legislator with "an extraordinary power," which allows him to "divine these hidden [*occultes*] forces and qualities that form the character of a nation, [and] the means to fertilize them, to put them into action and to draw from them the greatest resolution possible."[60] Throughout its history, the nation must always try to regain this inspiration.

It is at this point that the relationship between error and truth, difference and identity, becomes more apparent in the political sphere. Maistre's well-known critique of written constitutions and his dismissal of the idea that a nation can be properly formed through deliberation and discussion intersect with this basic difficulty. For Maistre, the codification and articulation of the constitution is both a result of human imperfection even at the origin of political order and a means to preserve some kind of order in the face of social dissonance. Writing, Maistre concludes, is a sign of weakness, or at least a sign of crisis. Fundamental principles exist before all written law, and in fact the most fundamental principle of all *must* remain unwritten if the constitution is to survive.[61] The history of a nation, then, is traced out in its constitutional framework. This history marks the various events with which the sovereign force has contended. As an example, Maistre offers the case of England: its constitution was never constructed a priori.

---

59. Maistre, *Considérations sur la France*, 125.
60. Maistre, *Etude sur la souveraineté*, 343–45.
61. Maistre, *Essai*, IX, 26.

The constitution is the work of circumstances, and the number of circumstances is infinite. Roman laws, ecclesiastical laws, feudal laws, Saxon, Norman, and Danish customs; the privileges, prejudices, and pretensions of all orders; wars, rebellions, revolutions, conquests, the Crusades; all the virtues, all the knowledge, all the errors, all the passions; all these elements, in conclusion, acting together and forming by their mixture and reciprocal action combinations multiplied by countless millions have in the end produced, after many centuries, the most complex unity and the finest balance of political powers ever seen in the world.[62]

Here is a central Maistrian image: the complex unity. Human order, at its best, is the complex interaction of divine power and concrete particularity, the intersection of universal unity and individual variation. As truth unfolds in the world, it meets with resistance, and the unity of a complex history lies in the continuity of the authentic force of order, a force that is expressed in many ways and by many organs.

Continuity, for Maistre, does not lie in the outward forms of political existence. What Maistre says is that the articulation of order, the promulgation of specific laws, and the elaboration of legal principles in writing are at best responses to the inevitable disruption introduced by disordering forces in the state. Maistre is of course drawing a parallel between political theory and the history of Christianity. As Maistre points out, Christ never codified the tenets of his thought, he never authored a foundational text that would provide a concrete guide for moral action. The New Testament, of course, was written after the death of the lawgiver, and even this text does not contain an imperative dogma. The symbols expressed in the biblical writing, Maistre explains, "are professions of faith for recognizing or contradicting the errors of the moment."[63] The text is a manifestation of truth in the face of momentary error.

The written constitution, it is not unreasonable to conclude, is the political version of the biblical texts, Maistre suggests. Looking again to England, he writes that its people "would not have sought the Magna Charta if the privileges of the nation had not been violated; but they also would never had demanded them, if the privileges had not existed before the Charter. With the Church as with the State: if Christianity had never been attacked, it would never have fixed dogma through writing." The problem is that once "truth" intervenes to combat error, this truth must take on concrete form: the specific clothing of particular laws. The truth, in other words, must make a local appearance. This action is two-

62. Ibid., xii, 30.
63. Ibid., xv, 33.

sided; although these defensive shields repel error, they also help conceal the purity of a universal truth.

> Faith, if sophistical opposition had never forced her to write, would be a thousand times more angelic: she weeps over these decisions that rebellion wrested from her, and that were always evils, since they all imply doubt or attack, and could arise only in the midst of the most dangerous disturbances. A state of war raised these venerable ramparts around the truth: they defend it, no doubt, but they conceal it; they have made [truth] unassailable, but as a result less accessible.[64]

Revelation is always a concealment. The inaccessibility of truth will always haunt human existence.

Ideally, the purity of life under God would bring all together in harmony; ideally, the inspirational foundation of the nation would keep all citizens together in political peace and prosperity for all time. Yet it is the nature of humanity to break away from the path of truth. And the task of regaining order in a fragmented world is one that cannot be accomplished through wishful nostalgia for past perfection, as the history of Christianity has shown, and the future of France has yet to prove, Maistre believed. The image of the rampart, then, is a significant one. Maistre saw history as a war, not just among nations but more profoundly between truth and error. The political theory Maistre outlined was not a template for establishing peaceful order: he knew that this idea was not only impossible but dangerous, since it ignored the inevitable differences that arise from the very structure of humanity after the Fall.

In the midst of differentiation and deviation, and in the absence of a fully visible truth, it was not possible simply to eradicate error. Error was not something sought out with the light of truth. If anything, the opposite was true, Maistre would suggest. Following the truth meant tracing its successive interactions (or confrontations) with error. What was clear to Maistre was that truth and error were not easily separated. The interaction was an intimate relationship. As Cicero had argued, every institution has its advantages and disadvantages, both of which were integral components. "The question is very difficult to resolve; the enumeration of inconveniences is a deceptive argument. What is bad in a constitution, what must even destroy it, constitutes nevertheless a part of it just as what is good."[65] That is, "every political constitution has its essential de-

---

64. Ibid., XVII, 35–37.
65. Maistre, *Considérations sur la France,* 140n.

fects, which derive from its nature and which are impossible to separate."[66]

Maistre here alludes to one of his central themes: the ever-present danger of violence erupting in the human world. As he wrote in the *Considerations on France:* "Unfortunately, history proves that war is, in a certain sense, the habitual state of humanity." War is the concrete manifestation of difference and disorder in the world. Violence is a characteristic of the imperfect organization of humanity. "There is nothing but violence in the world; but we are tainted by a modern philosophy which says that *all is good*, whereas evil has tarnished everything, and in a very real sense, *all is evil*, since nothing is in its place."[67] The problem, as Maistre interpreted it, was that it was beyond human power to put things in their place. Human sin, repeated with each generation, made any just order unstable and impermanent.

"There is nothing good in the world that evil has not tarnished or altered."[68] The ideal of reform, for Maistre, is not simply the extraction of the good and the elimination of the bad; not when human order is intrinsically corrupted. Social harmony, Maistre holds, is like the problematic harmony of the keyboard: "Tune the *fifths* rigorously and the *octaves* will clash, and conversely. Dissonance being thus inevitable, instead of eliminating it, which is impossible, it is necessary to *moderate* it by distributing it. Thus, in all the parts, *imperfection [le défaut] is an element of possible perfection*." As Maistre explains, the paradox is only a formal one: worldly order is inevitably errant or dissonant only because it can never equal the unique perfection of the divine, which nonetheless gives it whatever harmony it has. The problem that arises, the same problem that Rousseau, Condorcet, and the revolutionaries confronted when they admitted the inevitable discord that accompanies any community of individuals seeking the unity of the general will, is that it is difficult to distinguish the defect from the essence. In fact, if this were at all possible, discord would hardly be inevitable. Maistre writes:

> *But,* one might still say, *where is the rule for distinguishing the accidental defect from that which derives from the nature of things and which is impossible to exclude?* Men whom nature has given only ears [*des oreilles*] ask these sorts of questions, and those who have a good ear [*de l'oreille*] shrug their shoulders.[69]

66. Maistre, *Essai*, XLI, 73.
67. Maistre, *Considérations sur la France*, 87, 95.
68. Maistre, *Essai*, XL, 70.
69. Ibid., XLI, 74–75.

Insight into the singularity of divine truth is possible, but only if one can transcend the inherent multiplicity of human existence. This transcendence could be accomplished, if only in an imperfect sense, by trying to establish unity in the world and by trying to remain faithful to this self-imposed order.

INFALLIBILITY AND POLITICAL AUTHORITY

This effort to regain unity in the heart of difference is what grounds Maistre's discussion of interventional sovereignty, and it is here that the relation between truth and error becomes even more complex. The inevitability of error does not mean that we must deny the possibility of truth, even when truth is never self-evident. Political action is not abandoned to the mysteries of providential motion simply because legitimacy cannot easily be defined. In order to follow the path to human redemption, the discipline of unity and order must be self-consciously followed. Once society accepts the *transience* of the forms of human order, then total violence and destruction are the only outcome. Even if the purity of complete harmony is impossible (and dangerous in itself in a corrupted world), all humanity must give itself up to a higher authority if any order is to be preserved, and this inevitably meant that society must give itself up to the worldly agents of divine power: the temporal sovereigns. What Maistre makes clear, though, is that it is not the human being that we submit to, but the commissioned office.

This leads us to Maistre's rigorous analysis of the papacy and its relations (both concrete and theoretical) with political states. "*Infallibility* in the spiritual order and *sovereignty* in the temporal order are two perfectly synonymous words. Both express this highest power, which dominates all others, from which all others derive: who governs and is not governed; who judges and is not judged."[70] No matter what institutional or other order may be in question, Maistre argues, there must always be a certain decisive force that cannot be disputed:

> In the judicial order, which is nothing but a section of the government, can we not see that it is absolutely necessary to come to a power that judges and is not judged, precisely because it pronounces in the name of the supreme power, of which it is deemed to be only the organ and voice? Go about it as you will, give this high judicial power any name you want, there will always have to be one to whom it cannot be said: *You have erred* [*Vous avez erré*].[71]

70. Maistre, *Du Pape*, 27.
71. Ibid., 28.

As Maistre describes it, the highest authority cannot be questioned simply because to question this authority is to begin dismantling the entire structure. In other words, every system of authority needs a point at which all appeals stop; otherwise, no decision could ever be final and no continuing order could be preserved.

And so Maistre defines infallibility (that is, the state of not being subject to error) as a "necessary consequence of *supremacy,* or rather, it is absolutely the same thing under two different names."[72] Here Maistre concludes, in effect, that the infallibility of the pope is not really a theological problem, but more a direct consequence of the political structure of his authority. It is simply a fact that "error could not be charged against the Pope, even if it were possible, just as it cannot be charged against the temporal sovereigns who have never claimed infallibility." What Maistre is suggesting is that once claims to truth cannot be measured against objective and clearly visible standards, the problem of error is no longer an epistemological concern.[73] One can be charged with error only if some measure of objectivity exists. This standard is obviously lacking in political contexts, something even Condorcet had to confront with his political mathematics. Maistre's response is to insist: "It is in effect absolutely the same thing in practice, not to be subject to error, or not to be able to be accused of it." With this sentence Maistre seems to reveal an essentially *decisionist* definition of sovereign authority: the proper decision is simply any decision that cannot be reviewed by a higher authority. Government must be absolute: "From the moment one can resist it under the pretext of error or injustice, it no longer exists." More clearly, he writes: "It is the same thing *in practice* to be infallible or to be wrong [*se tromper*] without appeal."[74]

This, perhaps, is the main reason that Maistre believed it always necessary to shroud these authorities in mystery, so as to make any analysis of their operation extremely difficult. The sacred dimension of authority

72. Ibid., 30.
73. On this point, see Freund, *L'essence du politique:* "The possibility of error characterizes every will by definition, since choice consists of an adherence to a conviction or a belief that is not logically necessary. When we say that the sovereign is infallible, it must be understood by this not that he is exempt from errors or injustices, but that his decision is without appeal or, in the worst case, that every government is good when it has been established, if it is true that politically (and not at all from a moral point of view) it is more important that a decision intervenes, whatever the manner in which it is made" (127).
74. Maistre, *Du Pape,* 30, 27, 194n. Cf. Bonald, *Théorie de pouvoir,* 563: "An authority can be considered fallible only as long as a superior authority can make it clear that it has failed [*failli*]."

could be interpreted as a mere practicality. And it has been said that for Maistre "man obeys as he believes: because power, like God, is absurd." Sovereignty is arbitrary for Maistre and hence any decision is good as long as it is made by the established authority, an idea taken up by Carl Schmitt, the constitutional theorist and Nazi apologist who often cited Maistre's work on decision.[75] Maistre certainly seems to head in this direction when he concludes this section on error with this remark: "It is not only a matter of knowing if the Pope *is* but if he *must be* infallible."[76] The right to accuse the pope (or any other sovereign power) of being wrong is the right to disobey, and for Maistre, this clearly is a contradiction.

At no time, however, did Maistre equate the infallibility of sovereign powers with a total, and totally arbitrary, authority. The idea of limitation was extremely important to him. For Maistre, sovereignty was not at all limited within the limits of what he called its "legitimate exercise."[77] The boundaries of its operation were set by the sacred fundamental laws establishing any particular political identity. Sovereignty, in other words, must take on a certain form appropriate to the specific nation, and subsequently not transgress that form. "The forms of sovereignty . . . are not at all the same everywhere: they are fixed by the fundamental laws, whose true foundations [*bases*] are never written." Legitimacy, then, is a function of political forms, not of content. The sovereign is not confined to any set of particular actions within the circle of its domain, yet it can never leave that circle. The unwritten (and therefore absent) origin of any nation is what founds the authority of the sovereign, through the formation of institutional spaces. In the course of history, the specific laws enacted within political institutions are "above" the sovereign only in the sense that this authority must obey what it has in fact itself created.[78] It is not simply the actions of the particular sovereign that preserve order; there is a fundamental continuity within the institutional and legal frameworks as well.

However, Maistre approaches the problem of authority not from a desire merely to justify monarchical forms and the Catholic Church. In an important sense, the problem of authority stems from the problematic

75. See Massimo Boffa, "La contre-Révolution, Joseph de Maistre," in *The French Revolution and the Creation of Modern Political Culture*, vol. 3: *The Transformation of Political Culture, 1789–1848*, ed. François Furet and Mona Ozouf (Oxford, 1989), 305. As well, see Schmitt, *Political Theology,* 56.

76. Maistre, *Du Pape,* 30. Cf. Bonald, *Théorie du pouvoir,* 564. "If infallibility belongs to the body of ministers, it cannot be attributed to any one individual."

77. Maistre, *Du Pape,* 136.

78. Ibid., 44.

relation between truth and error. If truth (in all its forms) were self-evident, then decisions would no longer be decisions, they would simply be applications. On the other hand, if all faith in truth were abandoned, then any decision would simply be a matter of force and would hardly require elaborate justification, except as propaganda. Although Maistre and Bonald have of course been accused of this latter course, it is hardly possible to question their faith. In other words, it seems more likely that Maistre was attempting a theory of action in a condition of perpetual error. The discipline of order and authority was a way of keeping to a path that would in time lead to the expiation of humanity, or at least keep alive the possibility of that future state.

> There can be no human society without government, or government without sovereignty, or sovereignty without infallibility; and this last right [*privilège*] is so absolutely necessary that we are forced to presume infallibility even in temporal sovereigns (where it does not exist), under threat of seeing the association dissolve.[79]

The actual sovereign is not necessarily free from error, but it must assume this air of infallibility if in the course of time order is going to prevail. The discipline of unified authority allows the irregularities to work themselves out eventually, rather than multiply until total chaos ensues. "The essential point for each nation is to maintain its particular discipline." Often the fact of the decision was more important than its content: "Our interest is not at all that it be decided in this or that manner, but that it be done without delay and without appeal."[80] The emergency decision, however, was not a celebration of dictatorial power. If the historical dimension of Maistre's thought is attended to, we can see that there is a sacrificial aspect to the dialectic between violence and interventional order in human experience.

As the sovereign maintains order within the boundaries of the nation, Maistre believed that the pope could use his power to intervene when these international orders were threatened. For Maistre, authority did not impose a structured order, it intervened to preserve a continuity. Throughout history the popes had tried to maintain the unity of European civilization.

> The popes in no way interfered so as to impede the wise princes in the exercise of their functions, still less interrupt the order of sovereign successions,

79. Ibid., 123.
80. Ibid., 121, 122.

as long as things were going according to ordinary and recognized rules; it is when there was a great abuse, great crime or large doubt that the Sovereign Pontiff intervened with his authority [*interposait son autorité*].[81]

The popes, moreover, had, Maistre believed, continually made the effort to expand human civilization through the missionary enterprise.[82]

This formal organization of unity in the midst of national variation characterized the Catholic Church, the paradigmatic example of identity within a diversity of forms. Maistre never saw the Protestant churches as legitimate expressions of a larger unity. Although he once commented that there is no such thing as an entirely false religion, the schismatic churches were not, for Maistre, simply variant forms of a unified Christian movement. They were actually forces of destruction. The very name gives proof of this, Maistre believed. The names of the Protestant churches have no relation to unity, and "that which excludes all idea of unity consequently excludes truth."[83] The invention of a name proves its inauthenticity, and it is significant, Maistre writes, that all the schismatic churches have two names: the one they call themselves and the one by which outsiders call them. Only the Catholic Church, which also has survived as an institution for almost eighteen centuries, has only one name, used by all, both within and without. For this reason, Maistre sees the Catholic Church as the necessary center of human organization, the one disciplined authority that can bring an errant humanity together into one whole, however many different national forms may exist. "Hydra-headed error will be vanquished before indivisible Truth: God will reign in the Temple as He reigns in heaven, in the blessed communion of his Saints."[84]

In another context, Maistre once remarked on the coming reintegration of human societies, the result, he believed, of the rapid exploration and emerging interconnection of the world. In its ignorance, humanity often makes mistakes concerning its future goals and the means to achieve them, yet "Providence never hesitates, and it is not in vain that it agitates the world. Everything announces that we are marching toward a grand unity that we must *hail from afar*."[85]

81. Ibid., 188.
82. Ibid., bk. 3, chap. 1.
83. Ibid., 318.
84. The translation of this particular passage (which concludes *Du Pape*) is by Harold J. Laski, in "De Maistre and Bismarck," in *Studies in the Problem of Sovereignty* (New Haven, 1917), 231.
85. Maistre, *Soirées de Saint-Petersbourg*, 121.

VIOLENT SACRIFICE

The optimistic tone of these passages cannot direct attention from Maistre's profound pessimism, or at least his insistence that violence must always attend this progression toward harmony. The progress was transformative, the movement of discontinuous cultures and peoples, the historical motion of internally dissonant nations; this movement was always a painful one. As he said, humanity is often ignorant of this historical direction, and through its own errant course often resists. Providence, acting itself out through chosen instruments, must inevitably intervene to sort out the disorders of individual actions. As Maistre put it, "humanity [*le genre humain*] may be considered as a tree that an invisible hand constantly prunes and that often gains from this operation. In truth, if one damages the trunk or overprunes, the tree may die; but who knows the limits of the human tree?"[86] It is hardly coincidental, Maistre thought, that throughout history violence has been the preparation for the emergence of new orders. The birth of every nation, Maistre claims, is accompanied by violent war. Moreover, the progress of the national identity is furthered by violent upheaval. "We know that nations never reach the highest point of greatness of which they are capable except after long and bloody wars," he wrote.[87] Blood fertilizes genius, as he put it. Maistre's version of providential intervention is that the inevitable errors of humanity will produce discord, and this discord will either be decided by a respected authority or be worked out through violent conflict.[88] Obviously, the best path is the one of self-discipline. But history shows that conflict is hardly a rare occurrence, especially in the international sphere. Everything is out of place and dissonant. "The keynote of our system having been lowered, all the others have been lowered proportionately, following the rules of harmony. *All creation groans,* and moves, with pain and effort, toward

---

86. Maistre, *Considérations sur la France,* 92. See Rom. 11:17–21: "But if some of the branches were broken off, and you, a wild olive shoot, were grafted in their place to share the rich root of the olive tree, do not boast over the branches. If you do boast, remember that it is not you that support the root, but the root that supports you. You will say, 'Branches were broken off so that I might be grafted in.' That is true. They were broken off because of their unbelief, but you stand only through faith. So do not become proud, but stand in awe. For if God did not spare the natural branches, perhaps he will not spare you."

87. Maistre, *Considérations sur la France,* 91–92.

88. For a detailed analysis of sacrifice in Maistre's work, see Owen Bradley, *A Modern Maistre: The Social and Political Thought of Joseph de Maistre* (Lincoln, Neb., 1999), chap. 2.

another order of things."[89] Disorder (error) can lead to order (truth), but the preparation for this movement toward order can lessen the violence.

It is this structure that forms the basis of Maistre's interpretation of the French Revolution. The miracle of the Revolution is the fact of its great success, but this success was an explosive dissipation of the energy built up from years of error. Providence did not want to punish only a few guilty men, as if the revolutionary leaders were solely responsible for these events. "It was necessary that the great purification be accomplished, and that eyes were opened [*frappés*]; it was necessary that the metal of France, freed from its bitter and impure dross, come cleaner and more malleable into the hands of the future king."[90] The Revolution was a pruning of the French nation, which would lead to a new political order once the storm had passed. In a sense, France was repeating the experience of England: a bloody civil disruption that would found a stronger national identity. For Maistre, history could be understood as a series of transformative repetitions that revealed at each step the progressive course of human destiny.

This perhaps explains why he concluded his *Considerations on France* with a curious chapter titled "Fragment of a History of the French Revolution by David Hume," which pieced together parts of Hume's *History of England* to draw parallels between the two countries' revolutionary experience. It was only after Maistre's death that this title was changed, for some reason (presumably because of the incongruity), with "English Revolution" being substituted for "French Revolution."[91] Maistre's intention in this chapter was, however, precisely to penetrate the hidden continuity of the historical process in Europe, which took many different forms in different national contexts but where the spirit was in its essence the same. The epigraph for this conclusion was, appropriately enough, "Eadem mutata resurgo" (I rise again, transformed but the same). The transformations Maistre depicted were painful births, sacrificial events. "All creation groans," he wrote, in anticipation of the final revelation. With this allusion to St. Paul,[92] Maistre refers, in a note, to the concept of palingenesis, the idea that history is a series of rebirths, an ongoing regeneration of human (and natural) identity in the transforma-

89. Maistre, *Considerations sur la France*, 95.

90. Ibid., 74.

91. See the editor's note in the critical edition of *Considérations sur la France*, 185n. This title change is maintained in the English translation.

92. See Rom. 8: 18–25.

tive contexts of evolutionary time.[93] This situates Maistre's disruptive history of repetition in a line of thought that leads back into the eighteenth century, to Charles Bonnet and philosophical palingenesis, and forward into the Restoration, to Pierre-Simon Ballanche's later theory of social palingenesis.

93. Maistre, *Considérations sur la France*, 95n.

CHAPTER 8

Deviant Repetitions: Birth and
Rebirth in Biology and History

When Maistre alluded to both St. Paul and Charles Bonnet in the *Considerations on France* (and again in his *Soirées de Saint-Petersbourg*), he was articulating a vision of the natural and social world that stressed its invisible foundational structures. As St. Paul often said, the world should be considered the visible manifestation of an essentially invisible reality. Maistre introduced a Platonic variation of the Pauline ontology. The surface of appearance, for Maistre, was a kind of distortion, or aberration, of a reality that was essentially spiritual and therefore intangible. In his own work, Maistre explicitly linked this idea to the problem of error: the truth of this hidden, invisible reality often emerges in our profane world to combat the dangers of error. Yet in making this appearance in the visible world, this spiritual reality itself must take on an appearance; it must, in other words, take on an aberrant physical form. So living on the borders of the spiritual and the physical, humanity was caught in the constant presence of error and aberration, hoping for insight even as the truth of the spiritual presence could never appear directly within our experience.

From Bonnet's Enlightenment naturalism, Maistre adopted the idea of a certain kind of historical evolution that structured the forms of life. Bonnet believed that the evolution of individual species was part of a vast transformational process that drew on the energy of the spiritual world, a process that was organized by the comprehensive divine unity of the universe. Each species was repeatedly "reborn" in new forms of outward appearance—this was the movement of palingenesis (from the Greek *palin*, again). Maistre envisioned the history of humanity in a similar way, again with emphasis on the importance of error in the process.

210

Each stage of historical development, in each particular human culture or nation, revealed in a distorted form the true nature of humanity, a humanity defined by its perfect relation to the higher unity and harmony of the divine reality. This theory was extended and amplified by the early nineteenth-century writer Pierre-Simon Ballanche, who explicitly transformed Bonnet's early ideas on natural evolutionary change into a theory of history in the postrevolutionary context, describing in his many complex works how "humanity" was a fragmented individual condemned to an errant temporal experience as a way of expiating an original crime.

So from Bonnet to Ballanche, a certain theological understanding of identity grounds a historical approach to the problem of error and aberration. These deviations, in other words, were not simply momentary wanderings from normative forms, but instead a temporal process of becoming. The truth that defined the straying of error was no longer metaphorically hovering on the horizon of knowledge, but instead waiting at the end of time. And like the truth in Enlightenment epistemological theory, this historical truth made its fleeting appearances, as Maistre indicated. This historical approach to error was not, however, confined to the Christian tradition exemplified in figures like Bonnet, Maistre, and Ballanche. The concept of palingenesis, used in medical and alchemical traditions since the Renaissance to mean "the process of being born again," was explicitly invoked by these three authors to make sense of the repetitions of error that marked the transformations of the social and natural world. But in the eighteenth century, this link between aberration and temporal change was already being explored in a more philosophical and secular context. The rediscovery of an eschatological conception of error in postrevolutionary theological writers was part of a broader line of thought that was already transforming the conceptualization of aberration as historical during the Enlightenment.

ABERRATIONS OF ORDER IN ENLIGHTENMENT NATURAL HISTORY

For Europeans, the rapid expansion of world trade, the exploration of exotic locales, along with new explorations of their own continent by geologists, all generated a rapid increase in the flow of information in natural history. This influx was extremely disruptive intellectually, for the new discoveries challenged traditional models by which the order of nature was understood. Conceptual schemes could not contain the proliferation of new species of plants and animals brought to the attention of European scientists, and the whole notion of a hierarchy of creation seemed less obvious, given a better understanding of the global multiplicity of complex beings. New geological discoveries interfered with complacent natural theology, since it was clear by the eighteenth century that the earth was much older than it had been thought to be, and that it had its own history of cataclysmic upheavals, a series of geological ages. The new acquaintance with fossil remains raised new questions about the order of nature, for it was not easy to explain why so many species had become extinct.

In the first half of the eighteenth century, these questions were still being formulated, and there was no one clear framework for organizing all these problems. The very source of order in the world of nature was no longer clearly identifiable. The traditional ordering of discrete creatures was no longer adequate, if only because there were so many of them to be classified and ordered, and visual signs of hierarchy were not obvious. As Jean Ehrard has pointed out, before 1750 the metaphysically vague concept of a "chain" of being coexisted uneasily alongside new mechanical notions of natural law inherited from the physical sciences. After 1750, the issue became much more confrontational, with a clear opposition between those who believed in the divine origin of order and those who thought that the laws of nature were enough to explain the profound complexity of the visible (and increasingly invisible) universe.[1] This debate was somewhat unproductive, however, since it was difficult to argue about the origins of order when the very existence of that order was in doubt. What was the identity unifying the vast complexity of the natural world? Whether this was a strictly theological question or a naturalist problem in science, it was first necessary to *locate* order and identify its variations and (possible) aberrations before the question of origin could be addressed. Was God (or nature) really a fundamental set of laws that structured the world, or was this hidden reality more a productive, interventional force that could create radically new entities? The Enlightenment was faced with the task of identifying the continuities and discontinuities of the natural order as a way of settling the debate. Of course, this was not a purely empirical matter, and depending on the starting point, there were many ways to approach this search for the inner unity or harmony of the natural world. This was a decision not between religion and science but about the very order that would be designated divine or merely natural.

As is well known, the origins of modern classificatory schemes lie in the eighteenth century. Faced with the sheer complexity and variety of

1. Jean Ehrard, *L'idée de nature en France dans la première moitié du XVIIIe siècle*, 2 vols. (Paris, 1963), 1: 197.

material, many working scientists abandoned any idea of a linear hierarchy and focused on figuring out the many relationships among specimens. Linneaus, the heroic figure of Enlightenment classification, worked out these relationships by closely observing discrete characteristics of individual specimens, then mapping out the networks of resemblance.[2] These chains of resemblance were organized into larger categories of "species," "genus," and "family." No one organism was really higher than another. Rather, each individual organism belonged to broader and broader forms of identity. Although modern biologists see these groupings as merely taxonomic, for Linneaus and his many eighteenth-century followers they marked the boundaries of an essential natural identity. Any one example was, metaphysically, a member of these groups. As such, these identities were understood to be fixed. Variation or deviation was contained within these parameters. In fact, any individual variation was ascribed to the merely "accidental" causes that affected the essential character of the individual organism.[3] The order of nature, for Linneaus and many others, was to be found in the complex interaction (and fundamental harmony) of all these created forms of life. Even if Linnaeus was forced to admit the possibility that new species might arise from hybridization,[4] he could see the divine order in the large, complex plan of nature, with the details only filled in by these small-scale transformations. For the most part, the infertility of most hybrid forms convinced scientists that the order of nature was largely determined from the start. Of course, the problem of the extinction of species, made pressing by renewed interest in fossil discoveries, was still evaded in this Linnaean framework. Or rather, it had to be explained how this supposedly divine order could ever degenerate, or alternatively, how this complex order unfolded over time.

These questions became even more acute as botanists, for example, began to encounter examples of nonaccidental variation in nature; in other words, variations that became permanent features. Also puzzling was the existence of homogeneous characteristics distributed spatially in radically diverse conditions. Consequently, many began to look for some inner causes that might explain both the production of variations and the continuity of identity. In other words, as Caspar Friedrich Wolff was

2. On Linnaeus, see James L. Larson, *Reason and Experience: The Representation of Natural Order in the Work of Carl von Linné* (Berkeley, 1971).

3. James L. Larson, *Interpreting Nature: The Science of the Living Form from Linnaeus to Kant* (Baltimore, 1994), 68.

4. See Bentley Glass, "Heredity and Variation in the Eighteenth-Century Concept of the Species," in *Forerunners of Darwin, 1745–1849*, ed. Bentley Glass, Oswei Temkin, and William L. Strauss Jr. (Baltimore, 1959), 144–51.

arguing, the identity of the species, its essential character, might actually *condition* the visible variations an organism exhibited.[5] However, this concept raised an even more difficult question. Where exactly was this essential character located? To measure variation, one had to have a clear understanding of identity. And if identity was not, as Linnaeus had believed, found in the external characteristics themselves, an alternative site had to be established. Or, as Buffon once noted, the very order of classification might be simply an arbitrary mode of ordering with no ontological significance. At what point did individual "variety" cross over into a new species altogether? What was the status of these groupings of actual individual entities?

Of course, as Buffon himself would argue in the monumental *Histoire naturelle,* there was another way of looking at the relationships among diverse individuals and between diverse species. He suggested that what linked all the varieties of species in nature was the same as what connected all the multiple examples of any one species in the first place: a common lineage. If a class of beings was not to be totally arbitrary, he said, then it must have a common origin that unites the individual organisms in their diversity.[6] In his own work, he argued that the vast number of animal species could be reduced to five basic starting points. From this perspective, Buffon could see that what had been called variation was better seen as aberration, a straying that was due to the prolonged "degeneration" of the original species prototypes over time. If Buffon's ideas were not well supported empirically and thus not accepted for the most part by the scientific community, the difficulties raised by his analysis persisted. It was important now to look not just at the external characteristics of individuals and groups in an effort to identify continuity and discontinuity, but at the historical identity of generation as well. Some would speculate, for example, that some kind of vice or aberration in reproduction might explain some of these nonaccidental variations.[7] If variations within species and across family groups were not examples of divine creation, perhaps they were the result of some physical force in the process of generation. Yet there was no clear understanding of this process that could help resolve the relationships of order, variation, and deviation.

In the middle of the seventeenth century, William Harvey had demonstrated that Aristotelian models of generation were no longer tenable.

5. Larson, *Interpreting Nature,* 68.
6. On Buffon's ideas concerning variety and diversity, see Jacques Roger, *Buffon: Un philosophe au Jardin du Roi* (Paris, 1989), chap. 18.
7. Larson, *Interpreting Nature,* 80–84.

Harvey had observed, from dissection of animals, that the fetus gradually developed on its own from its origin as an egg within the uterus. He could see no evidence that the egg was shaped in any way by external forces. Early preformationist theories that developed in the wake of Harvey's work theorized that the structure of the being was already delineated within the egg from the start. However, it was difficult to explain how this structure came into existence. Despite the success of the mechanical approach in the physical sciences, the problem of generation resisted purely physical explanations. It was held by some that these initial "germs" were created by God, and had existed from the beginning of Creation, in a series of encapsulations. Each new birth was really just a delayed development of a preexisting germ. This theory avoided the introduction of any spiritual or vitalist forces, and preserved a physical view of the process of development. Microscopic investigations seemed to confirm the preexistence of organs and limbs in the earliest stages of the embryo. Of course, the discovery of spermatozoa complicated the theory of generation considerably, since it raised the possibility of a male origin for the embryo. The debate between "ovists" and "animalculists" (those who believed that the germ of the animal was located in the spermatozoa) at the end of the seventeenth century centered on the question of origin. The discovery of plant sexuality only made the question more obscure (if more crucial), for it was in botany that it was discovered that the interbreeding of plants could form hybrids that reproduced, in effect creating new species. The possibility of the new species made preformationism of any sort less tenable. The intense study of variation in the eighteenth century only strengthened this doubt. It was difficult, perhaps even impossible, to explain variation and deviation within a preformationist model.[8]

By the mid–eighteenth century, generation itself was beginning to be explained mechanically, that is, as a result of forces acting on matter to produce certain entities. This framework best resolved the problem of variation (or deviation), because it greatly reduced the significance of this change by making it the almost chance result of minor perturbations at the microscopic level. Such aberration was not, then, "unnatural" and disruptive of a preexisting order. Rather, order was reduced to a series of physical processes, which may or may not go astray, depending on particular circumstances. The earlier preformationist theories, while ex-

8. This paragraph relies on Jacques Roger, *Les sciences de la vie dans la pensée française au XVIIIᵉ siècle: La generation des animaux de Descartes à l'Encyclopédie*, 3d ed. (Paris, 1993), chaps. 2–3; and Elizabeth Gasking, *Investigations into Generation, 1651–1828* (Baltimore, [1967]), chaps. 2–5.

plaining much of the new evidence, could not easily account for the many examples of deviation. Yet if a mechanical philosophy was beginning to reconfigure the search for order in nature in terms of basic physical processes, it was immediately clear to eighteenth-century scientists that generation was still a fundamental mystery. A mechanical concept of matter did demystify variation and aberration, perhaps, but it did not convincingly demonstrate how such complex organizations developed in the first place. How did matter organize itself into sophisticated organisms, then replicate so perfectly?[9] For there to be order in what was the otherwise dead matter of mechanical philosophy, some kind of transcendent organizing force was necessary. Maupertuis, for example, suggested that matter had its own appetites and aversions (as Leibniz had thought earlier).[10] Buffon speculated that there were "inner molds" that shaped matter.[11] Others revived the preformationist idea of the "germ" as a kind of inner structure that shaped the physical organization of concrete matter, or argued that there were "formative forces" or inner identities in play.[12]

At any rate, Enlightenment natural history began to separate the inner process of order from the actual results of that process. Concrete variety could be interpreted as a surface effect of inner identity. Once the variety of organic forms was identified both across space and in history, it was possible to look for identity in something other than visible structures. The origin of natural life could perhaps reside in this process of transformation rather than in a singular act of multiple formation. And so Jean Baptiste Robinet, in the *Considérations philosophiques sur la gradation naturelle des formes de l'Etre, ou Les Essais de la nature, qui apprend à former l'homme* (1768), would describe all the existing natural forms (including rocks, animals, and human beings) as multiple *variations* of some originary prototype. Robinet saw these widely different entities as, literally, experimental attempts (*essais*) by a productive nature to develop the individual species in higher and higher forms. Process and the multiplicity of effects had been effectively separated.

Monsters and Enlightenment Aberration

By the late eighteenth century, the monster no longer demonstrated the exceptional singularity, the marvel that was, in a sense, out-

9. See Roger, *Les sciences de la vie*, 475, and Larson, *Interpreting Nature*, 63.

10. Ernst Cassirer, *The Philosophy of the Enlightenment*, trans. Fritz C. A. Koelln and James P. Pettegrove (Princeton, 1951), 87. Cf. Larson, *Interpreting Nature*, 134.

11. See Roger, *Buffon*, 187–91.

12. Roger, *Les sciences de la vie*, 648; Larson, *Interpreting Nature*, 91, 97, explores the theories of Wolff and Blumenbach.

side of nature altogether.[13] Yet the existence of rare "errors" of nature still challenged any theory of natural order, especially one that put divine harmony at its center.[14] Monsters, those aberrations of natural animal and human forms, what Bacon called "errors of nature . . . where nature deflects and declines from its usual course,"[15] were a longstanding problem in natural history. But the Enlightenment did not simply mark a new, "rational" theory of monstrosity to replace older theological explanations of these phenomena. What was new in the Enlightenment was a desire to study more closely actual examples of aberration in order to understand their place in nature. The eighteenth century saw a marked increase in dissections and accurate pictorial representations. It was no longer acceptable to speculate on monsters that one had not actually studied carefully. The massive amount of information collected on monsters in this period precluded any simple comprehensive explanation. In fact, early in the century, it was difficult to explain the existence of monsters in any way. Given the dominant theory of generation, the preexistence of germs, it seemed as if monstrous germs must exist. The idea is not in itself so irrational, but it implied that God must have created monsters, a conclusion that many could not really accept. As Roger comments, this very consequence forced some to abandon the germ theory.[16] In the end, though, an explanation was offered that preserved the germ theory and absolved God of direct responsibility for monsters. The monster, it was argued, resulted from the accidental aberration of the germ itself. The monster (which had always been classified in relation to normal forms) was stripped of its singularity and reintroduced into the natural order.[17] The question now was how to explain this accidental variation of form. One of the more notorious theories was a resurrected belief that the maternal imagination could affect the fetus in the womb, producing deformities. The philosopher Nicolas de Malebranche defended this view against the idea that God may very well have included monsters in his divine plan of nature. "The female organs," as Marie-Hélène Huet comments, were often identified as "the source of errors" into the eighteenth century.[18]

13. See Lorraine Daston and Katherine Park, *Wonders and the Order of Nature, 1150–1750* (Cambridge, Mass., 1998), chap. 5, and their earlier contribution, "Unnatural Conceptions: The Study of Monsters in Sixteenth- and Seventeenth-Century France and England," *Past and Present* 92 (1981): 20–54. See as well Marie-Hélène Huet, *Monstrous Imagination* (Cambridge, Mass., 1993), pt. 1.

14. Larson, *Interpreting Nature,* 61.

15. Francis Bacon, *The New Organon,* ed. Lisa Jardine and Michael Silverthorne (Cambridge, 2000), bk. 2, aphorism XXIX, p. 148.

16. Roger, *Les sciences de la vie,* 397, 398.

17. Daston and Park, *Wonders,* 205.

18. See Huet, *Monstrous Imagination,* 57.

There was no clear decision, though, on the question whether monsters were discrete creations or aberrations of normal organisms. It was easier, in fact, to suggest that monsters were special cases, since there was no real evidence for any biological process of aberration. At this time, the idea of the preformed germ could account for all monstrous births. While many had speculated on these alternate theories, in the early eighteenth century the two opposing views were debated in French scientific circles by Louis Lémery and Jacques-Bénigne Winslow. Lémery denied the preexistence of monstrous germs and in 1724 proposed that monsters resulted from the accidental "deformation" of the germ. Either the germ was mutilated in some way (and produced a *monstre par défaut*) or, he said, two germs accidentally fused (resulting in a *monstre par excès*).[19] He would go on to develop this theory in a series of memoirs at the Academy of Sciences. Lémery took the idea that individual variation in normal organisms was produced by accidental causes and applied it to the problem of monsters by suggesting that an excessive accidental variation had breached the very identity of the species.[20] Monsters were the products of chance at its most extreme, and not miracles or the products of direct intervention.[21] The monster thereby enters the field of medical diagnostics. As Lémery argued, the fetus was subject to some organic malady and became deformed in some way. It was just difficult to locate this malady before birth, since its development was hidden from direct observation.[22] Winslow rejected Lémery's claims as pure speculation. There was, he said, no real evidence of these accidental infractions of the laws of generation. With a profound knowledge of anatomy, Winslow showed that this theory could not in fact explain many monsters. Still, Lémery's observations were powerful. So many monstrous births seemed to be clearly aberrations of the norm, with no purpose imaginable.[23] For Lémery, it seemed implausible that God could have designed such "disorganization, disorder, disturbance, confusion, and faulty executions."[24] Winslow, for his part, refused to believe that the universe was just one big clock that contained the occasional faulty mechanism. The monster, he argued, was a marvel that could not always be explained.[25] He pointed to the example of one "monster," a soldier

19. Louis Lémery, "Sur un foetus monstrueux," *Mémoires de l'Académie des Sciences,* 1774, 44–62.

20. Patrick Tort, *L'ordre et les monstres: Le débat sur l'origine des déviations anatomiques au XVIIIᵉ siècle* (Paris, 1980), 110.

21. See Ehrard, *L'idée de nature,* 1: 213–14.

22. Tort, *L'ordre et les monstres,* 111–12, 128.

23. Roger, *Les sciences de la vie,* 408–18.

24. Quoted and translated in Huet, *Monstrous Imagination,* 63.

25. Roger, *Les sciences de la vie,* 414, 417.

with an inverted distribution of organs. Here there was no evidence of accident and in fact a perverse kind of harmony. Confronted with this example, even Lémery had to admit that this individual was not really a monster. As Patrick Tort suggests, Lémery's faith in order, unity, and functionality as signs of identity convinced him that unusual (even unique) forms were not necessarily "monstrous."[26]

It is possible to see the reemergence of vitalist theories in the eighteenth century in this context. If aberrations could exemplify the functions of life as well as "normal" forms, perhaps the identification of this life force was more important than classifying the visible order in some kind of hierarchy. The physical form of the monster was not the crucial factor. The order of nature could be found in its productive forces. Just as variation (within species, within nature as a whole) might be the surface effects of more fundamental laws and forces, the monstrous aberration might be yet another "surface variation."[27] For Enlightenment scientists, a new question emerges from the study of variation and its radical cousin, monstrosity. How are both monsters and normal forms produced and replicated in the world, and what constitutes their organizational identity? Lémery's speculations mark the origin of this new approach, one that in the very effort to explain monstrous aberration normalizes the deviation by folding it back into the very order of nature.[28] The subsequent discovery that, according to the new sciences of probability, monsters were in fact *not* completely accidental further integrated aberration and norm even as it condemned Lémery's germ theory of accidental aberration. There was, it seems, something within nature that *regularly* produced both monsters and the normal variety of organisms.[29] This observation only intensified the search for an adequate theory of generation, one that would explain the organization of all beings, normal and monstrous, without merely attributing that order to mysterious or divine sources.

Despite its lack of empirical support, Buffon's idea of degeneration resolved many of these questions. Buffon invoked the "errors" of nature to explain both the existence of monsters and the variety of species, since both were in fact examples of "degeneration" of original prototypical examples.[30] The origins of all degeneration, then, would lie in the process of generation. What exactly were these errors of nature? It was

26. Tort, *L'ordre et les monstres*, 130–38.
27. See Roger, *Les sciences de la vie*, 418–39.
28. See Ehrard, *L'idée de nature*, 1: 214; Daston and Park, *Wonders*, 205; Larson, *Interpreting Nature*, 63.
29. Tort, *L'ordre et les monstres*, chap. 11.
30. Buffon's approach is discussed in Tort, *L'ordre et les monstres*, 229.

clear to Buffon that the history of various species was really a process of transformative reproduction, and not the continuous expression of one relatively static identity. Buffon, unlike most eighteenth-century naturalists, theorized that both parents "reproduced" themselves in the embryo, a process that would explain family resemblances. The possibility of inheriting acquired characteristics also suggested a mechanism of transformation (or degeneration).[31] Pierre-Louis Maupertuis, who shared Buffon's rejection of "parental singularity," to use Marie-Hélène Huet's phrase, sought the explanation of monstrous aberration, resemblance, and variety in a theory of inheritance. One particular "monster," an albino Negro child in Paris who had two normal black parents, stimulated Maupertuis's thoughts on generation and aberration. In his dissertation on this case, Maupertuis noted that offspring usually inherit characteristics from both parents, and often exhibit "mixed" ones as well (in skin color, for example). This observation seemed to argue against any preformationist account of generation. Maupertuis, drawing on recent experiments in chemical affinity, suggested that embryos were formed from maternal and paternal secretions that came together to produce structures. These secretions might contain particles from the adult organs, he argued in works such as *Vénus physique* (1745). Particles from both parents mingled together to form the new organs of the child. In this way, certain monsters could be formed, Maupertuis claimed. Monsters *par excès*, for example, might have acquired extra particles. This theory of inheritance could also explain the albino Negro. The particles of a distant white ancestor could have remained hidden, though passed on from parent to child, if the particles of another parent had dominated in the formation of the fetal organs. Or, he pointed out, the white Negro could be the first of its type, a kind of monstrous "mutation."[32]

Maupertuis's theory of heredity and his application of this idea to the problem of the origin of individual species links the idea of error with the manifestation of difference. What Maupertuis claimed was that all change in the forms of similar species could be the result of accumulated error transmitted between early generations. The origin of the new species, for him, was to be found at the moment of deviation in the reproductive cycle. The aberrant offspring, Maupertuis suggested, was the consequence of imperfect *sémences* from the two parents. The result would be some kind of monster or a being lacking normal features. Nor-

31. Roger, *Buffon*, 179, 183–84.
32. On the white Negro and Maupertuis's theory of generation, see Gasking, *Investigations into Generation*, chap. 6.

mally, this kind of imperfection would block reproduction of any "monstrous" offspring, but this was not necessarily the case, Maupertuis believed. As he wrote in the *Système de la nature:*

> Could we not explain in this way how, from two single individuals, the multiplication of the most dissimilar species might have sprung? They would have owed their first birth [*première origine*] only to a few chance productions, in which the elementary particles would not have retained the order that they had in the father and mother animals: each degree of *error* would have created a new species; and by dint of repeated divergences [*écarts*] would have come about the infinite diversity of animals that we see today, which will perhaps still increase with time, but to which the passing of centuries brings only imperceptible increments.[33]

In Maupertuis's vision, error introduces variation, and the entire history of the natural world might be seen as a vast table of errors, all stemming from an originary error in reproductive transmission. Maupertuis also speculates that these errors might have something to do with environmental crisis: we should not be surprised, he wrote, if, after the earth suffers a global disruption such as a flood or conflagration, new elements are formed and new plants and animals produced.[34] Here Maupertuis suggests that the error of variation may actually serve to adapt a species to a new environment. The fixity and predictability of any one specific organization would work against long-term survival: the very diversity of errant offspring in changing world conditions could be seen as a positive feature. The error of transmission could serve to protect the underlying (or remaining) identity, preserving continuity in a hostile environment. Maupertuis here resolves Lémery's difficulty. Regularity is not to be found in the organism itself but in the laws of nature. The monster, through infraction, reveals this law perhaps even more clearly than the normal example. As another medical scientist wrote in 1761, "errors of nature themselves are often instructive, and can serve to clarify an infinity of interesting points, which would be forever enigmas in their natural state."[35] The white Negro was not an object of wonder but an "error" of nature that leads us to the very truth of generation.

33. Pierre-Louis Moreau de Maupertuis, *Système de la nature: Essai sur la formation des corps organisés,* in *Oeuvres,* 4 vols. (Lyon, 1756), 2: 148* [164]; my emphasis. This volume of this particular edition has duplicated pagination after p. 160; the number in square brackets refers to the interpolated page number, while the starred figure represents the repeated page number.

34. Ibid., 2: 154* [170].

35. Quoted in Tort, *L'ordre et les monstres,* 239.

Diderot's Errant Nature

Of course, when the monster was redefined as "a simple variant in the interplay of familiar norms,"[36] as just another example of error, the very idea of aberration could easily lose its value without a redefinition of identity.[37] By defining variation in terms of biological error, Maupertuis locates identity in some mythical (perhaps biblical) parental unit: the error of difference must, after all, be measured against an original order of some kind. The difficulty of actually penetrating this privileged order interested Diderot in his own evolutionary speculations.[38] The more Diderot studied the problems, the less it seemed entirely clear that the various forms of being in nature should be seen as aberrant versions of some master prototype, the variant product of some pure beginning. He began to question the interaction between error and the defining context of environmental order.

Diderot saw that within a dynamic framework, variety was simply a response to continual change and disruption. That is, Diderot saw the complex variety of forms not as deviations from order but as productive expressions of a natural force that was essentially blind. "It seems that nature has been pleased to vary the same mechanism in an infinity of different ways. It abandons a species [*genre*] of productions only after having multiplied the individuals under all possible aspects." Nature was a process of trial and error. We now observe only the successful versions of all kinds of species that exist as prototypes; not ideal forms, but prototypes in a more modern industrial sense: a vehicle for testing. The exterior forms of beings could be interpreted as "successive metamorphoses of the prototype's envelope," wrote Diderot. Nature, then, was less an ordered whole than a whole that constantly formed new orders. Forms, Diderot suggested, were essentially "transitory."[39] As a consequence, the world of nature was marked by "a rapid succession of beings that follow one another, advance, and disappear; a transient symmetry; a momentary order." The variety of species, thought Diderot, was a vast experimental procedure aimed at testing forms that might or might not succeed in this impermanent, unstable environmental context. The human being, far from being a perfected development (as Robinet

36. Huet, *Monstrous Imagination*, 102.
37. This seems to be the implication of Michel Foucault's *Les mots et les choses: Une archéologie des sciences humaines* (Paris, 1967).
38. Lester G. Crocker analyzes the evolution of Diderot's evolutionary thinking in "Diderot and Eighteenth-Century French Transformism," in Glass et al., *Forerunners of Darwin*, 114–43. The analysis is grounded by modern genetic evolution theory.
39. Denis Diderot, *Pensées sur l'interprétation de la nature* (1753), in *Oeuvres complètes*, ed. Herbert Dieckmann et al. (Paris, 1975–), 9: 35–36, 43.

may have thought), was merely a successful one, Diderot suggested. As he wrote, if man had at the beginning of his existence suffered from a blocked larynx or a lack of appropriate food, the species would have quickly vanished.[40]

And so while Diderot speculates, in the manner of Maupertuis, as to how variations in species might come about through defective reproductive material, he ultimately argues that the error of the transformation, the aberration of the monster or defective offspring, can be defined as a deviant failure only in relation to a specific set of circumstances. Diderot was less interested in the idea of error in the genetic material than in the idea that all beings were the chance result of random combinations.[41] The aberrant being is really only a momentary incompatibility in the complex order of natural transition. As human beings, we can hardly experience the vastness of the temporal order, and so the survival of our own human species is by no means guaranteed. If the conditions of existence were to change, humanity could simply disappear. The "order" is always in a state of flux, and just as there have been species before us that no longer exist, in the future there will be new ones. Everything in nature is transitory.[42]

Diderot refuses to define variation in terms of any kind of standard. The error Maupertuis identified is only the product of blind chance for Diderot, a chance that governs all "production." The variation is a defect only if it does not survive; otherwise it can be legitimately seen as a development. Diderot asked: "What is a monster? A being whose life is incompatible with the existing order." The monster was just unsuccessful, and not perverse or evil, something Holbach argued as well. Norm and deviation had no stable context of reference. The challenge, for Diderot, was to rethink the norm itself as "monster."[43]

> But the general order is always changing. The advantages and disadvantages [*vices et vertus*] of the preceding order have led to the existing order, whose advantages and disadvantages will lead to the order that follows, without our being able to say that the whole is improving or worsening.

40. Diderot, *Lettre sur les aveugles, à l'usage de ceux qui voient,* in *Oeuvres complètes,* 4: 50–52.

41. Huet, *Monstrous Imagination,* 90. Huet cites Jay Caplan's *Framed Narratives: Diderot's Genealogy of the Beholder* (Minneapolis, 1985), 65–66, for this distinction between error and chance.

42. Diderot, *Le rêve de d'Alembert,* in *Oeuvres complètes,* 17: 128.

43. See Huet, *Monstrous Imagination,* 89–90. Cf. Ehrard, *L'idée de nature,* 1: 214, 234; and Emita B. Hill, "The Role of 'Le Monstre' in Diderot's Thought," *Studies on Voltaire and the Eighteenth Century* 97 (1972).

The idea of the monster, then, is entirely relative. "Why should man, why should all the animals not be regarded as slightly more enduring species of monsters? . . . The universe sometimes seems to be only a collection of monstrous beings." Success and failure define what is "normal" and aberrant in this context. As Diderot writes: "The world is the house of the strongest."[44] There is no essential order in the world, only an interaction of transient, infinitely variable forms. As Kant would later speculate, perhaps nature was irreducibly diverse, resisting any pattern of internal order.[45] Past and future bear no relation to one another in this chaotic interaction. Nature is defined in terms of difference, not identity. At the end of the century it was possible, in fact, to define monstrosity as a function of abnormal *resemblance*.[46] Robinet, in his *De la nature* (1761), wrote: "The existence of Nature is necessarily successive. . . . A state of permanence does not befit it. . . . In this continual vicissitude, there are no two points in the existence of Nature precisely similar in whole or in part. Though always the same, it is always different."[47] The continuity of the forms of nature was evident in the analogical similarities revealed through comparative study, yet these various forms arrayed in grids of resemblances were themselves transitory.

PALINGENESIS AND THE TRANSFORMATION OF BEING

Awareness of radical natural variety led Diderot inevitably to a belief in essential indeterminacy, the idea that any one form is really aberrant or monstrous, and only relatively successful. Yet variety did not have to be strictly defined in terms of a static (and comprehensive) order for there to be continuity between variant forms. As Maupertuis suggested, perhaps change itself could be the result of a crisis or disruption. It is not the case, then, that Diderot's "deconstructed" natural order could be opposed only by some kind of continuing general order, which would be defined systematically. If the error of variation was both a deviation and, in a sense, an adaptation, then it was possible to identify a line of continuity between radical disjunctures. Maupertuis failed to explore this line of thought, however.

The Swiss naturalist Charles Bonnet, though, did develop a theory of transformational development that celebrated this kind of continuity.

44. Diderot, *Eléments de physiologie*, in *Oeuvres complètes*, 17: 444, 517.

45. See Larson, *Interpreting Nature*, 173.

46. Jacques-André Millot, *L'art de procréer les sexes à volonté, ou Système complet de la génération* (1800), discussed in Huet, *Monstrous Imagination*, 95–102.

47. Quoted and translated in Arthur Lovejoy, *The Great Chain of Being: A Study of the History of an Idea* (Cambridge, Mass., 1936), 274–75.

With Bonnet there is an attempt to link the obvious diversity of natural forms with the equally apparent unity of the universe, a unity that in Diderot's scheme could in the end be defined only as the containing border of a chaotic proliferation. The error of difference Maupertuis identified becomes in Bonnet the means of transition to a higher order of existence altogether. What Bonnet did was introduce the future back into the formal organization of natural life. Robinet and Maupertuis saw natural forms as being pushed forward in time in greater degrees of complexity or differentiation. Diderot denied any order to this "progression" either across space or through time. Bonnet, however, tried to explain how these forms were in a sense *drawn* into the future, and were therefore involved in a process of becoming.

In Bonnet's conception, the universe was united spatially and temporally in a series of interrelated chains, where nothing was isolated and every event was linked to the most distant occurrence.[48] This arrangement was a dynamic one; the universe was not a fixed, hierarchical order for all time. Although each species maintained its identity, as the circumstances of existence changed, the forms of beings could change accordingly. Humanity was not, therefore, limited to its present state, nor was any other identity. What distinguished Bonnet's theory from many eighteenth-century speculations was the idea that the external form was a variable "envelope" for an essential human identity that was in itself incorruptible. "Man is thus not at all essentially [*en soi*] what he appears to us to be. What we discover of him here on earth is only the crude envelope." These crude forms that cover humanity were not, however, the result of some blind experimentation (as Diderot believed). The form was, in a sense, the sacrificial vessel that preserved human identity in a corporeal condition: "The husk [*envelope*] of grain perishes, the Seed remains, and assures Man his immortality."[49]

Bonnet suggests here that while a material existence will always be subject to transformations, there exists a whole other plane of spiritual existence, and humanity must be understood as dwelling in both spheres. Therefore, the constant change of human (and other natural) form, he said, should not lead us to the conclusion that identity is merely a function of momentary success. For Bonnet, the radical transformation of species, races, even mineral organizations, were all opportunities for

48. Charles Bonnet, *Contemplation de la nature,* new ed., 3 vols. (Hamburg, 1782), 1: 7. For a contextualization of Bonnet's theory of palingenesis and a discussion of the intellectual differences between Bonnet and Ballanche on this topic, see Arthur McCalla, "*Palingénésie philosophique* to *Palingénésie sociale:* From a Scientific Ideology to a Historical Ideology," *Journal of the History of Ideas* 55 (1994): 421–39.

49. Bonnet, *Contemplation de la nature,* 1: 207.

progress, leading to the eventual liberation from corporeal form alto-gether. This process was described as a kind of continual rebirth, which Bonnet called "palingenesis."

This word Bonnet adopted from the Greek, "signifying *new birth,* and which could be rendered by the French word *renaissance.*" This defini-tion expressed Bonnet's belief (shared by Maupertuis and other eigh-teenth-century naturalists) that the earth had undergone drastic revolu-tionary changes in its geological existence. Bonnet rejected the idea that the book of Genesis was really an account of some original creation. In-stead, he saw this narrative as the description of the beginning of the most recent "epoch" of the earth's history.[50] Clearly, the magnitude of change involved in these epochal revolutions was extraordinary. Bonnet would suggest that the variety of species in existence at any one time could survive these radically new circumstances only by transforming their bodily shape. The variety of forms, then, could not be measured as deviations from "original" forms. Any particular form was a temporary version encapsulating the true identity of the species. For this reason Bonnet was critical of contemporary natural science for the belief that it might be possible to trace the forms of beings to their original "proto-types." The envelope of any being is not the true essence of its being, Bonnet asserted. The animal is not merely a "collection" of its parts, to be analyzed and compared in minute detail. In fact, the envelope is a kind of mask that not only protects the essential being in its worldly existence but at the same time conceals it from our view. The impenetrable core of identity is hidden by the transient form it takes. Bonnet can then argue that humanity is immortal, that it never changes, despite the fact it is constantly transformed with every new global epoch.

What Maupertuis saw as errors of difference Bonnet integrates into a theory of progress. The immense variety of physical forms are all linked together as a series of steps that immortal beings ascend over time. But this theory of palingenesis reintroduces the concept of error in a new context. The progression within the divine order, the ongoing rebirth of the human essence in newer and higher forms of existence, places hu-manity (in its past and present forms, at least) in an errant condition: hu-manity is displaced from the highest order of knowledge, and can only glimpse the superficial effects of the universal reality as it wanders over

50. Charles Bonnet, *La palingénésie philosophique, ou Idées sur l'état passé et sur l'état futur des êtres vivans* (1770), in *Oeuvres d'histoire naturelle et de philosophie,* 18 vols. (Neuchatel, 1779–83), 15: 171n, 255. Bonnet believed that the vast diversity of the universe, the fact that there was an infinite number of suns and worlds with the potential for life, made the central significance of our particular planet's creation an especially absurd idea. (See ibid., 258.)

the globe. If, as Bonnet said, the universe is an immensely complex chain linking diverse formal expressions of hidden internal identities, the human mind can know only a few of them, and even then it cannot really be sure of their ultimate order: "We follow this admirable progression only very imperfectly and through thousands and thousands of detours." At our point of development, it is clear that humanity is denied entrance to what Bonnet calls the "Temple" of truth, and must be content with observing only the surface effects of things. "Man lives only in the farthest courtyards of this Temple where he adores the GREAT BEING." The beauty of the inner sanctums are made for higher intelligences, Bonnet declares, whose "sublime faculties" not only allow them to avoid the intrinsic aberrations marking human perception, but "who travel without losing their way [s'*égarer*] through the shadowy Labyrinths [*Dédales*] of Nature, and who, penetrating their deepest depths, draw from there endless new truths." For these intelligences, Bonnet writes, Leibniz, Haller, all the great human thinkers would seem like mere Hottentots.[51]

And yet according to Bonnet, humanity will eventually gain this knowledge, living more and more in the intellectual realm, and freed from its crude corporeal form, just as certain animals will ascend to humanity's place in this world during the next global revolution. "One day we will draw all light from the ETERNAL SOURCE, and instead of contemplating the WORKER in the work, we will contemplate the work in the WORKER. *At present, we see things confusedly, and as if in a dim glass; but then we will see face to face.*"[52] The goal of the revolutionary progress of the species is reintegration with the eternal being who never changes. The intermediate forms all cloud and distort our vision of the true reality. In the middle of this voyage up the ladder of being, humanity is caught between the mere transience of corporeal existence and the purity of intellectual being: this state defines human errancy ("wandering" over the surface of appearances) and a human potential to gain the truth (the inner workings of nature as part of God's thought). Each step in the ongoing palingenesis is a preparation for future insight; each step prepares a movement toward truth.

The line of thought Bonnet follows here links natural history with human history. If Bonnet was interested in the cosmic problem of diversity and progress measured on a vast universal scale, the same approach to the relationship between variety and identity could be applied to human existence within this particular cosmic epoch—which for Bonnet began with the story of Genesis and will end with global destruction by

51. Ibid., 16: 502–3, 27–29.
52. Bonnet, *Contemplation de la nature*, 3: 444.

fire, as predicted in the New Testament.[53] Social forms, like natural forms, could be seen as variations of an original, united community, or, alternatively, as the chance organization of isolated individuals. The unity of humanity is problematic because social organization by definition marks the separation of peoples, races, cultures, languages. While mainstream thought in the human sciences might have looked to the study of the individual as a physiological and psychological being as one way of penetrating this common identity, it was possible to work out this problem in a more historical context.

When Rousseau, for example, sought the origin of human inequality, he was forced to address the difficult problem of how to identify the essential characteristics of humanity, characteristics that had perhaps been obscured through generations of modification and even degradation. Rousseau asked, in the preface to the *Second Discourse:*

> How will man manage [*viendra-t-il à bout de*] to see himself as Nature formed him, through all the changes that the succession of time and circumstances must have produced in his original constitution, and so distinguish what is connected to his own foundation from that which circumstances and his progress have altered or added to his primitive state? Like the statue of Glaucus, which time, the sea, and storms had so disfigured that it resembled less a god than a ferocious beast, the human soul altered in the heart of society by a thousand ever-recurring causes, by the acquisition of a multitude of knowledge and errors, by the changes taking place in the constitution of bodies, and by the continual impact of the passions, has, as it were, changed in appearance to the point of being almost unrecognizable.[54]

This problem of separating the continuity of humanity's true identity from the deviant modifications introduced over the course of his historical existence leads Rousseau to the controversial method to be employed in the essay: the description of "natural man" on the brink of entering society. Here Rousseau formulates a conjecture to clarify the question, not resolve it, since the reality of humanity's natural state is not open to observational techniques. Rousseau makes no attempt to penetrate the natural origin. What he tries to do is construct an admittedly artificial picture of human identity, an image free from the disruptive particularities of actual historical forms. The knowledge gained, however, will be

53. Bonnet, *La palingénésie philosophique,* 181: "And this new creation will introduce here a new order of things, completely different from that which we contemplate at present."

54. Rousseau, *Discours sur l'origine et les fondemens de l'inégalité parmi les hommes,* in *Oeuvres complètes,* ed. Bernard Gagnebin and Marcel Raymond, 5 vols. (Paris, 1964–95), 3: 122.

real, but it will be of a "state that no longer exists, that perhaps never existed, and that will probably never exist, and yet of which it is necessary to have just ideas to judge our present state well." Rousseau's anthropology uses an ideal-type structure to penetrate identity (which for him is the divine supernatural gift of reason and language) in the midst of degeneration and error. Here Rousseau crystallizes an important concept in Enlightenment thought: the idea of an invisible continuity within a history of radical disruption.

What Rousseau says about the evolution of humanity in the *Second Discourse* could be applied to the whole natural world in the eighteenth century.[55] The problem of identity and difference, in particular the idea that unity could be translated into diversity, linked the structures of natural evolution with human historical movement. Of course, the historical development could be approached in many ways in this period. The variety of social forms, like the variety of species, could have resulted from an imperfect transmission of original traditions, from a separation or fragmentation due to geographical disruptions early in our history, or even from blind chance. But it is, I think, worth tracing another alternative, one suggested by the approach of writers like Bonnet and Rousseau. Rather than trying to reconcile the overwhelming diversity of peoples and customs, or the vast arrays of natural forms, throughout historical time or across all global spaces, by defining these differences with respect to one singular foundational moment, or one shared universal characteristic, some intellectuals made identity a function of the temporal process itself. This move to history, so important in the postrevolutionary era, originated in the Enlightenment. Diversity, for some thinkers, was accepted as part of a *movement* of a hidden identity as it expressed itself at any one time in history. As Bonnet suggested, the complex form of any situated being was a function of both a contingent material history and a future-oriented identity. What needed to be explained was less the origin of this identity than the origin of this temporal complexity: how did the original identity of humanity, for example, become fractured into diverse forms, and what path would lead to a reintegration of those forms into one unitary form of being? The very

55. One philosopher, also a translator of Bacon, wrote a book whose "sole idea," the key to all other ideas (which were only "transformations"), was that "all particular phenomena are only transformations of the unique phenomenon that reveals the Universe, and of which this idea is only the representation." The "visible universe" is "only one sole movement varied by the circumstances of time, place, quantity, figure, situation, distance, etc.": Antoine de La Salle, *La balance naturelle, ou Essai sur une loi universelle appliquée aux sciences, arts et métiers, et aux moindre détails de la vie commune* (London [i.e. Paris], 1788), ix, xiii–xiv.

multiplicity of beings, as Bonnet indicated, concealed the essential unity, and this meant that unity would be rediscovered only fleetingly in moments of transformation. If difference marked the aberrant translation of a divine unity into time and space, then this unity would be found not within these errors but only in the gaps between them.

NATURAL REVOLUTION AND SOCIAL FRAGMENTATION

This line of thought was engaged in the Comte de Nogaret's *Essais sur les montagnes* (1785), an unusual but revealing text that can serve as a bridge between Bonnet's concept of natural palingenesis and postrevolutionary historical understanding, like Ballanche's theory of social transformation. Taking as its point of departure eighteenth-century natural history, Nogaret's text attempted to integrate commonplace conceptions of radical disruption and violence in the natural world with traditional religious approaches to the fragmentation of human identity and its possible redemption. For the most part, as is evident from his title, Nogaret tried to theorize about the formation of mountains, and did so within the expected framework of eighteenth-century natural history. The world, we are told, has undergone radical disordering events, such as great floods, and these events have caused radical upheavals in the surface features of the globe. However, near the end of this complicated explication of geographical transformation Nogaret described the effect of these *bouleversements* on human societies. Unlike such naturalists as Bonnet and Maupertuis, who discussed how the *species* might be transformed in the course of these radical events, Nogaret worked out provocative ideas on the diversity of social groups within the history of the human race as a whole.

Like so many Enlightenment figures, Nogaret addressed the difficult problem of explaining the plurality of human languages and the unity of human speech. Here he argued that global geographical disruptions fragmented the original shared identity of the human community. That identity having been "transformed many times" in the course of renewal, the common bonds of society and language had been broken. The pressures of change had weakened the links between individuals. Just as the natural world was no longer the same, having suffered great violence in its past, its inhabitants were no longer "one people" and had become as inconstant as the earth's surface. Variety here becomes the mark of degeneration for Nogaret. "Separated peoples" were forced to form new signs for new ideas, new ideas generated by new conditions introduced by geological revolution. "Their language has weakened; it has taken varieties, new turns; . . . it has been formed from disfigured dialects, relative to local circumstances and new needs." As Nogaret explained, languages are necessarily perverted in this adaptation to "local circumstances," which vary as much as the geographical regions of the earth. "All the signs of thoughts, all the accents of the heart, all the expressions of ideas are mutilated and debased imitations of the same model. It is the hundredth copy, by a hundred apprentices, of a Raphael painting."[56] Each change, each reproduction introduces an errant variation until the original is no longer even visible.

The kind of radical variation Nogaret locates within humanity points again to a familiar structure: we see here the vision of a lost identity that cannot by definition be regained simply through an analysis of these deviant fragments. Reintegration is impossible in a present state of aberration, yet the very sense of aberration holds out the ideal as a possibility. This is how Nogaret addressed the problem. A universal language, he said, cannot be recreated from the fragmented, perverted remains of the original language lying hidden in "mutilated" dialects. However, any attempt to construct an arbitrary new identity would result only in a false unity with no genuine foundation. A true integration required the remaking of humanity in its entirety. The critical problem, Nogaret observed, was that having lost our identity with our origin after generations of errant wandering on the globe, we often think that the diversity and imperfection we see in the world are inevitable and natural to our being. As Nogaret wrote:

We are like the descendants of wandering travelers [*voyageurs égarés*], and were long ago cast by storms into new lands, under an unknown sky, who . . . have lost any memory of the native land and the happiness of their fathers; so, not conscious enough of the impression that remains of their former state, they come in the end to the opinion that they were born in that region, and that the ailments associated with their constitution are natural and inseparable from their condition.[57]

Unlike Bonnet, who described the almost automatic progress of humanity in each transformative act of palingenesis, Nogaret claimed that the more glorious human past would have to be actively regained if the fu-

56. Comte de Nogaret, *Essais sur les montagnes*, 2 vols. (Amsterdam, 1785), 2: 472–73, 482.

57. Ibid., 606. Nogaret's text has much in common with Nicolas-Antoine Boulanger's *L'antiquité dévoilée par ses usages* (1766), where the radical fragmentation of the world caused by the great flood is discussed. Boulanger writes that the floodwaters completely changed the geography of the earth's surface, and man was abandoned in this disrupted environment: "He erred in obscurity in the debris of his dwelling place": *Oeuvres*, 6 vols. (Amsterdam, 1794), 2: 320–21.

ture integration were to be accomplished: "[Humanity's] renewal has made it forget what it was; it cannot compare itself with itself." Europe had become the "land of error [*patrie des erreurs*]," Nogaret claimed, precisely because it refused to acknowledge its essential aberrations. Only when it did so could it even begin to seek the path forward.

For Nogaret, the past state was not something to be reestablished in its original purity, since both humanity and its material context had been irreversibly transformed. Yet the traces of our origin, however faint, however fleeting, still remained within us, and could be the starting point of recovery, the instrument for the reestablishment of peace and order in the world. Here the differentiation and variability of human social forms could become the tool for the rediscovery of our essential unity as human beings. Repeated change was, for Nogaret, a path toward stability, since the world we lived in was itself not at all stable. Unity would be rediscovered as the spiritual continuity between human beings in varied contexts; the memory of unity, not its concrete original expression, would found a new order of existence.[58] The errors of the prototypical social form, unlike the errors of physiological change, could be overcome, but only if those faint traces of identity were recognized. Again, for Nogaret as for so many others in the Enlightenment, it was the very condition of error that opened up the space for insight into a lost truth.

BALLANCHE'S SOCIAL PALINGENESIS: HISTORY AS ERRANCY

Writing in the wake of the massive social disruptions and violence that scarred Europe during the revolutionary period, Pierre-Simon Ballanche outlined a vast and ambitious theory of social transformation that brought together the Enlightenment discourse of error, theological speculation, and the structural conditions of natural history and evolution in the eighteenth century. Looking back to Bonnet's concept of palingenesis, which he explicitly invoked, Ballanche saw that the errancy of human history was linked to an original error, one that had fragmented a unified human identity. The historical process generated by this original error would, he thought, constitute a process of expiation that would lead ultimately to a reintegration of humanity, with itself and with the divine. Ballanche drew from Bonnet the central idea of a continuing identity that was manifested in particular and transient externalized forms. What Bonnet had done for "man" as an individual physical being Ballanche declared he would do for humanity understood as a social being. Bonnet, whom Ballanche called the "Brahmin" of natural sci-

58. Nogaret, *Essais sur les montagnes*, 2: 612–32.

ence, had shown in *La palingénésie philosophique* how "even during his transient existence, the mortal being can manifest in himself the immortal being, how the imperishable and incorruptible being is contained in the corruptible and perishable being," wrote Ballanche. Now Ballanche himself would set out to show the same structure for the *homme collectif*, tracing "under varied and sometimes symbolic forms the image of every transformation of human societies."[59] This was the foundation of a social palingenesis: the recovery of a human identity veiled by both the spatial fragmentation of peoples and the particular historical transformations each of them was undergoing over time.

Ballanche's own working method, emblematic of his theory of transformation, provides a concrete example of this idea of "hidden" identity. Introducing his own work, he explained that the successive nature of literary exposition always leads to a diversity of expressions and explanations, but the discontinuity of these wanderings does not really vitiate the essential unity of their inspiration. This principle applied not just to individual works, Ballanche says, but also to the complete body of writing over the course of a life. Fittingly, Ballanche throughout his career rarely finished complete, discrete works; they were always being rewritten, expanded, and republished in ever new forms. Moreover, every work invariably contained elaborate plans for ever greater, more comprehensive examinations of human history and tradition.

The *Palingénésie sociale*, for example, the text we will focus on here, was essentially a series of introductory essays that would function as only the preparation for a vast, multivolume historical philosophy. In this text he warned that any wandering in the organization of the ideas was not to be taken as evidence of any incoherence in thought. "Irregularity" in the course of ideas was only apparent, he advised. The actual book would be successive and fragmented, perhaps, but the main idea would be "perfectly unified, perfectly identical, perfectly homogeneous," and the impression for the reader ought to be equally perfect. The book was the same thought, or the same "sentiment," clothed in "different forms." The true book, then, is not at all written in concrete texts, it exists as this "general impression" formed by each reader after he has followed the diverse paths of the texts.[60] Ballanche's description of his own writing echoes Bonnet's earlier discussion of the biblical texts, texts that seem on first reading to be so disjointed, even contradictory,

59. Pierre-Simon Ballanche, *Palingénésie sociale: Prolégomènes*, in *Oeuvres complètes* (1833, 6 vols.; reprint [1 vol.] Geneva, 1967), 4: 9 [304]. Numbers in brackets refer to the page of the reprint edition, each of which contains four pages of the original edition cited.
60. Ibid., 4: 18–21 [306–7].

and therefore so inconclusive. A great part of *La palingénésie philosophique* was in fact devoted to a discussion of textual "unity" in the Scriptures, with Bonnet trying to show that a correct reading would clearly reveal the truth of the texts' common origin. He relates that after setting out to read the Bible "impartially," he saw "the oppositions disappear, the shadows grow dim, the light burst forth from the heart of obscurity, Faith unites with Reason, and forms with it from then on only the same unity."[61]

Ballanche's own textual unity had to be "discovered" in a similar fashion. And what Ballanche invited the reader to do for his own work he attempted to do for human history as a whole. Humanity, like the text, was a real entity, an ideal reality that existed only in the variety of expressions in each historical epoch. The wanderings of history had to be retraced if the "general impression" of human identity was to be felt. Ballanche believed that there was a common origin for humanity, and that this original life had left traces in each of the particular histories of individual peoples and civilizations. These particular forms would not themselves lead to a common point of departure. The manifestation of different human societies was not a gradual evolution; it was, Ballanche said, a break that subsequently makes any return to the origin impossible. There is always a point reached in the historical past where it is impossible to penetrate the clouds veiling early formations. Nonetheless, the origin persists as a kind of mythic presence. Our historical sense forces us to think temporally, yet the true beginning lies outside the structure of time. The human mind cannot think this origin yet it knows it must exist.

> There is thus a state of humankind anterior to that which is contained in history, or which is deduced from history. This anterior state is itself decreed in another sort of history, [a] fantastic history whose details we are not familiar with, clothed in ungraspable forms, which has a chronology, but an ideal chronology, which amounts to either a dogma or a myth, according to traditions and beliefs.[62]

These traditional stories and ideas are strange, aberrant visions of a prehistorical state. Ballanche's goal is to work through these symbolic forms in all their irreconcilable variety and penetrate this original state. As he later described his work on palingenesis, it was a matter of "divining, under the veil of local and particular traditions, the genius of general traditions."[63] Ballanche was tracing a "difficult route" and attempting, as he

---

61. Bonnet, *La palingénésie philosophique*, 473.
62. Ballanche, *Palingénésie sociale*, 4: 75 [320].
63. Ballanche, *La ville des expiations, et autres textes*, ed. P. Michel (Lyon, 1981), 154.

put it, "to explain the ruins" observed along the way.[64] Human mythology was a series of ruins to be interpreted in light of their original living forms.

And so Ballanche embarked on an ambitious voyage through the myths of antiquity in order to reveal the common source of all early traditions. He believed that he had found evidence of this mark of continuity. "Each people has had, if one can speak this way, a translation of general traditions of the human species that it has applied." Working through Egyptian, Greek, and Oriental traditions, Ballanche found that each historical form was a kind of transformation of another. These identities within traditions, suggested Ballanche, "are perhaps nothing but the very forms of human intelligence diversely manifested according to the variety of languages."[65] The universal facts of human existence are expressed in specific national identities. Even if there is a "mistranslation," the germ of this common origin is preserved, and so Ballanche can, for example, write: "False religions exist, without doubt, only through the force of tradition, which links them to true revelations; and they are in a way a very emanation of these revelations. Truth alone can always live on [*subsister*]."[66] Here the error is a revelation of a lost truth, a truth that in a sense lives on through the error.

In fact, the truth that Ballanche believed he had discovered in his historical and literary analysis was this: the origin of human history was always traced to the idea of error. Humanity, according to all religions, was undergoing a series of tests, a process of expiation linked to some original transgression. Ballanche concluded that humanity had been condemned to a historical existence that was in fact a form of punishment. This idea led Ballanche to the theory that humanity "could be regarded as the same individual passing through a series of palingeneses." The division of mankind is understood to be the result of a lost continuity, since the common memory of a past identity is preserved, however dimly, in all cultures. "Man, that is to say intelligence, the human essence, has been taken from the domain of eternity in order to live in the domain of time. Thought has thus become successive."[67]

The reason for this fall into time (one that echoes Condillac's own phenomenological fall of the self into time and space) is related by Ballanche in his synthesis of mystic and Christian doctrine, *La vision d'Hébal*, a strange text that recounts the revelations of a young Scottish clansman as a way of introducing a "history" of humanity. There Ballanche described

64. Ballanche, *Essai sur les institutions sociales*, in *Oeuvres complètes*, 2: 118 [132].
65. Ballanche, *Palingénésie sociale*, 4: 93, 47 [325, 313].
66. Ballanche, *Institutions sociales*, 2: 59–60 [117].
67. Ballanche, *Palingénésie sociale*, 4: 14, 36–37 [305, 310–11].

how, even before the birth of man, error—that straying from truth—was introduced into the world with the fall of the angels: "Among the intelligent substances a few erred, and a place became necessary in order to invest them with a form, a form that had to serve to regenerate them by trial."[68] This was the origin of matter. When the universal man, who exists wholly within God's thought, is set free to be responsible in the world, a similar error is committed, and it is here that the universal man is imprisoned in material forms and his identity divided. The initial division of the sexes is, for Ballanche, the emblem for all human difference, and also serves as an image of succession, since this original division is repeated through propagation. History, as Ballanche interprets it through the medium of the originary myths of ancient tradition (and included in these traditions is Christianity, a religion that Ballanche believed to have existed in early forms long before the appearance of Christ), is the fall into successive material existence, which serves to expiate the error that defines human alienation from the divine. Man is divided in order to be expiated (divided quite literally, into male and female), but he does not therefore cease to be identical to himself.[69] "Broken unity produces succession."[70] This unity can still be revealed in the midst of its fragmentation, if perceived in the proper way.

The division of peoples that is represented by the plurality of human languages is one basic form of this problematic. "Human language was broken and divided; the human races share among themselves the debris of human language."[71] Ballanche writes that the unity of humankind and the unity of human language are "two identical unities." "Languages are the forms of the human spirit." The various tongues are the expressions of what constitutes and characterizes distinct social groups. Despite the diversity of their expression, then, Ballanche stresses that it should always be understood that these diversities leave intact the idea of "a sole human essence."[72] The commonalities identified in a general grammar attest to linguistic continuity. It is important, though, to recognize that these diverse forms are not only related, but related in a particular way: each tongue is a version of a more primitive, perfect means of expression, and while each maintains some connection with this lost original (otherwise, speech would be mere sound, entirely transient), we have at present only a "confused" memory of this past state of being.[73]

68. Ballanche, *La vision d'Hébal*, ed. A.-J.-L. Busst (Geneva, 1969), 125–26, 135–38.
69. Ballanche, *Palingénésie sociale*, 4: 78–80 [321].
70. Ballanche, *La vision d'Hébal*, 137.
71. Ibid., 147.
72. Ballanche, *Palingénésie sociale*, 4: 181, 36–37 [347, 310–11].
73. Ballanche, *Institutions sociales*, 2: 241–42, 308–9 [163, 179–80].

The fragmentation of language is the trace of the human fall into the world, the effect, that is, of a disjuncture introduced between the divine word and the human word. Echoing Maistre, Ballanche says that human beings may wish to create lasting monuments by means of the name, but they have lost this power and therefore nothing they create will truly last.[74] "The prerogative of naming," wrote Ballanche, "is in a sense a participation in the creation." When Adam was granted the right to name the animals in the Garden of Eden, an "intimate knowledge" of nature was revealed to him, the very essence of all the created beings.[75] Having "succumbed" to temptation, however, humanity is exiled from this intimacy. No longer seeing things from within, "man," Ballanche tells us, sees only "the relations of things to himself." This is a position of "exteriority": "Man, successive being, has need of a sign" to know even his own self. Subjective and objective are no longer "simultaneous," and this disjuncture estranges humanity from the absolute knowledge of divine law and the Creation. Our errors in the sphere of knowledge mirror a more fundamental moral straying from God's will.

> The moral law is thus essentially absolute and unconditional. But man, in his present existence, in a relation of exteriority with the world of creation, can sense it only conditionally and gradually. It is through an effort of human reason assimilated with divine reason that he knows that the moral law is absolute.[76]

For this reason, Ballanche maintains, dissonance and errancy in the world are not easily overcome. It will not be possible to reconcile the multiplicity of human expression, since the "essential and fundamental" difference between people is a consequence of their very individuality, related to their very modes of thought.[77] The human being, who lapses into a successive mode of being as an individual fragment of "universal man," is inevitably discontinuous in his relations with others. As Ballanche writes, animals, who live solely in the present, may come together at times to accomplish a task, but it is always a collection of individuals who resemble one another exactly and simply do the same work in a group. Humanity works through the "conjunction of diverse acts." Human activity is essentially organic, and genuine difference is part of its structure. "Unity for man is in man himself" (that is, as a collective being expressed in diverse parts), whereas animals must be unified by a higher force (God), which brings discrete entities together. Their unity is

74. Ibid., 236 [161].
75. Ballanche, *Palingénésie sociale*, 4: 125 [333].
76. Ballanche, *La ville des expiations*, 133.
77. Ballanche, *Institutions sociales*, 2: 22, 180 [108, 147].

only temporary and imposed.[78] Only humanity is a true collectivity, and not a mere collection of parts.[79] The human being is at once individual and collective, free yet subordinate to a fate shared by all humanity throughout its temporal existence.

The essential discontinuity of human expression means, for Ballanche as it did for Maistre, that perfection is not attainable: imperfection is a part of any actual perfection. Or rather, the very imperfection is what allows for the possibility of perfection in the first place. The task is not to perfect identity at any one time but to keep to the course of development, preserving continuity, preserving the possibility of unity. France, for example, has been subjected as a nation to many changes in habits and customs, but the historical forms of a people do not extinguish or vitiate an inner continuity. And so the French people, Ballanche says, are "similar to these noble characters whose very errors are generous," who are degraded neither by their faults nor by their "infidelities."[80] A nation's "meaning," like that of the text, persists even within the digressions and contradictions of particular events and actions.

Ballanche's theory of social palingenesis assumes that particular societies are the forums for human expiation. The historical process was not, strictly speaking, a mode of punishment, since it was for the most part a means for rehabilitation. In *La ville des expiations* (1823) Ballanche sketched a vision of a prison city designed to provide for the reform of the criminal. This ideal city, Ballanche pointedly noted, was to be seen as an emblem of human social existence in general.[81] Society has been imposed on humanity in its divided, successive condition in order to allow it to regenerate. Given responsibility, human beings must be allowed the opportunity to repair their errant action. A way must be opened to expiate the "painful error," as Ballanche wrote at another time, on capital punishment.[82] The prison city Ballanche envisioned in *La ville des expiations* was a Spartan environment with strict discipline and attention to duties rather than freedom. Those who had strayed entered the city with a new identity and worked to overcome their deviation, and after a period of rehabilitation, they were released into society. The need for this social form was a direct result of human imperfection, the essential lack that stems from the very individuality of the human race.[83] "In another

78. Ballanche, *Réflexions diverses*, in *Oeuvres complètes*, 6: 259 [545].
79. Ballanche, *Palingénésie sociale*, 4: 357 [391].
80. Ballanche, *Institutions sociales*, 2: 23–24 [108].
81. Ballanche, *La ville des expiations*, 24, 35.
82. Ballanche, *Palingénésie sociale*, 4: 305 [378].
83. Ballanche, *Institutions sociales*, 2: 221–28 [158–59].

life, individuality will be more perfect; in this life below, it cannot avoid a thousand reefs."[84]

Ballanche showed that the forms of these expiatory societies in the historical development of humanity are not fixed, but constantly change according to the various stages of the collective being inhabiting them. As Ballanche wrote in his *Orphée:* "Peoples are successively savages, nomads, hunters, farmers, laborers, tradesmen. All these different and successive states demand different and successive laws, emanating from general laws applicable to all."[85] Since the social form is what preserves the identity of humanity, that form is often destroyed to facilitate a new order of life. "Diverse" and "successive" societies "are only variable forms of humanity, one, identical, immortal, marching to its definitive destinies through suffering, trial, expiation."[86] The human spirit passes through these variable forms, which are constantly regenerating themselves, constantly taking on new shapes in new circumstances. Like the Phoenix that rises again from the ashes of destruction, something always survives the death of a society.[87] The successive and diverse forms are vehicles of preparation: "The immutable, situated in time, is obliged to express itself through the mobile organs of time, and thus suffers a successive incarnation. Eternal truth . . . employs progressive expressions, as does the progressive being to whom it is addressed."[88]

In this context, Ballanche thought it was possible to analyze a social form (in its local, particular incarnation) as it is related to the collective being of humanity by using this structural relation between error and truth. "Principles are invariable and absolute, but applications change," wrote Ballanche, repeating Bonald's formulation. The contingency of the world guarantees difference, even deviation. "There is no absolute truth at all . . . no absolute justice in this contingent and conditional world."[89] But the error of the conditional is not to be eliminated. Significantly, Ballanche tells us that "sometimes errors themselves lead to the truth," or, perhaps more accurately, error can be seen as a kind of vehicle for an absolute truth's sojourn in this world, its means of preservation, its *progressive* expression in a contingent reality. In an image that was most likely borrowed from Bonnet, Ballanche comments that "truth often rests after all on error, as the seed of a delicate fruit is protected by the hard cover-

84. Ballanche, *La ville des expiations*, 32.
85. Ballanche, *Orphée*, in *Oeuvres complètes*, 6: 78 [502].
86. Ballanche, "Seconde elégie," in *La Ville des expiations*, 141.
87. Ballanche, *Institutions sociales*, 2: 52 [115].
88. Ballanche, *Palingénésie sociale*, 4: 362–63 [392].
89. Ballanche, *La ville des expiations*, 38, 52.

ing [*enveloppe*] of the kernel."[90] The error itself can survive only if it is in a sense grafted onto truth: "An error always has at its root a truth; without this it could not survive."[91] If the truth of humanity resides in its essential unity over history, then the specific social forms it takes during this time might be seen as the errors continually preserving this inner identity.

As Ballanche tells us: "The present exists only as a condition of the past and future, or rather is only the mysterious assimilation of the past and the future." Once past, present, and future are linked into a peculiarly contemporaneous whole, the outlines of which we cannot wholly perceive, it is possible to see the errors of successive existence as the developing forms of a future state. Society was always painfully moving toward something it was, in a sense, already connected with. This is why the momentary forms of organization were often sacrificed to this movement. "Human passions, violent acts, murders, often serve as the exterior form [*enveloppe*] for the future thought hidden in the present; this future thought triumphs through blood and tears, as the seed hidden in the grain of wheat triumphs through the destruction of the grain itself."[92] The resistance of forms to necessary change results in this violent transformation. Ballanche describes how each particular social form may be appropriate at any one time, even though at a future moment it will be only an error. This is not to say, as some did in the eighteenth century, that every system is perfectly good according to its relative context; rather, the error must serve the truth, which is the general law established for universal humanity in its totality. Whatever function slavery and the caste system may have served, at some point their persistence is unjust: "that which is preparatory became definitive."[93] Inevitably, the system will then collapse, as it did eventually in France with the Revolution.

Like the Phoenix, human societies die and are reborn, but this Phoenix also searches in the ashes for something that must be retained in the new order, trying to find "in the intimate elements of a now stationary principle the seed of a new progressive principle."[94] In a way, this is what drove Ballanche's own work, for he believed that the truth of human identity was expressed in all of its forms, however degraded or far away in the past, and if this "seed" were recovered, a new order could be better prepared. His retellings of traditional narratives such as those of *Or-*

90. Ballanche, *Institutions sociales*, 2: 49 [115].
91. Ballanche, *Palingénésie sociale*, 4: 339 [386].
92. Ballanche, *Réflexions diverses*, 6: 288–89, 290–91 [552, 553].
93. Ballanche, *Palingénésie sociale*, 4: 339–42 [386–87].
94. Ballanche, *Orphée*, 6: 78 [502].

pheus and *Antigone* were ways of recovering such veiled truths. "Man," Ballanche wrote, "is constantly occupied in remaking the past, and the past belongs to him by the same right as the future." He went on to say that each "palingenesic crisis" revealed most clearly the operation of the general laws, as one form died and a new one was prepared. This new order, then, could benefit from an intimate study of past crises. "Man is thus forced to foretell the past, to reconstruct it in accordance with the idea that lies sleeping in monuments, in accordance with the general law that reveals itself at every palingenetic crisis."[95]

For Ballanche, human perfectibility lies in this "reconstruction of being," a great goal worth the inevitable pain and suffering.[96] Although we may at times be ignorant of our ultimate goals, traveling along "obscure paths,"[97] humanity would be redeemed. The path of progress was hardly painless. The difficulties could be directly attributed to the eternal "vicissitudes" of human life, where "nothing is stable."[98] "Feebleness and unhappiness, that is the whole of our history." Ballanche laments that man is constantly subject to error, and always seems to be ignorant of his true interests.[99] "In the heart of the desert we painfully traverse, we sometimes lose sight of the luminous side of this miraculous cloud that is our guide; but still we always see this cloud, and from time to time rays of light emerge from it to enlighten us."[100] Here Ballanche invokes the imagery of Enlightenment as we encountered it in d'Alembert, Castilhon, and Condillac. The shadowy world of error, the clouds and mists of human epistemological travel, become in the end a concrete connection with the ephemeral light of truth obscured by those same obstacles.

In an essay on palingenesis, the nineteenth-century French writer Charles Nodier noted: "I have understood that the life of derision and error we lead on earth, which would appear to be no more than the ironic game of an evil spirit, was on the contrary all that it must be in the ever living and ever progressive system of a creation that is continuing."[101] Movement is here possible and perfection attainable only if we are first capable of error. If humanity was, in all of its individual incarnations, not subject to error ("infallible"), then, as Ballanche wrote, the in-

95. Ballanche, *Réflexions diverses,* 6: 288–89 [552].

96. Ballanche, *Orphée,* 6: 263–64 [546].

97. Ballanche, *Antigone,* in *Oeuvres complètes,* 1: 328–29 [88].

98. Ballanche, *La ville des expiations,* 63.

99. Ballanche, *Fragments,* in *Oeuvres complètes,* 1: 347, 355 [92, 94].

100. Ballanche, *Institutions sociales,* 2: 77 [122].

101. Charles Nodier, "De la palingénésie humaine et de la résurrection," in *Oeuvres,* 12 vols. (1832–37; reprint Geneva, 1968), 5: 344.

dividual "would be just an animal with an elevated intellectual instinct; he would be without merit."[102] Humanity may err in its travel through time, but in the end will merit its accomplishments, for to know the endpoint of any journey makes the path leading there a mere instrument instead of a process of true discovery.

102. Ballanche, *Palingénésie sociale*, 4: 371 [394].

Epilogue: Modern Error

Patterns of historical periodization are at the same time so productive as heuristic devices yet so demonstrably aberrant.

PAUL DE MAN, "The Epistemology of Metaphor" (1978)

In 1807 Bernardin de Saint-Pierre, author of *Paul et Virginie*,
published *La chaumière indienne*. In the preface, writing about truth and
its relationship with human forms of knowledge, he said: "We could
not see the light of the sun if it did not fall upon bodies or at least
clouds. . . . It is the same with truth: we would not be able to seize it if
it did not settle [*se fixer*] in sensible events, or at least in metaphors and
comparisons that reflect it. A body is necessary for it to be reflected."
Why not simply stare at the light itself? This direct illumination would
be blinding, he tells us. The reflection distances us from the origin yet
reveals it to us in a way that is not overwhelming. Our ignorance, he
says, is a kind of eyelid that shields us from the direct light of truth.
"Ignorance is therefore as necessary to truth as shadow is to light."[1]
Neither immersed in darkness nor fully aware of the divine truth, humanity wandered between light and shadow, searching for insight in
the reflections and clouds. We lived in a fundamentally metaphorical
reality, though truth inhabited this reality indirectly. Like Ballanche,
Bernardin de Saint-Pierre never pretended that the human mind could
dispel all the shadows and reveal the pure truth. Humanity was condemned to work through error and fragmentation with the hope of future knowledge. What grounded this hope was the intimate relationship between truth and error. Error was the concrete form of truth for
the human mind. The reflection is an aberration, yet it is a reflection

1. Jacques-Henri-Bernardin de Saint-Pierre, *Oeuvres complètes* (Paris, 1818), 6: 222–23.

243

and aberration of something. Any particular errant manifestation has truth as its origin.

These reflections on light and knowledge take us back to the Enlightenment visions of truth that were our starting point. In late eighteenth-century France, it was understood that human reason was limited, that our organization of experience was always in error because of this limitation. Yet these errors were not mere mistakes. Error was characterized as a more fundamental condition of human existence: without the tangible destination of absolute truth in sight, humanity was wandering, erring in unknown territory. And yet this wandering was not totally random and without value. Enlightenment thought seized on the connection between truth and error. If error could be defined only in terms of truth, then the identification of error was also, in a way, a manifestation of truth. The Enlightenment believed that through error (the error of abstraction, the error of classification, the error of language) truth made its appearance. Following the often ambiguous traces of truth in error was the task of human inquiry.

The psychological error of judgment was, for mainstream Enlightenment figures, understood within the framework of a sensationalist model of the human mind. Here, it would seem, error is difficult to isolate, because of the isolation of the mind itself in relation to a world it can experience only indirectly. The major figure of eighteenth-century sensationalist psychology, Condillac, evades this problem by redefining the context of human experience. For Condillac, the fragmentation of our experience into discrete sensations is, like the fragmentation of the universe into discrete elements and objects, a condition of loss. Our original unity and identity of self, like the original divine unity of the universe, has been lost in this fragmentation, yet the disorder of experience points toward the original unity: it is not mere chaos. So, as Condillac explains, if our efforts to order sensations and manipulate them through language are always somewhat errant, since experience must be "violated" in order to be organized in this way, this organization also points to that original unity that has been lost, though it can never reach it entirely, because of the spatial and temporal limitations of our experience. Error, for Condillac, is the mark of both our epistemological failure and our promise.

The error of the fragment, the truth of divine unity: this basic theological structure reveals itself in secular frames of thought in the late Enlightenment. Rousseau, already secularizing the religious notion of the general will, envisioned a political identity that would guide the decisions of the community. And yet this community was never fully present anywhere at any one time. It could speak, Rousseau said, only through the individual citizens that made up this higher identity. By definition, however, the individual was potentially in error. The interests of any one individual resisted the interests of this higher collective entity. So Rousseau is left with a difficult problem: how to work through this inevitable errancy without any clear idea of the truth that defines political aberration. Condorcet took up this challenge, and attempted to resolve the difficulty with a combination of mathematics and political metaphysics. He hoped to show, first of all, that error could be minimized if political procedures were properly organized. Yet Condorcet was aware that error could never be eliminated, given the ineffability of truth in politics. He thought that error was an inevitable aspect of human progress, a part of our basic historical condition. Again, like other thinkers in this period, Condorcet stressed the need for *preparation* of a space of possible insight. Truth may have been evasive in its essence, yet it emerged and could be recognized if the individual was educated and purged of any intellectual "aberrations." The voice of common reason would speak to the enlightened individual.

The problem Rousseau and Condorcet addressed was not merely intellectual. By 1789, through various political actions and interventions, the idea of the general will and a perfect national unity emerged in France with the Revolution. The abbé Sieyes articulated the consequences of this turn even before the Estates General were transformed into the National Assembly. The nation, as a singular identity, was the measure of political truth. The task of the revolutionaries was to create the proper institutions that would effectively find this identity and voice its will. Early in the Revolution, as the constitution was being shaped, political actors tried to answer this challenge. Since the truth in this context was only partially realized and remained imperfectly known, there was no fundamental agreement on how best to express the will of the nation, the general will of this diverse French identity. Sieyes and others framed this question in terms of error, for they realized that what was at stake was not so much the definition of truth (which was impossible in this situation, as Rousseau had pointed out) as the elimination or at least reduction of error. A space had to be made that would allow the general will to emerge as clearly as possible. This meant finding a way to work through the errors of individual citizens or politicians. The question facing these early revolutionaries, then, was how to decide who was least subject to error. Political divisions were generated by this question. Monarchists had faith in inherited authority as a voice of the general will, radicals had faith in the "people" on the streets, while moderates like Sieyes and Condorcet thought that intellectual training would greatly reduce the chance of error in politics. At any rate, the problem of "representing" something that could never be represented—the sovereignty of the nation as a singular entity—meant that error was intrinsic to the creation of political space in France during the Revolution. However, Sieyes and other early revolutionaries failed to construct a political space that would guard against error, and the constitution (of 1791) that did create a political structure was a failure even before it went into effect. The very notion of popular sovereignty opened up the possibility of legitimate destruction of imperfect political institutions, and in the wake of August 1792, the definition of political space was again in question.

The Terror, the emergency state that eventually filled this space, is almost always approached first as a pathology (of the Revolution, of the Enlightenment, of individual and collective psychology). It is true, however, that Robespierre, early in the Revolution, framed the basic political questions in much the same way as other, less radical figures did. Robespierre understood that the general will was threatened by error; like Sieyes, he thought that a political space had to be formed that would allow this will to be voiced as purely as possible. Robespierre was, in fact, a master at manipulating all the latent ambiguities of sovereignty and the errors of its representation. For Robespierre, depending on the circumstances, any group or individual was potentially in error. The rise of the Terror can be understood in this framework. Robespierre attacked all the political errors before finally gaining the opportunity to institute a new political space. The difference was that this new Jacobin political space that was to reduce error was not fundamentally an institutional one. The new politics of the Terror was an internal and inevitably a moral space. Yet essentially, the structure of revolutionary politics, the relation between errant individuality and perfect collective identity, was not compromised. It was compromised when Robespierre collapsed the fragile relation between error and truth and proclaimed himself the privileged agent of truth, the one who could, without fail, discern error, crime, and virtue.

Postrevolutionary thinkers, shaken by the extreme violence of the Revolution and especially the violence of the Terror, looked to resolve the problem of political order in another context altogether. For theological writers like Maistre and Bonald, the error of the revolutionaries was their belief that through human effort alone order could be established. Human beings were, because of original sin, always in error, always faced with the unknown and the unpredictable. For Maistre, truth could come to humanity only if error was accepted with humility, if we submitted ourselves to an authority that did not represent human sovereignty but instead represented our *lack* of authority. In other words, if we assumed that those in power were infallible and acted accordingly, then the boundaries of our errancy would be fixed and limited. Humanity could move forward in history with less disaster. Still, because of our imperfections, this movement would always be violent and disruptive. Maistre's Augustinian view of humanity is taken up and transformed by Ballanche, another postrevolutionary who experienced the Revolution as a violent and radically disordered event. Ballanche took this larger view of humanity as a collective entity, moving in time as a fragmented version of itself, and reconnected the higher identity (humanity) and the errant fragments (individual societies and individuals). In the violent transformations of human history, perhaps we could glimpse the higher reality as old forms were dying and new ones were being born. The errors were always present, but in the presence of multiple errors perhaps the truth that inhabited them would appear, however fleetingly.

The line of thought I have traced is united by a conceptualization of error as an aberration, or to put it another way, an aberrant manifestation, of truth. The diversity of formulations stems from the different ways truth can be understood: the true judgment, the true voice of the nation, the true nature of humanity or God, all refer to different conceptions of truth. What unites these variations of error and truth is a shared understanding of truth's essential intangibility for limited human minds. In this line of thought, truth is always on the horizon of human knowledge, and therefore, if progress is going to be made toward truth, it must be recognized that any knowledge gained is always structured as error. This error will not be overcome with the sudden revelation of truth. The search for truth is itself an errant voyage of discovery. The problem is how to exploit this connection between truth and error, so that unproductive wandering is avoided and insight prepared.

Seen from the perspective of error, the Enlightenment can hardly be identified as the origin of a ruthless instrumental logic, one that forced the human and natural worlds into rigid formulations, founded on an assumed homogeneity. This raises an interesting question. Where can we locate the origins of a more destructive rationality? At this point, I can offer only a tentative answer. By sketching out a possible history of error after the Enlightenment, we can at least imagine an alternative narrative of modernity.

ERROR AFTER ENLIGHTENMENT

Although it has been long assumed that post-Enlightenment thinkers reacted against the rigidity and dogmatism of eighteenth-century thought by introducing systems that allowed for difference, conflict, and even error, we need to question this turn in modern thought. The Enlightenment figures I have studied were more than aware of the problem of error, its inevitability, its inherently problematic structure. What distinguishes this line of thought from fundamentally new positions that emerge in the nineteenth century is an awareness of the *fragility* of the relation between truth and error. By its very nature, the errant path was, for the late eighteenth-century writers I have analyzed, unpredictable and therefore dangerous. Truth remained highly mysterious; at best, we could prepare the way for the possible appearance of truth, though this insight was by definition exceptional, outside the normal framework for knowledge. By the nineteenth century, however, this almost mystical epistemology, which persists through the revolutionary period and into early Romantic forms of thought, was challenged by a number of positive, often scientific methods of gaining direct access to this ephemeral truth.

The discovery of the error curve in mathematics is emblematic of this shift in consciousness. When Pierre-Simon de Laplace, at the turn of the century, reworked Carl Friedrich Gauss's method of least squares into a comprehensive theory of the distribution of errors, it suddenly became possible to work systematically backward from seemingly disordered experience to the hidden truth revealed by the graphic average.[2] Laplace himself was interested only in observational error, that is, the human error that was introduced into astronomical data, for example. In these cases, there was no question that truth existed: it was simply the accurate position of any one star. But the error curve soon broke out of this limited framework altogether. It was discovered that many examples of variation and difference, in nature and in the human world, obeyed the error curve. The emergence of statistical sciences comes with the awareness that what was thought to be random, disconnected, unpredictable, in fact obeyed the newly discovered law of errors. Adolphe Quetelet, a Belgian astronomer turned statistical sociologist, first applied this Gaussian normal curve to human variation (physical characteristics such as height, criminal activity, marriage frequency) and realized that these variations could be understood as a kind of error, or aberration, with respect to the metaphysical "truths" revealed by the error curves. According to Quetelet, the analysis of human aberration led to the discovery of what he called the *homme moyen*, which became the norm for measuring all variation. This hidden mean, only now revealed by mathematical

2. On Laplace and the development of error theory, see Stephen Stigler's comprehensive *History of Statistics: The Measurement of Uncertainty before 1900* (Cambridge, Mass., 1986), esp. 109–38 and chap. 4.

analysis, gained ontological status.[3] Truth and error coexisted unproblematically.

Of course, Quetelet's social statistics was just one method of discovering tangible order in the midst of disorder, truth in the midst of error,
identity in the midst of aberration. Nineteenth-century thought had as
its object the concrete identification, by means of rigorous methods, of
what was for the Enlightenment an essentially mysterious truth whose
revelations would always be somewhat aberrant. After the Enlightenment, thinkers wanted to straighten the errant path by finding the secret
key that would unlock the truth hiding in error. The error curve was only
one such technique, though perhaps the most elegant and the most
lucid. But I think we can understand a variety of modes of thought that
are emblematic of the early nineteenth century in a similar fashion.
Many intellectuals outlined specific techniques for reaching the truth.
Looked at from the perspective of error and truth, the Romantic insight,
Hegelian dialectic, positivist sociology, laissez-faire political economy,
Darwinian evolutionary biology, statistical analysis, Marxist economics,
all were systematic ways of, if not eliminating error and aberration from
the world, at least reducing it (epistemologically) to mere appearance.
The regularity of "law" or "process" demystified the seemingly disruptive reality of error and aberration in human experience. Inevitably the
identification of these "norms" would lead to attempts to reimpose them
on an imperfect, aberrant reality, or even, in the case of someone like
Francis Galton, to improve these norms with scientific human breeding
programs.[4] Once error and aberration were "tamed,"[5] epistemologically,
some nineteenth-century thinkers thought they could perhaps be eliminated altogether. It was only in the nineteenth century, and not in the Enlightenment, as we usually assume, that some direct access to truth was
thought to be possible.

While this kind of radical positivism would persist well into the twentieth century, critical voices late in the nineteenth century resisted this

3. Two key works are Adolphe Quetelet, *Sur l'homme et le développement de ses facultés,
ou Essai de physique social* (Paris, 1835) and *Du système social et des lois qui le régissent* (Paris,
1848). On Quetelet and the emergence of statistical analysis, see Theodore M. Porter, *The
Rise of Statistical Thinking, 1820–1900* (Princeton, 1986), esp. chaps. 2 and 4. For a broader
context of this development in thinking about error and norms, see Paul Rabinow, *French
Modern: Norms and Forms of the Social Environment* (Cambridge, Mass., 1989) (esp. 66 for
Quetelet).

4. See, for example, Michel Foucault's brilliant *Discipline and Punish: The Birth of the
Prison,* trans. Alan Sheridan (New York, 1979), and Porter, *Rise of Statistical Thinking,*
chaps. 5 and 9.

5. To paraphrase the title of Ian Hacking's treatment of statistics in the nineteenth century: *The Taming of Chance* (Cambridge, 1990).

desire to reduce the concrete particularity of reality to systematic and regular laws. This critical turn can, in light of my reading of an Enlightenment line of thought on truth and error, be understood as a rediscovery of error and a renewed respect for the mystery of truth. To name only three of the most prominent figures, Durkheim, Nietzsche, and Freud all sought, in varied ways, to reintroduce complexity in response to simplistic and overly determinist models of understanding human nature, society, and nature, without abandoning the ideal of truth. It is significant, I think, that for these three key individuals, error and aberration were central to their rethinking of science and truth. Durkheim did, it is true, believe that sociology could be a science—he did, in other words, believe in the *reality* of social forces that lay behind the concrete individual actions of individuals—yet he knew that these forces could be studied only as they appeared in concrete spaces. And Durkheim always recognized that these concrete individual human beings often resisted or even "perverted" these collective forces.[6] The individual action was never entirely predictable. The tension between individual and social reality meant that the truth the sociologist sought was never quite fully present.

At the same time, Nietzsche identified truth as a kind of totality, the comprehensive totality of reality, only to point out that this was something forever inaccessible to limited intelligences that were, he said, shaped by the immediate exigencies of mere biological survival. Nietzsche thus redefined all perspectives on truth as varieties of error. Truth, for human understanding, was not so much the opposite of error as the "posture of various errors in relation to one another."[7] In other words, truth is nothing more than the effective implementation of limited, errant perspectives. Our truth is essentially in error, yet for us it is truth, and must be respected. Error, he would say in various contexts, is necessary for life itself. The worst mistake is to inflate these errant and particular truths to a position of absolute universal truth; this is the greatest error of Western philosophy and religion. Nietzsche's alternative philosophy was one rooted in error: self-consciousness, the very origin of the search for truth, was itself a radical error, an illusion.

In a way, Freud rediscovered error in the wake of Nietzsche, in that he investigated error as a form of truth (or at least a possible site for truth's

6. Durkheim wrote, for example, that "every civilization has its organized system of concepts that characterize it. . . . Because they are collective by nature, they cannot be individualized without being reformed, modified, and, consequently, perverted [*faussées*]": Emile Durkheim, *Les formes élémentaires de la vie religieuse* (Paris, 1960), 622.

7. Friedrich Nietzsche, *The Will to Power*, trans. Walter Kaufmann and R. J. Hollingdale (New York, 1967), 290.

appearance). For Freud, the psychological error (a slip of the tongue, a mistaken judgment, a misreading, a misperception) was important not as a "mistake" in relation to some truth but as a disguised appearance of the unconscious. By its nature, Freud believed, the unconscious can never speak directly in any way; it must appear obliquely, occluded in the blinding clarity that is the forms of conscious thought. If the unconscious ever emerges, it must be essentially transformed; it emerges, that is, only as an aberration of its most important feature—unconsciousness. For this reason, the error of conscious thought cannot be eliminated in any search for the truth; there is no distillation process, mathematical analysis, or dialectical predictability. All expressions of the unconscious are necessarily *not* what they really are, they are aberrations that can, precisely because they are aberrations, break through into consciousness. The error, then, is the only path to a truth that can never be isolated and studied, since every new appearance is unpredictable and unique to the situation. The unconscious can be observed only as the repetitive manifestations of unpredictable forms of contingent error.[8]

This brief look at some key transitional figures in modern thought is meant only to suggest that there was a rediscovery of error in this period, a turn marked by a genuine respect for the essential mystery of truth and a desire for methodological rigor. This observation sets up a possible relationship with eighteenth-century forms of thought that has not been explored. As in the Enlightenment, the new scientific methodology of inquiry in thinkers like Freud and Durkheim is not opposed to the mystery of an ephemeral truth. Rather, science organizes knowledge and prepares the ground for future insight. Science does not represent truth, nor does it constitute a direct path to the truth beyond the horizon that limits our perspective. It does, however, make possible the recognition of truth's novel and fleeting appearances. Error is a mark not of total failure but of *limitation,* and the very concept of limitation reveals a faith in the unlimited, that which simply is in itself, even as error is seen as constantly occluding this essential identity. Modernist thought emphasizes the almost tragic nature of this predicament, the fragmentary experience of something that is no longer with us.

A remarkable parallel can be found even in disciplines associated with

8. See, in particular, Sigmund Freud, "Errors," in *The Psychopathology of Everyday Life,* vol. 6 of *The Standard Edition of the Complete Psychological Works of Sigmund Freud,* trans. James Strachey et al., 24 vols. (London, 1953–). On Freud and the rejection of nineteenth-century models of demystification, see Paul Ricoeur, *Freud and Philosophy: An Essay on Intepretation* (New Haven, 1970). On the necessity of repetition for understanding the unconscious, see Neil Hertz, "Freud and the Sandman," in *The End of the Line: Essays on Psychoanalysis and the Sublime* (New York, 1985).

absolute faith in ultimate truth. Early twentieth-century theology, at least in its more revolutionary manifestations in figures such as Karl Barth, affirms the fragility of the relationship between human error and divine truth by focusing on the radical "alterity" of God, the absolute absence of Christ, and the essential unpredictability of our historical path to redemption. Martin Heidegger was perhaps the first to articulate this basic theological relationship in philosophical language: he defined human existence as a kind of errancy, a wandering across the reality of Being, which functions as a truth that is essentially concealed, yet even in its concealedness is revealed, in a strange way, in the form of error. Writing on the problem of truth in a famous transitional piece of the 1930s, Heidegger repeated, in a surprising way, some of the ideas we see present in eighteenth-century thought. Truth, he said, is this "what-is" revealed, yet this truth is always revealed in error, as a multiplicity of concrete beings in the world. We cannot, he said, find this truth (as so many nineteenth-century forms of thought tried to do) by simply seeking out what is common and universal to these concrete beings—to find what is hidden behind the surfaces of appearance, whether in space or in time. These concrete beings are, for Heidegger, more like fragments, always imperfect and always in error. As he wrote, "the disclosure of beings as such is simultaneously and intrinsically the concealing of being as a whole. In the simultaneity of disclosure and concealing, errancy holds sway. Errancy and the concealing of what is concealed belongs to the primordial essence of truth." For Heidegger, error is not something we fall into, like a ditch at the side of the road, to use his metaphor. Errancy, he says, is part of our inner constitution because we live in space and time, among the multiplicity of beings, and yet the very awareness of errancy and the recognition that there are "beings" in the world force us to ask ourselves the question of Being; that is, we ask (we are forced to ask) what is disclosed, even as it remains concealed in its totality, by the concrete reality in which we live.[9]

There is of course no easy answer to this question. Like his Enlightenment precursors, Heidegger speaks of creating a space, a "clearing" for the future appearance of Being, something understood to be unpredictable, essentially ephemeral, ungraspable. In Heidegger's late work, this clearing is the space of language. But again, the real danger, for Heidegger and for so many other thinkers of his generation, lies in the belief that we can ultimately control the world and ourselves through reason.

9. Martin Heidegger, "On the Essence of Truth," in *Basic Writings*, ed. David Farrell Krell (San Francisco, 1977), 137.

The danger, in other words, is that human beings will not respect the radical mystery of truth and the repetition of error in all its forms. Here, of course, lies the origin of the critique of the Enlightenment project in postmodernist thought: the eighteenth century is identified as the origin of "instrumental reason" and naive faith in human progress. My reading of a French Enlightenment discourse on error does, I think, force us to locate the origins of a more brutal instrumental reason elsewhere, most likely in the nineteenth-century turn to technologies of truth that banished true error in the name of predictability.

Now, the connection between a Heideggerian vision of human errancy in the face of the mysterious nature of Being and an Enlightenment line of thought on error and the spaces of insight is tantalizing. Most important, though, is that this connection points us to a historical problem that needs to be resolved. What explains the apparent continuity between these vastly different intellectual periods? This question leads back to the beginning of this study. "Postmodern" thought in particular has criticized the Enlightenment project as a source of violence and oppression, and has located the origin of this project in a desire to know truth absolutely, and to establish this truth as "universally" valid. The postmodern celebration of difference and fragmentation opposes itself to this supposedly blind Enlightenment faith in reason. Yet what has been lost in this postmodern turn is precisely the mystery of truth we have found in Enlightenment thought, and in figures such as Heidegger.

However much influenced by thinkers like Heidegger, postmodern thought has generally repressed any conception of truth in its own terms. If truth is essentially ephemeral and emerges only in momentary flashes, which themselves appear only in error, what faith can we have that this truth is in any way real?[10] In fact, error and errancy become, in the postmodern context, something that can liberate humanity from the illusion of truth, or even frustrated expectations of truth. "When nostalgia is gone and waiting is over, one can delight in the superficiality of appearances," notes the author of a book on postmodern "erring."[11] Ro-

10. Perhaps the best example of this difference between modernist and poststructural thought is Paul de Man's reading of Walter Benjamin's famous essay on translation. "This movement of the original," writes de Man, "is a wandering, an *errance,* a kind of permanent exile, but it is not really an exile, for there is no homeland, nothing from which one has been exiled." If the original is known only through fragments, "for all intents and purposes there has never been one." See Paul de Man, "Conclusions: Walter Benjamin's 'The Task of the Translator,'" in *The Resistance to Theory* (Minneapolis, 1986), 92, 91.

11. Mark C. Taylor, *Erring: A Post-Modern A/theology* (Chicago, 1984), 15–16.

mantic wandering is celebrated in its own right, and disconnected from any notion of truth that could limit or define it.[12] As Paul de Man once wrote, "truth and error" (at least in the realm of the text) "exist simultaneously, thus preventing the favoring of one over the other."[13] Similarly, a Derridean "iteration" that produces the illusion of continuity necessarily deviates from this continuity in the moment of its repetition.

Yet even here we can note an interesting parallel between poststructural approaches and the philosophical tradition they critique. If the ephemeral appearance of some metaphysical Being is denied as a function of language's own deceptive aberrations, language itself becomes the sphere of "otherness," a reality that cannot be denied even as it cannot be known or even directly experienced. Language never "appears" as itself, but appears only as concrete embodiments or performances, specific events that never exhaust the always ungraspable "meaning" of language. Essentially unpredictable, language generates its effects, according to poststructural thought, through a kind of productive aberration.[14] Emancipating itself from even a trace of metaphysics, the postmodern turn to language is not really an escape from the *structure* of error as we have defined it—it is simply a new version, a new localization of its appearance.

If the postmodern condition characteristic of later twentieth-century thought has fallen into crisis, owing in part to its inability to cope with the political and economic realities of our present age, a return to the Enlightenment has great potential. Not to rediscover models of consensus that would erase radical differentiation, and not to rediscover some universal truth that would bind humanity into one oppressive order. Yet a return to the problem of error and knowledge might indicate a new way of conceptualizing truth within contemporary realities. By bringing together the seemingly discordant concepts of error and enlightenment we have seen that these categories were far from being opposed. Thinkers in late eighteenth- and early nineteenth-century France in particular recognized the intimate connection between the inevitably aberrant diversity of our condition (whether epistemological, social, political, or historical) and at the same time the possibility of "illumination" in error. Without returning to specifically Enlightenment conceptions of insight (which I

12. One can compare two works in literary studies: Jean-Pierre Mileur, *The Critical Romance: The Critic as Reader, Writer, Hero* (Madison, Wis., 1990), e.g. 33, 113–14; and David Collings, *Wordsworthian Errancies: The Poetics of Cultural Dismemberment* (Baltimore, 1994).

13. Paul de Man, "Literary History and Literary Modernity," in *Blindness and Insight: Essays in the Rhetoric of Contemporary Criticism,* 2d ed., rev. (Minneapolis, 1983), 165.

14. The classic reference here is Jacques Derrida, "Signature Event Context," in *Margins of Philosophy,* trans. Alan Bass (Chicago, 1982).

have shown were radically diverse even at the time), it is worth tracing this more foundational relationship between error and truth. A truth that in its essence is beyond any one particular human experience, beyond any direct human control, a truth that nonetheless inhabits the fragmentary, disordered, and aberrant world in which we live, is a truth worth rediscovering. The historical task is to find that particular line of thought and prepare its reappearance in new conditions. The unraveling of its late eighteenth-century complexities is, I hope, one step in this process.

Index

257

Enlightenment Aberrations